Golf Rules

ILLUSTRATED

2010
EDITION

hamlyn

► CONTENTS

► FOREWORD

This edition of *Golf Rules Illustrated* deals with the Rules of Golf that are effective from 1 January 2008. There have been a number of changes made in the most recent review of the Rules themselves, mainly aimed at simplifying and clarifying certain Rules that have caused difficulty in the recent past. These changes are incorporated in this edition, together with the substance of a number of official Decisions to help interpret and implement the Rules.

Whereas the *Rule Book* itself is necessarily as concise as possible and designed to be carried easily in the pocket or golf bag, *Golf Rules Illustrated* is intended more as a reference document and companion to the *Rule Book*. It is designed to improve awareness and understanding of the Rules of Golf through the use of many photographs, drawings and descriptions of actual incidents in tournament golf.

This is the 14th edition of *Golf Rules Illustrated*. Its style and format continue to evolve, based on the feedback from golfers who have used earlier editions. We very much hope that you will enjoy and benefit from this new edition.

We would also like to draw your attention to the four-page 'Quick Guide to the Rules of Golf' set out for the first time in the 2008 *Rule Book*. Those who master the contents of the Quick Guide are a long way down the road to mastering the *Rule Book* itself.

ALAN W. J. HOLMES
Chairman, Rules of Golf Committee,
R&A Rules Limited

R&A Rules Limited
With effect from 1 January 2004, the responsibilities and authority of The Royal and Ancient Golf Club of St Andrews in making, interpreting and giving decisions on the Rules of Golf were transferred to R&A Rules Limited.

Gender
In the Rules of Golf, the gender used in relation to any person is understood to include both genders.

Golfers with Disabilities
The R&A publication entitled *A Modification of the Rules of Golf for Golfers with Disabilities* contains permissible modifications of the Rules of Golf to accommodate disabled golfers; it is available through The R&A.

PRINCIPAL CHANGES INTRODUCED IN THE 2008 CODE

General

The changes to the Rules generally fall into two broad categories: (1) those that improve the clarity of the Rules and (2) those that reduce the penalties in certain circumstances to ensure that they are proportionate.

Definitions

Advice

Amended to allow the exchange of information on distance, as it is not considered to be "advice".

Lost Ball

Amended to clarify substituted ball issues and to include the concept of "stroke-and-distance" (see corresponding changes to Rules 18-1, 24-3, 25-1c, 26 and 27-1).

Matches

Definition withdrawn and replaced by the two new Definitions, "Forms of Match Play" and "Forms of Stroke Play".

Rules

Rule 1-2. Exerting Influence on Ball
Note added to clarify what constitutes a serious breach of Rule 1-2.

Rule 4-1. Form and Make of Clubs
Amended to reduce the penalty for carrying, but not using, a non-conforming club or a club in breach of Rule 4-2, from disqualification to the same as carrying more than 14 clubs.

Rule 12-1. Searching for Ball; Seeing Ball
Amended to include searching for a ball in an obstruction.

Rule 12-2. Identifying Ball
Amended to allow a player to lift his ball for identification in a hazard (see corresponding change to Rule 15-3, removing the exemption from penalty for playing a wrong ball in a hazard).

Rule 13-4. Ball in Hazard; Prohibited Actions
Exception 1 amended for clarification; Exception 2 amended to refer to Rule 13-2 and to eliminate the reference to assistance in the player's subsequent play of the hole; Exception 3 added to exempt a player from penalty under Rule 13-4a (testing the condition of the hazard) in certain circumstances.

Rule 14-3. Artificial Devices, Unusual Equipment and Unusual Use of Equipment
Amended to refer to the unusual use of equipment (see also new Exception on use of equipment in a traditionally accepted manner) and new Exception added for players with a legitimate medical reason to use an artificial device or unusual equipment. Note added to clarify that a Local Rule may be introduced allowing the use of distance measuring devices; previously authorised by Decision only.

Rule 15-2. Substituted Ball
Exception added to avoid a "double penalty" when player incorrectly substitutes ball and plays from the wrong place (see corresponding change to Rule 20-7c).

Rules 15-3. Wrong Ball
Amended to remove the exemption from penalty for playing a wrong ball in a hazard (see corresponding change to Rule 12-2, allowing a player to lift a ball for identification in a hazard).

Rule 16-1e. Standing Astride or on Line of Putt
Exception added to apply no penalty if act was inadvertent or to avoid standing on another player's line of putt; previously authorised by Decision only.

Rule 18. Ball at Rest Moved
Penalty statement amended to avoid a "double penalty" when a player lifts his ball without authority and incorrectly substitutes ball (see related changes to Rules 15-2 and 20-7c).

Rule 18-1. Ball at Rest Moved; by Outside Agency
Note added to clarify procedure when ball might have been moved by an outside agency.

Rule 19-2. Ball in Motion Deflected or Stopped by Player, Partner, Caddie or Equipment
Amended to reduce the penalty in both match play and stroke play to one stroke.

Rule 20-3a. Placing and Replacing; By Whom and Where
Amended to reduce the penalty for having the wrong person place or replace a ball to one stroke.

Rule 20-7c. Playing from Wrong Place; Stroke Play
Note added to avoid a "double penalty" when player plays from the wrong place and incorrectly substitutes ball (see corresponding change to Rule 15-2).

Rule 24-1. Movable Obstruction
Amended to allow a flagstick, whether attended, removed or held up, to be moved when a ball is in motion.

Rule 24-3. Ball in Obstruction Not Found;

Rule 25-1c. Ball in Abnormal Ground Condition Not Found;

Rule 26. Water Hazards (including Lateral Water Hazards);

Rule 27-1. Stroke and Distance, Ball Out of Bounds; Ball Not Found Within Five Minutes

In the above Rules, the term "reasonable evidence" has been replaced by "known or virtually certain" when determining whether a ball that has not been found may be treated as in an obstruction (Rule 24-3), an abnormal ground condition (Rule 25-1) or a water hazard (Rule 26-1). See corresponding changes to Definition of Lost Ball and Rule 18-1.

Appendix I

Seams of Cut Turf
New specimen Local Rule added.

Temporary Immovable Obstructions
Clause II of the specimen Local Rule amended to include an additional requirement that, for intervention relief to be granted, the temporary immovable obstruction must be on the player's line of play.

Appendix II

Adjustability
Amended to allow forms of adjustability other than weight adjustment, subject to evaluation by The R&A.

Clubhead; Plain in Shape
Amended to clarify meaning of "plain in shape" and list some of the features that are not permitted; previously detailed in guidelines on equipment Rules.

Clubhead; Dimensions, Volume and Moment of Inertia
Sections added on moment of inertia and putter head dimensions; previously detailed in guidelines on equipment Rules and test protocols.

Clubhead; Spring Effect and Dynamic Properties
New section added on spring effect. The limit, as detailed in the Pendulum Test Protocol, now applies to all clubs (except putters) and in all forms of the game; previously covered by condition of competition.

HOW TO USE THE RULE BOOK

It is understood that not everyone who has a copy of the Rules of Golf will read it from cover to cover. Most golfers only consult the Rule book when they have a Rules issue on the course that needs to be resolved. However, to ensure that you have a basic understanding of the Rules and that you play golf in a reasonable manner, it is recommended that you at least read the Quick Guide to the Rules of Golf and the Etiquette Section contained within this publication.

The following points will assist you in using the Rule book efficiently and accurately:

UNDERSTAND THE WORDS
The Rule book is written in a very precise and deliberate fashion. You should be aware of and understand the following differences in word use:

- "may" (e.g. the player may cancel the stroke) means the action is optional
- "should" (e.g. the marker should check the score) means the action is recommended but is not mandatory
- "must" (e.g. the player's clubs must conform) means it is an instruction and there is a penalty if it is not carried out
- "a ball" (e.g drop a ball behind the point) means you may substitute another ball (e.g. Rules 26, 27 and 28)
- "the ball" (e.g. the player must lift the ball and drop it) means you must not substitute another ball (e.g. Rules 24-2 and 25-1)

KNOW THE DEFINITIONS
There are over 50 defined terms (e.g. abnormal ground conditions, through the green, etc) and these form the foundation around which the Rules of Play are written. A good knowledge of the defined terms (which are italicised throughout the book) is very important to the correct application of the Rules.

THE FACTS OF THE CASE
To answer any question on the Rules you must consider the facts of the case in some detail. You should identify:

- The form of play (e.g. match play or stroke play, single, foursome or four-ball)
- Who is involved (e.g. the player, his partner or caddie, an outside agency)
- Where the incident occurred (e.g. on the teeing ground, in a bunker or water hazard, on the putting green)
- What actually happened
- The timing of the incident (e.g. has the player now returned his score card, has the competition closed?)

REFER TO THE BOOK
If in doubt on any of the Rules, play the course as you find it and play the ball as it lies. On returning to the Clubhouse, you can refer the matter to the Committee and it may be that reference to the *Decisions on the Rules of Golf* will assist in resolving any queries that are not entirely clear from the Rule book itself.

As golf is a self-regulating game, all golfers should have a good understanding of the fundamental Rules, as contained in this guide. However, this guide is not a substitute for the Rules of Golf, which should be consulted whenever any doubt arises. For more information on the points covered in this guide, please refer to the relevant Rule.

GENERAL POINTS

Before commencing your round:
- Read the Local Rules on the score card or the notice board.
- Put an identification mark on your ball. Many golfers play the same brand and model of ball and if you can't identify your ball, it is considered lost. (Rules 12-2 and 27-1)
- Count your clubs. You are allowed a maximum of 14 clubs. (Rule 4-4)

During the round:
- Don't ask for "advice" from anyone except your partner (i.e. a player on your side) or your caddies. Don't give advice to anyone except your partner. You may ask for information on the Rules, distances and the position of hazards, the flagstick, etc. (Rule 8-1)
- Don't play any practice shots during play of a hole. (Rule 7-2)

At the end of your round:
- In match play, ensure the result of the match is posted.
- In stroke play, ensure that your score card is completed properly and return it as soon as possible. (Rule 6-6)

THE RULES OF PLAY

Tee Shot (Rule 11)

Play your tee shot from between, and not in front of, the tee-markers.

You may play your tee shot from up to two club-lengths behind the front line of the tee-markers.

If you play your tee shot from outside this area, in match play there is no penalty, but your opponent may require you to replay your stroke; in stroke play you incur a two-stroke penalty and must correct the error by playing from within the correct area.

Playing the Ball (Rules 12, 13, 14 and 15)

If you think a ball is yours but cannot see your identification mark, with the permission of your marker or opponent, you may mark and lift the ball to identify it. (Rule 12-2)

Play the ball as it lies. Don't improve your lie, the area of your intended stance or swing, or your line of play by moving, bending or breaking anything fixed or growing, except in fairly taking your stance or making your swing. Don't improve your lie by pressing anything down. (Rule 13-2)

If your ball is in a bunker or a water hazard, don't touch the ground in either type of hazard, or touch water in the water hazard, with your hand or club before your downswing and don't move loose impediments. (Rule 13-4)

You must swing the club and make a stroke at the ball. It is not permissible to push, scrape or spoon the ball. (Rule 14-1)

If you play a wrong ball, in match play you lose the hole; in stroke play you incur a two-stroke penalty and you must then correct the mistake by playing the correct ball. (Rule 15-3)

On the Putting Green (Rules 16 and 17)

You may mark, lift and clean your ball on the putting green. The ball should always be replaced on the exact spot. (Rule 16-1b)

You may repair ball marks and old hole plugs, but not any other damage to the putting green, such as spike marks. (Rule 16-1c)

When making a stroke on the putting green, you should ensure that the flagstick is removed or attended. The flagstick may also be removed or attended when the ball lies off the putting green. (Rule 17)

Ball at Rest Moved (Rule 18)

Generally, when the ball is in play, if you accidentally cause your ball to move, lift it when not permitted or it moves after you have addressed it, add a penalty stroke and replace your ball. However, see the exceptions under Rule 18-2a. (Rule 18-2)

If someone else moves your ball at rest or it is moved by another ball, replace it without penalty to you.

Ball in Motion Deflected or Stopped (Rule 19)

If a ball struck by you is deflected or stopped by you, your partner, your caddie or your equipment, add a penalty stroke and the ball is played as it lies. (Rule 19-2)

If a ball struck by you is deflected or stopped by another ball at rest, there is no penalty and the ball is played as it lies, except in stroke play where you incur a two-stroke penalty if your ball and the other ball were on the putting green before you played. (Rule 19-5a)

Lifting, Dropping and Placing the Ball (Rule 20)

Before lifting a ball that has to be replaced (e.g. when the ball is lifted on the putting green to clean it), the position of the ball must be marked. (Rule 20-1)

When the ball is being lifted in order to drop or place it in another position (e.g. dropping within two club-lengths under the unplayable ball Rule), it is not mandatory to mark its position although it is recommended that you do so.

When dropping, stand upright, hold the ball at shoulder height and arm's length and drop it.

A dropped ball must be re-dropped if it rolls to a position where there is interference from the condition from which free relief is being taken (e.g. an immovable obstruction), if it comes to rest more than two club-lengths from where it was dropped, or if it comes to rest nearer the hole than its original position, the nearest point of relief or where the ball last crossed the margin of a water hazard.

There are nine situations in total when a dropped ball must be re-dropped and they are covered in Rule 20-2c.

If a ball dropped for a second time rolls into any of these positions, place it where it first struck the course when re-dropped. (Rule 20-2c)

Ball Assisting or Interfering with Play
(Rule 22)

You may lift your ball or have any other ball lifted if you think the ball might assist another player.

You must not agree to leave a ball in position in order to assist another player.

You may have any ball lifted if it might interfere with your play.

A ball that is lifted due to it assisting or interfering with play must not be cleaned, unless it is lifted from the putting green.

Loose Impediments (Rule 23)

You may move a loose impediment (i.e. natural loose objects such as stones, detached leaves and twigs) unless the loose impediment and your ball are in the same hazard. If you remove a loose impediment and this causes your ball to move, the ball must be replaced and (unless your ball was on the putting green) you incur a one-stroke penalty. (Rule 23-1)

Movable Obstructions (Rule 24)

Movable obstructions (i.e. artificial movable objects such as rakes, tin cans, etc.) located anywhere may be moved without penalty. If the ball moves as a result, it must be replaced without penalty.

If a ball is on a movable obstruction, the ball may be lifted, the obstruction removed and the ball dropped, without penalty, on the spot directly under where the ball lay on the obstruction, except that on the putting green, the ball is placed on that spot.

Immovable Obstructions and Abnormal Ground Conditions (Rules 24-2 and 25-1)

An immovable obstruction is an artificial immovable object such as a building or an artificially-surfaced road (but check the Local Rules for the status of roads and paths).

An abnormal ground condition is either casual water, ground under repair or a hole, cast or runway made by a burrowing animal, a reptile or a bird.

Except when the ball is in a water hazard, free relief is available from immovable obstructions and abnormal ground conditions when the condition physically interferes with the lie of the ball, your stance or your swing. You may lift the ball and drop it within one club-length of the "nearest point of relief" (see Definition of "Nearest Point of Relief"), but not nearer the hole than the nearest point of relief (see diagram on page 9).

If the ball is on the putting green, it is placed at the nearest point of relief.

There is no relief for intervention on your line of play unless both your ball and the condition are on the putting green.

As an additional option when the ball is in a bunker, you may take relief from the condition behind the bunker under penalty of one stroke.

The diagram on page 9 illustrates the term "nearest point of relief" in Rules 24-2 and 25-1 in the case of a right-handed player.

Water Hazards (Rule 26)

If your ball is in a water hazard (yellow stakes and/or lines) you may play the ball as it lies or, under penalty of one stroke:

- play a ball from where you hit the ball into the hazard, or
- drop any distance behind the water hazard keeping a straight line between the hole, the point where the ball last crossed the margin of the water hazard and the spot on which the ball is dropped.

If your ball is in a lateral water hazard (red stakes and/or lines), in addition to the options for a ball in a water hazard (see above), under penalty of one stroke, you may drop within two club-lengths of, and not nearer the hole than:

- the point where the ball last crossed the margin of the hazard, or
- a point on the opposite side of the hazard equidistant to the hole from the point where the ball last crossed the margin.

Ball Lost or Out of Bounds; Provisional Ball
(Rule 27)

Check the Local Rules on the score card to identify the boundaries of the course.

If your ball is lost outside a water hazard or out of bounds you must play another ball from the spot where the last shot was played, under penalty of one stroke, i.e. stroke and distance.

You are allowed five minutes to search for a ball, after which, if it is not found or identified, it is lost.

If, after playing a shot, you think your ball may be lost outside a water hazard or out of bounds you should

NEAREST POINT OF RELIEF

Direction of play
(right-handed player)

A P1 B1

Road
or
GUR

B2

P2 C

B1	= position of ball on road, in ground under repair (GUR), etc.
P1	= nearest point of relief.
P1 A–A	= shaded area within which ball to be dropped, radius of one club-length from P1 measured with any club.
B2	= position of ball on road, in ground under repair (GUR), etc.

-----	= notional stance required to play ball at P2 with club which player would expect to play the stroke.
P2	= nearest point of relief.
P2 C–C	= shaded area within which ball to be dropped, radius of one club-length from P2, measured with any club.

play a "provisional ball". You must state that it is a provisional ball and play it before you go forward to search for the original ball.

If it transpires that the original ball is lost (other than in a water hazard) or out of bounds, you must continue with the provisional ball, under penalty of one stroke. If the original ball is found in bounds, you must continue play of the hole with it, and must stop play with the provisional ball.

Ball Unplayable (Rule 28)
If your ball is in a water hazard, the unplayable ball Rule does not apply and you must proceed under the water hazard Rule if taking relief. Elsewhere on the course, if you believe your ball is unplayable, you may under penalty of one stroke:

- play a ball from where the last shot was played, or
- drop a ball any distance behind the point where the ball lay keeping a straight line between the hole,

the point where the ball lay and the spot on which the ball is dropped, or
- drop a ball within two club-lengths of where the ball lies not nearer the hole.

If your ball is in a bunker you may proceed as above, except that if you are dropping back on a line or within two club-lengths, you must drop in the bunker.

Etiquette
If you have not already done so, you should also read the Etiquette Section – not more Rules as such, but a practical guide to getting around the course safely, in good time, with consideration for others and having taken good care of the course.

ETIQUETTE; BEHAVIOUR ON THE COURSE

Introduction

This section provides guidelines on the manner in which the game of golf should be played. If they are followed, all players will gain maximum enjoyment from the game. The overriding principle is that consideration should be shown to others on the course at all times.

The Spirit of the Game

Golf is played, for the most part, without the supervision of a referee or umpire. The game relies on the integrity of the individual to show consideration for other players and to abide by the Rules. All players should conduct themselves in a disciplined manner, demonstrating courtesy and sportsmanship at all times, irrespective of how competitive they may be. This is the spirit of the game of golf.

Safety

Players should ensure that no one is standing close by or in a position to be hit by the club, the ball or any stones, pebbles, twigs or the like when they make a stroke or practice swing.

Players should not play until the players in front are out of range.

Players should always alert greenstaff near by or ahead when they are about to make a stroke that might endanger them.

If a player plays a ball in a direction where there is a danger of hitting someone, he should immediately shout a warning. The traditional word of warning in such situations is "fore".

Consideration for Other Players

No Disturbance or Distraction Players should always show consideration for other players on the course and

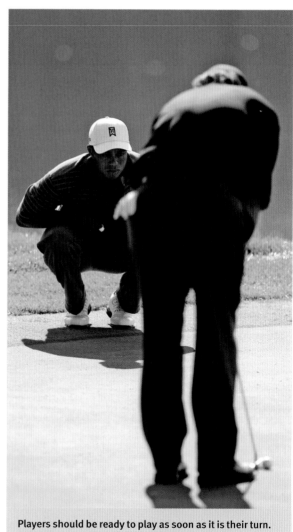

Players should be ready to play as soon as it is their turn. This can be achieved by lining up putts while other players are playing, provided there is no disturbance or distraction for them. Here Phil Mickelson putts out while Tiger Woods prepares for his putt.

should not disturb their play by moving, talking or making unnecessary noise.

Players should ensure that any electronic device taken onto the course does not distract other players.

On the teeing ground, a player should not tee his ball until it is his turn to play.

Players should not stand close to or directly behind the ball, or directly behind the hole, when a player is about to play.

On the Putting Green On the putting green, players should not stand on another player's line of putt or, when he is making a stroke, cast a shadow over his line of putt.

Players should remain on or close to the putting green until all the other players in the group have holed out.

Scoring In stroke play, a player who is acting as a marker should, if necessary, on the way to the next tee, check the score with the player concerned and record it.

Pace of Play
Play at Good Pace and Keep Up Players should play at a good pace. The Committee may establish pace of play guidelines that all players should follow.

It is a group's responsibility to keep up with the group in front. If it loses a clear hole and it is delaying the group behind, it should invite the group behind to play through, irrespective of the number of players in that group. Where a group has not lost a clear hole, but it is apparent that the group behind can play faster, it should invite the faster moving group to play through.

Be Ready to Play Players should be ready to play as soon as it is their turn to play. When playing on or near the putting green, they should leave their bags or carts in such a position as will enable quick movement off the green and towards the next tee. When the play of a hole has been completed, players should immediately leave the putting green.

Lost Ball If a player believes his ball may be lost outside a water hazard or is out of bounds, to save time, he should play a provisional ball.

Players searching for a ball should signal the players in the group behind them to play through as soon as it becomes apparent that the ball will not easily be found. They should not search for five minutes before doing

CARE OF THE COURSE

(1) Always repair divots, (2) carefully repair pitch-marks on the putting green and (3) smooth over footprints and other marks when leaving a bunker. (4) Do not lean on your putter when removing the ball from the hole.

so. Having allowed the group behind to play through, they should not continue play until that group has passed and is out of range.

Priority on the Course
Unless otherwise determined by the Committee, priority on the course is determined by a group's pace of play. Any group playing a whole round is entitled to pass a group playing a shorter round. The term "group" includes a single player.

Care of the Course
Bunkers Before leaving a bunker, players should carefully fill up and smooth over all holes and footprints made by them and any nearby made by others. If a rake is within reasonable proximity of the bunker, the rake should be used for this purpose.

Repair of Divots, Ball-Marks and Damage by Shoes
Players should carefully repair any divot holes made by them and any damage to the putting green made by the impact of a ball (whether or not made by the player himself). On completion of the hole by all players in the group, damage to the putting green caused by golf shoes should be repaired.

Preventing Unnecessary Damage Players should avoid causing damage to the course by removing divots when taking practice swings or by hitting the head of a club into the ground, whether in anger or for any other reason.

Players should ensure that no damage is done to the putting green when putting down bags or the flagstick.

In order to avoid damaging the hole, players and caddies should not stand too close to the hole and should take care during the handling of the flagstick and the removal of a ball from the hole. The head of a club should not be used to remove a ball from the hole.

Players should not lean on their clubs when on the putting green, particularly when removing the ball from the hole.

The flagstick should be properly replaced in the hole before the players leave the putting green.

Local notices regulating the movement of golf carts should be strictly observed.

Conclusion; Penalties for Breach

If players follow the guidelines in this section, it will make the game more enjoyable for everyone.

If a player consistently disregards these guidelines during a round or over a period of time to the detriment of others, it is recommended that the Committee considers taking appropriate disciplinary action against the offending player. Such action may, for example, include prohibiting play for a limited time on the course or in a certain number of competitions. This is considered to be justifiable in terms of protecting the interests of the majority of golfers who wish to play in accordance with these guidelines.

In the case of a serious breach of etiquette, the Committee may disqualify a player under Rule 33-7.

▶ ETIQUETTE

FREQUENTLY ASKED QUESTION

Q Does a single player have any standing on the golf course?

A Different players play at different speeds. Whilst players should not have to run round the course, they should be aware that there are other players on the course at the same time and should therefore act with common sense and courtesy towards those other players.

The Etiquette section suggests that, unless otherwise determined by the Committee, priority on the course is determined by a group's pace of play, and the term "group" includes a single player. The Pace of Play part of

the Etiquette section also states that, "It is a group's responsibility to keep up with the group in front. If it loses a clear hole and it is delaying the group behind, it should invite the group behind to play through, irrespective of the number of players in that group. Where a group has not lost a clear hole, but it is apparent that the group behind can play faster, it should invite the faster moving group to play through." Therefore, a slow group should give way, where possible, to a faster group, and single golfers should have the same rights as all other players.

DEFINITIONS

The Definitions are listed alphabetically and, in the *Rules* themselves, defined terms are in *italics*.

Abnormal Ground Conditions An "*abnormal ground condition*" is any *casual water*, *ground under repair* or hole, cast or runway on the *course* made by a *burrowing animal*, a reptile or a bird.

Addressing the Ball A player has "*addressed the ball*" when he has taken his *stance* and has also grounded his club, except that in a *hazard* a player has *addressed the ball* when he has taken his *stance*.

Advice "*Advice*" is any counsel or suggestion that could influence a player in determining his play, the choice of a club or the method of making a *stroke*.

Information on the *Rules*, distance or matters of public information, such as the position of *hazards* or the *flagstick* on the *putting green*, is not *advice*.

Ball Deemed to Move See "*Move or Moved*".

Ball Holed See "*Holed*".

Ball Lost See "*Lost Ball*".

Ball in Play A ball is "*in play*" as soon as the player has made a *stroke* on the *teeing ground*. It remains *in play* until it is *holed*, except when it is *lost*, *out of bounds* or lifted, or another ball has been *substituted* whether or not the substitution is permitted; a ball so *substituted* becomes the *ball in play*.

If a ball is played from outside the *teeing ground* when the player is starting play of a hole, or when attempting to correct this mistake, the ball is not in play and Rule 11-4 or 11-5 applies. Otherwise, *ball in play* includes a ball played from outside the *teeing ground* when the player elects or is required to play his next *stroke* from the *teeing ground*.

ADDRESSING THE BALL

Except in a hazard, a player has addressed the ball when he has taken his stance and grounded his club.

In a bunker or water hazard a player has addressed the ball when he has taken his stance.

The player has decided not to ground his putter. Therefore, he has not "addressed the ball" and cannot be penalised under Rule 18-2b should his ball move.

BUNKER

Tim Clarke plays out of one of the bunkers at Royal Liverpool at the 2006 Open Championship. A bunker face consisting of stacked turf, whether grass covered or earthen, is not part of the bunker.

Exception in match play: *Ball in play* includes a ball played by the player from outside the *teeing ground* when starting play of a hole if the opponent does not require the *stroke* to be cancelled in accordance with Rule 11-4a.

CADDIE

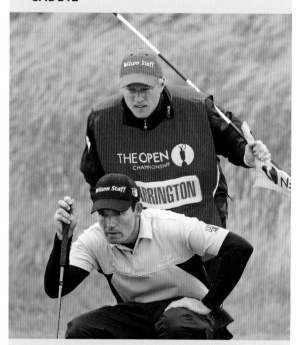

A caddie will carry a player's clubs and may offer advice on club selection, the direction of play and the line for putting.

Best-Ball See "*Forms of Match Play*".

Bunker A "*bunker*" is a hazard consisting of a prepared area of ground, often a hollow, from which turf or soil has been removed and replaced with sand or the like.

Grass-covered ground bordering or within a *bunker* including a stacked turf face (whether grass-covered or earthen), is not part of the *bunker*.

A wall or lip of the *bunker* not covered with grass is part of the *bunker*. The margin of a *bunker* extends vertically downwards, but not upwards.

A ball is in a *bunker* when it lies in or any part of it touches the *bunker*.

Burrowing Animal A "*burrowing animal*" is an animal (other than a worm, insect or the like) that makes a hole for habitation or shelter, such as a rabbit, mole, groundhog, gopher or salamander.

Note: A hole made by a non-burrowing animal, such as a dog, is not an *abnormal ground condition* unless marked or declared as *ground under repair*.

Caddie A "*caddie*" is one who assists the player in accordance with the *Rules*, which may include carrying or handling the player's clubs during play.

When one *caddie* is employed by more than one player, he is always deemed to be the *caddie* of the player sharing the *caddie* whose ball (or whose *partner's* ball) is involved, and *equipment* carried by him is deemed to be that player's *equipment*, except when the *caddie* acts upon specific directions of another player (or the *partner* of another player) sharing the *caddie*, in which case he is considered to be that other player's *caddie*.

Casual Water "*Casual water*" is any temporary accumulation of water on the *course* that is not in a *water hazard* and is visible before or after the player takes his *stance*. Snow and natural ice, other than frost, are either *casual water* or *loose impediments*, at the option of the player. Manufactured ice is an *obstruction*. Dew and frost are not *casual water*.

A ball is in *casual water* when it lies in or any part of it touches the *casual water*.

Committee The "*Committee*" is the committee in charge of the competition or, if the matter does not arise in a competition, the committee in charge of the *course*.

Competitor A "*competitor*" is a player in a stroke play competition. A "*fellow-competitor*" is any person with whom the *competitor* plays. Neither is *partner* of the other.

In stroke play *foursome* and *four-ball* competitions, where the context so admits, the word "*competitor*" or "*fellow-competitor*" includes his *partner*.

Course The "*course*" is the whole area within any boundaries established by the *Committee* (see Rule 33-2).

Equipment "*Equipment*" is anything used, worn or carried by the player or anything carried for the player by his *partner* or either of their *caddies*, except any ball he has played at the hole being played and any small object, such as a coin or a *tee*, when used to mark the position of a ball or the extent of an area in which a ball is to be dropped. *Equipment* includes a golf cart, whether or not motorised.

Note 1: A ball played at the hole being played is *equipment* when it has been lifted and not put back into play.

Note 2: When a golf cart is shared by two or more players, the cart and everything in it are deemed to be the *equipment* of one of the players sharing the cart.

If the cart is being moved by one of the players (or the *partner* of one of the players) sharing it, the cart and everything in it are deemed to be that player's *equipment*.

Otherwise, the cart and everything in it are deemed to be the *equipment* of the player sharing the cart whose ball (or whose *partner's* ball) is involved.

EQUIPMENT

Any small object, such as a coin or a tee, when used to mark the extent of an area in which a ball can be dropped is not equipment of the player.

CASUAL WATER

Casual water is an "abnormal ground condition" and a player may take relief from such a condition under Rule 25-1.

GROUND UNDER REPAIR

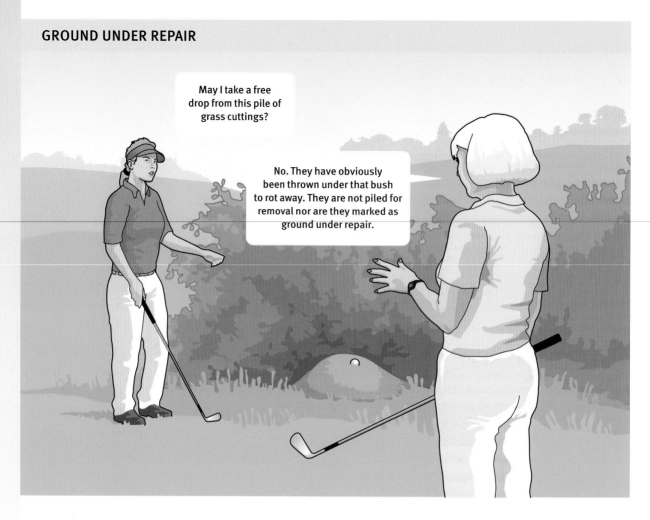

Fellow-Competitor See "*Competitor*".

Flagstick The "*flagstick*" is a movable straight indicator, with or without bunting or other material attached, centered in the *hole* to show its position. It must be circular in cross-section. Padding or shock absorbent material that might unduly influence the movement of the ball is prohibited.

Forecaddie A "*forecaddie*" is one who is employed by the *Committee* to indicate to players the position of balls during play. He is an *outside agency*.

Forms of Match Play
Single: A match in which one player plays against another player.
Threesome: A match in which one player plays against two other players, and each *side* plays one ball.
Foursome: A match in which two players play against two other players, and each *side* plays one ball.

Three-Ball: Three players play a match against one another, each playing his own ball. Each player is playing two distinct matches.
Best-Ball: A match in which one player plays against the better ball of two other players or the best ball of three other players.
Four-Ball: A match in which two players play their better ball against the better ball of two other players.

Forms of Stroke Play
Individual: A competition in which each *competitor* plays as an individual.
Foursome: A competition in which two *competitors* play as *partners* and play one ball.
Four-Ball: A competition in which two *competitors* play as *partners*, each playing his own ball. The lower score of the *partners* is the score for the hole. If one *partner* fails to complete the play of a hole, there is no penalty.
Note: For bogey, par and Stableford competitions, see Rule 32-1.

Four-Ball See "*Forms of Match Play*" and "*Forms of Stroke Play*".

Foursome See "*Forms of Match Play*" and "*Forms of Stroke Play*".

Ground Under Repair "*Ground under repair*" is any part of the *course* so marked by order of the *Committee* or so declared by its authorised representative. All ground and any grass, bush, tree or other growing thing within the *ground under repair* are part of the *ground under repair*. *Ground under repair* includes material piled for removal and a hole made by a greenkeeper, even if not so marked. Grass cuttings and other material left on the *course* that have been abandoned and are not intended to be removed are not *ground under repair* unless so marked.

When the margin of *ground under repair* is defined by stakes, the stakes are inside the *ground under repair*, and the margin of the *ground under repair* is defined by the nearest outside points of the stakes at ground level. When both stakes and lines are used to indicate *ground under repair*, the stakes identify the *ground under repair* and the lines define the margin of the *ground under repair*. When the margin of *ground under repair* is defined by a line on the ground, the line itself is in the *ground under repair*. The margin of *ground under repair* extends vertically downwards but not upwards.

A ball is in *ground under repair* when it lies in or any part of it touches the *ground under repair*.

Stakes used to define the margin of or identify *ground under repair* are *obstructions*.

Note: The *Committee* may make a Local Rule prohibiting play from *ground under repair* or an environmentally-sensitive area defined as *ground under repair*.

Hazards A "*hazard*" is any *bunker* or *water hazard*.

Hole The "*hole*" must be 4¼ inches (108 mm) in diameter and at least 4 inches (101.6 mm) deep. If a lining is used, it must be sunk at least 1 inch (25.4 mm) below the *putting green* surface unless the nature of the soil makes it impracticable to do so; its outer diameter must not exceed 4¼ inches (108 mm).

Holed A ball is "*holed*" when it is at rest within the circumference of the hole and all of it is below the level of the lip of the *hole*.

Honour The player who is to play first from the *teeing ground* is said to have the "*honour*".

Lateral Water Hazard A "*lateral water hazard*" is a *water hazard* or that part of a *water hazard* so situated that it is not possible, or is deemed by the *Committee* to be impracticable, to drop a ball behind the *water hazard* in accordance with Rule 26-1b. All ground and water within the margin of a *lateral water hazard* are part of the *lateral water hazard*.

When the margin of a *lateral water hazard* is defined by stakes, the stakes are inside the *lateral water hazard*, and the margin of the *hazard* is defined by the nearest outside points of the stakes at ground level. When both stakes and lines are used to indicate a *lateral water hazard*, the stakes identify the *hazard* and the lines define the *hazard* margin. When the margin of a *lateral water hazard* is defined by a line on the ground, the line itself is in the *lateral water hazard*. The margin of a *lateral water hazard* extends vertically upwards and downwards.

A ball is in a *lateral water hazard* when it lies in or any part of it touches the *lateral water hazard*.

Stakes used to define the margin of or identify a *lateral water hazard* are *obstructions*.

Note 1: That part of a *water hazard* to be played as a *lateral water hazard* must be distinctively marked. Stakes or lines used to define the margin of or identify a *lateral water hazard* must be red.

Note 2: The *Committee* may make a Local Rule prohibiting play from an environmentally-sensitive area defined as a *lateral water hazard*.

Note 3: The *Committee* may define a *lateral water hazard* as a *water hazard*.

Line of Play The "*line of play*" is the direction that the player wishes his ball to take after a *stroke*, plus a reasonable distance on either side of the intended direction. The *line of play* extends vertically upwards from the ground, but does not extend beyond the *hole*.

Line of Putt The "*line of putt*" is the line that the player wishes his ball to take after a *stroke* on the *putting green*. Except with respect to Rule 16-1e, the *line of putt* includes a reasonable distance on either side of the intended line. The *line of putt* does not extend beyond the *hole*.

Loose Impediments "*Loose impediments*" are natural objects, including:

- stones, leaves, twigs, branches and the like,
- dung, and
- worms, insects and the like, and the casts and heaps made by them,

provided they are not:

- fixed or growing,
- solidly embedded, or
- adhering to the ball.

Sand and loose soil are *loose impediments* on the *putting green*, but not elsewhere.

Snow and natural ice, other than frost, are either *casual water* or *loose impediments* at the option of the player.

Dew and frost are not *loose impediments*.

Lost Ball A ball is deemed "*lost*" if:

a. It is not found or identified as his by the player within five minutes after the player's *side* or his or their *caddies* have begun to search for it; or

b. The player has made *stroke* at a *provisional ball* from the place where the original ball is likely to be or from a point nearer the *hole* than that place (see Rule 27-2b); or

c. The player has put another ball into play under penalty of stroke and distance (see Rule 27-la); or

d. The player has put another ball into play because it is known or virtually certain that the ball, which has not been found, has been moved by an *outside agency* (see Rule 18-1), is in an *obstruction* (see Rule 24-3), is in an *abnormal ground condition* (see Rule 25-1c) or is in a *water hazard* (see Rule 26-1); or

e. The player has made a *stroke* at a *substituted ball*.

Time spent in playing a *wrong ball* is not counted in the five-minute period allowed for search.

Marker A "*marker*" is one who is appointed by the *Committee* to record a *competitor's* score in stroke play. He may be a *fellow-competitor*. He is not a *referee*.

Move or Moved A ball is deemed to have "*moved*" if it leaves its position and comes to rest in any other place.

Nearest Point of Relief The "*nearest point of relief*" is the reference point for taking relief without penalty from

LOOSE IMPEDIMENTS

Natural objects such as:

branches

pine cones

dead rat

stones

worm casts

leaves

insects

MOVABLE OBSTRUCTIONS

Artificial/manufactured objects such as:

litter

bottle

rake

booklet

tin can

score card

tee

BALL DEEMED TO MOVE

This ball is deemed not to have "moved" because, having left its original position, it rolled back into it again.

This ball is deemed to have "moved" because it has left its original position and come to rest in another place; the fact that it has moved vertically, rather than laterally, is irrelevant.

interference by an immovable *obstruction* (Rule 24-2), an *abnormal ground condition* (Rule 25-1) or a *wrong putting green* (Rule 25-3).

It is the point on the course nearest to where the ball lies:

(i) that is not nearer the *hole*, and

(ii) where, if the ball were so positioned, no interference by the condition from which relief is sought would exist for the *stroke* the player would have made from the original position if the condition were not there.

Note: In order to determine the *nearest point of relief* accurately, the player should use the club with which he would have made his next *stroke* if the condition were not there to simulate the *address* position, direction of play and swing for such a *stroke*.

Observer An "*observer*" is one who is appointed by the *Committee* to assist a *referee* to decide questions of fact and to report to him any breach of a *Rule*. An *observer* should not attend the *flagstick*, stand at or mark the position of the *hole*, or lift the ball or mark its position.

Obstructions An "*obstruction*" is anything artificial, including the artificial surfaces and sides of roads and paths and manufactured ice, except:

a. Objects defining *out of bounds*, such as walls, fences, stakes and railings;

b. Any part of an immovable artificial object that is *out of bounds*; and

c. Any construction declared by the *Committee* to be an integral part of the *course*.

An *obstruction* is a movable *obstruction* if it may be moved without unreasonable effort, without unduly delaying play and without causing damage. Otherwise, it is an immovable *obstruction*.

Note: The *Committee* may make a Local Rule declaring a movable *obstruction* to be an immovable *obstruction*.

Out of Bounds "*Out of bounds*" is beyond the boundaries of the *course* or any part of the *course* so marked by the *Committee*.

When *out of bounds* is defined by reference to stakes or a fence or as being beyond stakes or a fence, the *out of bounds* line is determined by the nearest inside points at ground level of the stakes or fence posts (excluding angled supports). When both stakes and lines are used to indicate *out of bounds*, the stakes identify *out of bounds* and the lines define *out of bounds*. When *out of bounds* is defined by a line on the ground, the line itself is *out of bounds*. The *out of bounds* line extends vertically upwards and downwards.

A ball is *out of bounds* when all of it lies *out of bounds*. A player may stand *out of bounds* to play a ball lying within bounds.

NEAREST POINT OF RELIEF

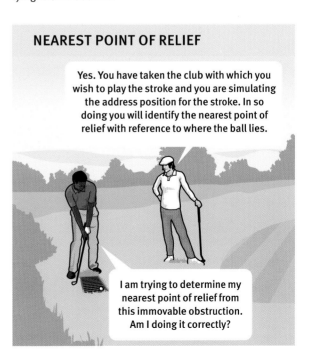

Yes. You have taken the club with which you wish to play the stroke and you are simulating the address position for the stroke. In so doing you will identify the nearest point of relief with reference to where the ball lies.

I am trying to determine my nearest point of relief from this immovable obstruction. Am I doing it correctly?

PARTNER

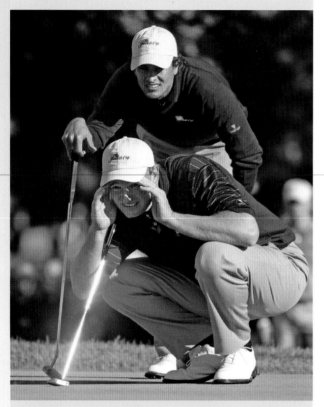

A partner is a player associated with another player on the same side.

Objects defining *out of bounds* such as walls, fences, stakes and railings are not *obstructions* and are deemed to be fixed. Stakes identifying *out of bounds* are not *obstructions* and are deemed to be fixed.
Note 1: Stakes or lines used to define *out of bounds* should be white.
Note 2: A *Committee* may make a Local Rule declaring stakes identifying but not defining *out of bounds* to be movable *obstructions*.

Outside Agency In match play, an "*outside agency*" is any agency other than either the player's or opponent's *side*, any *caddie* of either *side*, any ball played by either *side* at the *hole* being played or any *equipment* of either *side*. In stroke play, an *outside agency* is any agency other than the *competitor's side*, any *caddie* of the *side*, any ball played by the *side* at the hole being played or any *equipment* of the *side*. An *outside agency* includes a *referee*, a *marker*, an *observer* and a *forecaddie*. Neither wind nor water is an *outside agency*.

Partner A "*partner*" is a player associated with another player on the same *side*.

In *threesome*, *foursome*, *best-ball* or *four-ball* play, where the context so admits, the word "player" includes his *partner* or *partners*.

Penalty Stroke A "*penalty stroke*" is one added to the score of a player or *side* under certain *Rules*. In a *threesome* or *foursome*, *penalty strokes* do not affect the order of play.

Provisional Ball A "*provisional ball*" is a ball played under Rule 27-2 for a ball that may be *lost* outside a *water hazard* or may be *out of bounds*.

Putting Green The "*putting green*" is all ground of the hole being played that is specially prepared for putting or otherwise defined as such by the *Committee*. A ball is on the *putting green* when any part of it touches the *putting green*.

R&A The "*R&A*" means R&A Rules Limited.

Referee A "*referee*" is one who is appointed by the *Committee* to accompany players to decide questions of fact and apply the *Rules*. He must act on any breach of a *Rule* that he observes or is reported to him.

A *referee* should not attend the *flagstick*, stand at or mark the position of the *hole*, or lift the ball or mark its position.

DEFINITION OF A STROKE

At this point, as the player has not started his downswing, he has not begun his stroke. Once the player begins his downswing he is considered to have made a stroke, unless he checks his downswing voluntarily.

TEEING GROUND

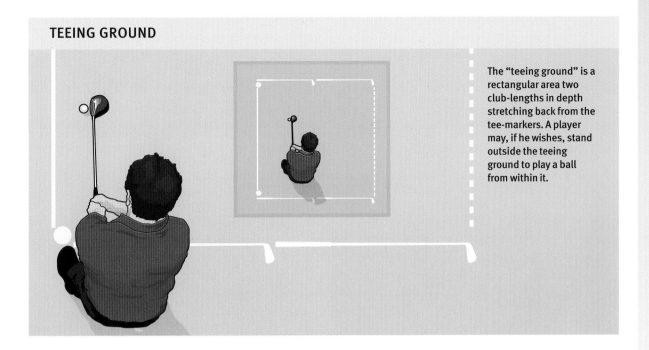

The "teeing ground" is a rectangular area two club-lengths in depth stretching back from the tee-markers. A player may, if he wishes, stand outside the teeing ground to play a ball from within it.

Rub of the Green A "*rub of the green*" occurs when a ball in motion is accidentally deflected or stopped by any *outside agency* (see Rule 19-1).

Rule or Rules The term "*Rule*" includes:
a. The Rules of Golf and their interpretations as contained in "Decisions on the Rules of Golf";
b. Any Conditions of Competition established by the *Committee* under Rule 33-1 and Appendix I;
c. Any Local Rules established by the *Committee* under Rule 33-8a and Appendix I; and
d. The specifications on clubs and the ball in Appendices II and III and their interpretations contained in "A Guide to the Rules on Clubs and Balls".

Side A "*side*" is a player, or two or more players who are *partners*.

Single See "*Forms of Match Play*" and "*Forms of Stroke Play*".

Stance Taking the "*stance*" consists in a player placing his feet in position for and preparatory to making a *stroke*.

Stipulated Round The "*stipulated round*" consists of playing the holes of the course in their correct sequence, unless otherwise authorised by the *Committee*. The number of holes in a *stipulated round* is 18 unless a smaller number is authorised by the *Committee*. As to extension of *stipulated round* in match play, see Rule 2-3.

Stroke A "*stroke*" is the forward movement of the club made with the intention of striking at and moving the ball, but if a player checks his downswing voluntarily before the clubhead reaches the ball he has not made a *stroke*.

Substituted Ball A "*substituted ball*" is a ball put into play for the original ball that was either *in play*, *lost*, *out of bounds* or lifted.

Tee A "*tee*" is a device designed to raise the ball off the ground. It must not be longer than 4 inches (101.6 mm) and it must not be designed or manufactured in such a way that it could indicate the *line of play* or influence the movement of the ball.

Teeing Ground The "*teeing ground*" is the starting place for the hole to be played. It is a rectangular area two club-lengths in depth, the front and the sides of which are defined by the outside limits of two tee-markers. A ball is outside the *teeing ground* when all of it lies outside the *teeing ground*.

Three-Ball See "*Forms of Match Play*".

Threesome See "*Forms of Match Play*".

Through the Green "*Through the green*" is the whole area of the *course* except:

a. The *teeing ground* and *putting green* of the hole being played; and

b. All *hazards* on the *course*.

Water Hazard A "*water hazard*" is any sea, lake, pond, river, ditch, surface drainage ditch or other open water course (whether or not containing water) and anything of a similar nature on the *course*. All ground and water within the margin of a *water hazard* are part of the *water hazard*.

When the margin of a *water hazard* is defined by stakes, the stakes are inside the *water hazard*, and the margin of the *hazard* is defined by the nearest outside points of the stakes at ground level. When both stakes and lines are used to indicate a *water hazard*, the stakes identify the *hazard* and the lines define the *hazard* margin. When the margin of a *water hazard* is defined by a line on the ground, the line itself is in the *water hazard*. The margin of a *water hazard* extends vertically upwards and downwards.

A ball is in a *water hazard* when it lies in or any part of it touches the *water hazard*.

Stakes used to define the margin of or identify a *water hazard* are *obstructions*.

Note 1: Stakes or lines used to define the margin of or identify a *water hazard* must be yellow.

Note 2: The *Committee* may make a Local Rule prohibiting play from an environmentally-sensitive area defined as a *water hazard*.

Wrong Ball A "*wrong ball*" is any ball other than the player's:

• *ball in play*;

• *provisional ball*; or

• second ball played under Rule 3-3 or Rule 20-7c in stroke play;

and includes:

• another player's ball;

• an abandoned ball; and

• the player's original ball when it is no longer *in play*.

Note: *Ball in play* includes a ball *substituted* for the *ball in play*, whether or not the substitution is permitted.

Wrong Putting Green A "*wrong putting green*" is any *putting green* other than that of the hole being played. Unless otherwise prescribed by the *Committee*, this term includes a practice *putting green* or pitching green on the *course*.

▶ DEFINITIONS

INCIDENT

During his quarter-final match with Thomas Levet at the 2004 HSBC World Match Play at Wentworth, Padraig Harrington's ball lay close to a tree on the 9th hole. The Irishman was concerned that the branches of the tree might interfere with the area of his intended swing, but seemed to have convinced himself prior to addressing the ball that there would not be any interference. On taking his backswing, the player's club struck a part of the tree and, although Harrington began his downswing, he decided during the downswing not to strike the ball. Although unable to stop the club before it reached the ball, the player adjusted his swing to intentionally swing over the ball.

Harrington advised the referee walking with the match that he had altered the path of the downswing deliberately in order to miss the ball. In accordance with the provisions of Decision 14/1.5, the referee decided

Padraig Harrington injures his hand in making a stroke at his ball close to a tree at Wentworth.

that Harrington had not made a stroke as his intention to strike the ball ceased during the downswing. In addition, as nothing had been done to improve the area of the player's intended swing when he clipped the tree, there was no penalty under Rule 13-2.

However, the incident did not end there. When Harrington actually came to play the stroke, his hand struck the tree on his follow-through. With the permission of the referee (under Rule 6-8a), Harrington discontinued play for a few minutes to receive medical attention for a bleeding thumb. Decision 6-8a/3 confirms that it would be reasonable for the Committee to allow a player 10 to 15 minutes to recuperate from such a physical problem.

▶ DEFINITIONS
FREQUENTLY ASKED QUESTIONS

Q How does a player establish the nearest point of relief?

A Say a player's ball lies on the fairway. The player would be entitled to relief without penalty if he has interference to the lie of the ball, or the area of intended stance or swing, from, for example, an abnormal ground condition (Rule 25-1). If the player opts to take relief, he is required to take relief from all three of these elements (that is, "complete relief"); he cannot choose to take relief from one but not the others. Thus, if his ball was in casual water (an abnormal ground condition), when determining his nearest point of relief, the player must ensure the ball is not in the casual water, and the casual water does not interfere with his stance or swing. He cannot take relief simply for the lie of the ball.

In order to determine the nearest point of relief accurately, the player should use the club with which he would have made his next stroke were the condition (the casual water) not there, and he should simulate the address position, direction of play and swing for such a stroke, making sure he is free of interference from the condition when doing so.

The nearest point of relief is the point on the course nearest to where the ball lies (i) that is not nearer the hole, and (ii) where, if the ball was positioned at that point, there would no longer be any interference from the condition, in this case, casual water.

Q What club must a player use to measure and to determine his nearest point of relief?

A In determining the "nearest point of relief" (see the definition of this term) the player should use the club with which he expects to play his next stroke. This is a recommendation, hence the use of the word "should" rather than "must", and the player cannot be penalised purely for failing to follow the recommendation.

However, if a player uses a different club, for example a club with which it would not be at all reasonable to expect the player to play his next stroke, he is in danger of identifying a spot that is not, in fact, his nearest point of relief. If the player does this, he may, as a consequence, drop his ball in a wrong place and, if he plays from there, he will be penalised for playing from a wrong place.

For example, say the player's ball lies 100 yards from the hole and he is standing in casual water. The player is entitled to relief without penalty from the casual water under Rule 25-1. The player should imagine that the casual water is not there and simply select which club he would normally hit with from that position – for example, a pitching wedge. The pitching wedge, therefore, would be the correct club to use in order to accurately determine the nearest point of relief.

On the other hand, in measuring a one- or two club-length dropping area (depending on the Rule), the player may use any club.

Some Rules – for example immovable obstructions (Rule 24-2), abnormal ground conditions (Rule 25-1) – require a player to drop a ball within one club-length of the nearest point of relief. Other Rules, such as unplayable ball (Rule 28), simply require a player to drop a ball within a certain number of club-lengths: in the case of Rule 28c, within two club-lengths of where the ball lies.

THE RULES OF PLAY

▶ RULE 1

THE GAME

DEFINITIONS
All defined terms are in *italics* and are listed in the Definitions section – see pages 13–23.

1-1 General

The Game of Golf consists of playing a ball with a club from the *teeing ground* into the *hole* by a *stroke* or successive *strokes* in accordance with the *Rules*.

1-2 Exerting Influence on Ball

A player or *caddie* must not take any action to influence the position or the movement of a ball except in accordance with the *Rules*.

(Removal of loose impediment – see Rule 23-1)

(Removal of movable obstruction – see Rule 24-1)

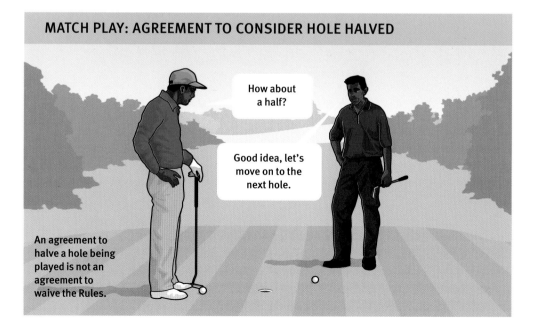

MATCH PLAY: AGREEMENT TO CONSIDER HOLE HALVED

How about a half?

Good idea, let's move on to the next hole.

An agreement to halve a hole being played is not an agreement to waive the Rules.

EQUITY: SOME EXAMPLES

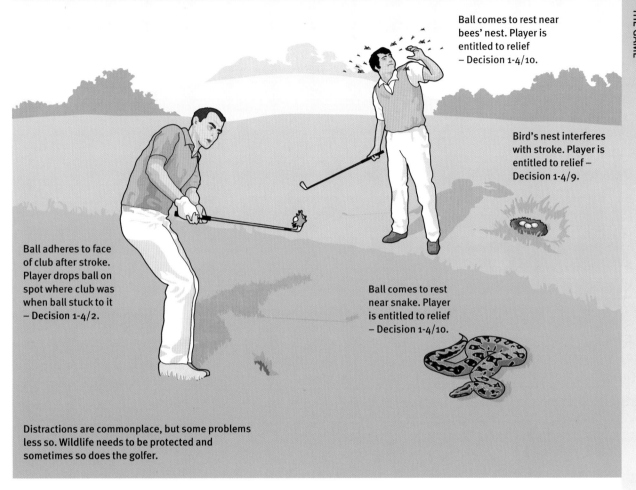

Ball comes to rest near bees' nest. Player is entitled to relief – Decision 1-4/10.

Bird's nest interferes with stroke. Player is entitled to relief – Decision 1-4/9.

Ball adheres to face of club after stroke. Player drops ball on spot where club was when ball stuck to it – Decision 1-4/2.

Ball comes to rest near snake. Player is entitled to relief – Decision 1-4/10.

Distractions are commonplace, but some problems less so. Wildlife needs to be protected and sometimes so does the golfer.

---

* PENALTY
For breach of Rule 1-2:
Match play – Loss of hole;
Stroke play – Two strokes.
* In the case of a serious breach of Rule 1-2, the *Committee* may impose a penalty of disqualification.

NOTE
A player is deemed to have committed a serious breach of Rule 1-2 if the *Committee* considers that his act of influencing the position or movement of the ball has allowed him or another player to gain a significant advantage or has placed another player, other than his *partner*, at a significant disadvantage.

1-3 Agreement to Waive Rules
Players must not agree to exclude the operation of any *Rule* or to waive any penalty incurred.

PENALTY

For breach of Rule 1-3:

Match play – Disqualification of both *sides*;

Stroke play – Disqualification of *competitors* concerned.

(Agreeing to play out of turn in stroke play – see Rule 10-2c)

1-4   Points Not Covered by Rules

If any point in dispute is not covered by the *Rules*, the decision should be made in accordance with equity.

▸ RULE 1

INCIDENT

The 2008 Open Championship at Royal Birkdale was defined by high winds on all four days, which caused a number of wind-related Rules incidents.

On the first day, at the 6th hole, Lee Westwood marked, lifted and replaced his ball on the green, but before he could play his next stroke, the wind blew his ball off the green and down the slope in front of it. Rule 20-3d states that, if a ball – when placed – comes to rest on the spot on which it is placed and subsequently moves, there is no penalty and the ball must be played as it lies, unless the provisions of any other Rule apply. Consequently, Westwood had to play the ball from its new position, off the green, although his mood brightened when he holed the chip shot for a five!

Playing on the third day during the windiest period of the week, Fredrik Jacobson's ball came to rest in a fairway bunker on the left side of the 10th fairway. Before entering the bunker to play his shot, Jacobson observed his ball move on two occasions, both times blown by the wind. In a bunker, a player is deemed to have addressed his ball simply when he has taken his stance, therefore

Jacobson was very concerned about entering the bunker and potentially incurring a penalty (under Rule 18-2b: Ball Moving After Address) should the ball move for a third time once he had entered the bunker and taken his stance.

After discussion with the referee accompanying the game, Jacobson entered the bunker and, having taken his stance, the ball did, in fact, move. Although there is normally a one-stroke penalty if a player's ball moves after he has addressed it (and the ball must be replaced), following further consultation with a roving rules official and David Rickman (Director of Rules, R&A), it was decided that, given the exceptional nature of the circumstances, and the fact that it was absolutely clear that Jacobson's actions had not caused the ball to move, in equity (Rule 1-4), no penalty would be applied and the ball would be played from its new position.

▸ RULE 1

FREQUENTLY ASKED QUESTION

Q What does the term "Equity" mean?

A Equity means to treat like situations alike. Some situations are not covered by the Rules of Golf, thus the decision must be made according to what is fair under the Rules. Equity is not a substitute for the proper application of a Rule, however.

▶ RULE 2

MATCH PLAY

2-1 General

A match consists of one *side* playing against another over a *stipulated round* unless otherwise decreed by the *Committee*.

In match play the game is played by holes.

Except as otherwise provided in the *Rules*, a hole is won by the *side* that *holes* its ball in the fewer *strokes*. In a handicap match, the lower net score wins the hole.

The state of the match is expressed by the terms: so many "holes up" or "all square", and so many "to play".

A *side* is "dormie" when it is as many holes up as there are holes remaining to be played.

2-2 Halved Hole

A hole is halved if each *side holes* out in the same number of *strokes*.

When a player has *holed* out and his opponent has been left with a *stroke* for the half, if the player subsequently incurs a penalty, the hole is halved.

DEFINITIONS

All defined terms are in *italics* and are listed in the Definitions section – see pages 13–23.

WINNER OF THE MATCH: HOLE BY HOLE PLAY-OFF

Good putt. That squares the match. We'll have to go back to the 1st for a sudden death play-off.

No. We started this match at the 10th hole, so that is our first extra hole. As before you'll get your handicap stroke.

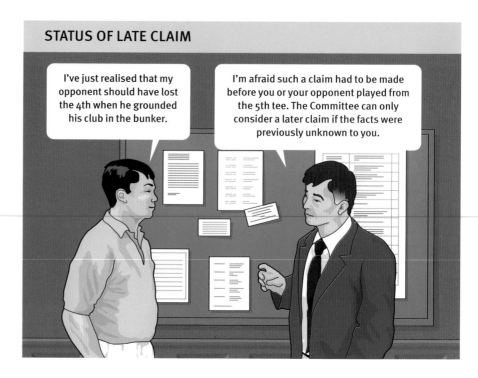

2-3 Winner of Match

A match is won when one *side* leads by a number of holes greater than the number remaining to be played.

If there is a tie, the *Committee* may extend the *stipulated round* by as many holes as are required for a match to be won.

2-4 Concession of Match, Hole or Next Stroke

A player may concede a match at any time prior to the start or conclusion of that match.

A player may concede a hole at any time prior to the start or conclusion of that hole.

A player may concede his opponent's next *stroke* at any time, provided the opponent's ball is at rest. The opponent is considered to have *holed* out with his next *stroke,* and the ball may be removed by either *side*.

A concession may not be declined or withdrawn.

(Ball overhanging hole – see Rule 16-2)

2-5 Doubt as to Procedure; Disputes and Claims

In match play, if a doubt or dispute arises between the players, a player may make a claim. If no duly authorised representative of the *Committee* is available within a reasonable time, the players must continue the match without delay. The *Committee* may consider a claim only if the player making the claim notifies his opponent (i) that he is making a claim, (ii) of the facts of the situation and (iii) that he wants a ruling. The claim must be made before any player in the match plays from the next *teeing ground* or, in the case of the last hole of the match, before all players in the match leave the *putting green*.

A later claim may not be considered by the *Committee*, unless it is based on facts previously unknown to the player making the claim and he had been given wrong information (Rules 6-2a and 9) by an opponent.

Once the result of the match has been officially announced, a later claim may not be considered by the *Committee*, unless it is satisfied that the opponent knew he was giving wrong information.

2-6 General Penalty

The penalty for a breach of a *Rule* in match play is loss of hole except when otherwise provided.

▶ RULE 2

INCIDENT

Jack Nicklaus' concession of Tony Jacklin's putt on the final hole during the final match of the 1969 Ryder Cup resulted in the event's first tie, and is hailed as one of golf's finest acts of sportsmanship.

Going into the final day's competition at Royal Birkdale Golf Club in Southport, England, the United States and Great Britain & Ireland were even at eight points apiece. That morning's singles matches resulted in a two-point lead for Great Britain & Ireland but the US responded in the afternoon to leave the matches tied at 15 points each with only the final match of Nicklaus and Jacklin still on the course. Eighteen of the 32 Ryder Cup matches went

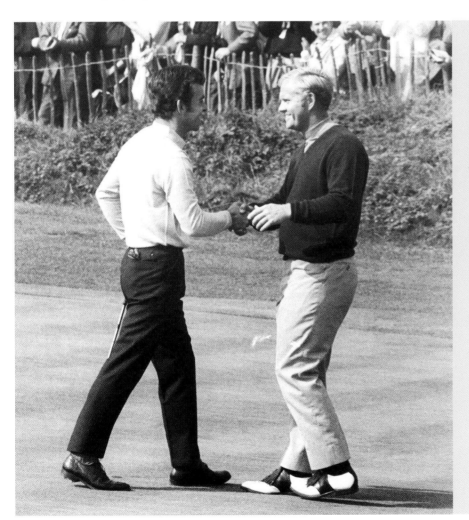

Tony Jacklin and Jack Nicklaus shake hands on the 18th green during the 1969 Ryder Cup at Royal Birkdale. The result of the overall match between Great Britain & Ireland and the United States had come down to the very last putt of the very last match. Sensing the importance of the moment Nicklaus conceded Jacklin's putt, resulting in the first tie in Ryder Cup history.

to the final hole that year, and it was there that the three-day competition would be ultimately decided.

Nicklaus seemed to have the upper hand as Jacklin fell behind on the back nine but the reigning Open champion Jacklin would not relent. Indeed, he eagled the 17th to go all square with Nicklaus.

At the par-5 18th, Jacklin missed his putt for birdie. Nicklaus holed his four-footer for par leaving Jacklin with a short putt to tie Nicklaus. If he holed the putt it would be a tie but a miss by Jacklin would result in an outright win by the Americans.

Before Jacklin could putt, Nicklaus conceded the Englishman's putt thereby ensuring a tie. "I don't think you would have missed that Tony," Nicklaus reportedly said, "but under these circumstances I'd never give you the opportunity."

"The length of the putt has varied after thirty years," Jacklin has stated recently to reporters. "It's been as long as four feet. But my recollection is 20 inches. Of course, I could have missed it; there are no guarantees in golf, especially in the crucible of the Ryder Cup, but I believe I would have made it. But Jack saw the big picture, two months before I had become the first British player in 18 years to win The Open, so there was very much a pro-British fervour at the Ryder Cup in England that year. Jack saw that the putt on the last hole in 1969 meant a heck of a lot more to the Ryder Cup than who won or lost that particular match. It was a great moment."

▶ RULE 2
FREQUENTLY ASKED QUESTION

Q In match play, if you are unsure how to proceed, can you play a second ball?
A No. If a member of the Committee is not available, you must continue the match without delay by proceeding in the manner that you believe is in line with the Rules.

If your opponent disagrees with this, the opponent can make a claim. The claim must be made before either player plays from the next tee or, in the case of the last hole of the match, before all players leave the putting green (Rule 2-5).

▶ RULE 3
STROKE PLAY

DEFINITIONS
All defined terms are in *italics* and are listed in the Definitions section – see pages 13–23.

3-1   General; Winner

A stroke play competition consists of *competitors* completing each hole of a *stipulated round* or rounds and, for each round, returning a score card on which there is a gross score for each hole. Each *competitor* is playing against every other *competitor* in the competition.

The competitor who plays the *stipulated round* or rounds in the fewest *strokes* is the winner.

In a handicap competition, the *competitor* with the lowest net score for the *stipulated round* or rounds is the winner.

3-2   Failure to Hole Out

If a *competitor* fails to hole out at any hole and does not correct his mistake before he makes a *stroke* on the next *teeing ground* or, in the case of the last hole of the round, before he leaves the *putting green*, **he is disqualified.**

DOUBT AS TO PROCEDURE IN STROKE PLAY

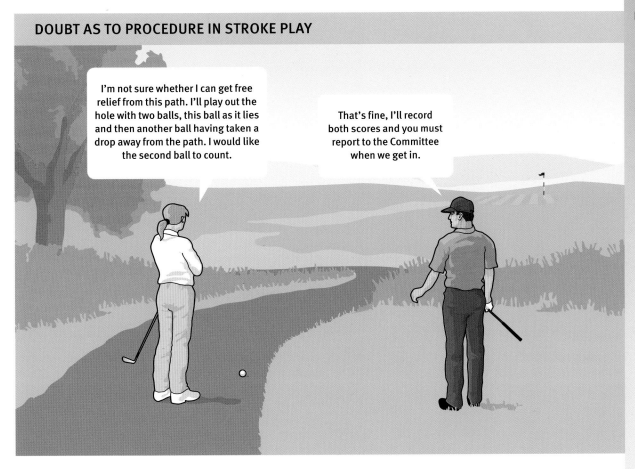

3-3 Doubt as to Procedure

3-3 a Procedure

In stroke play, if a *competitor* is doubtful of his rights or the correct procedure during the play of a hole, he may, without penalty, complete the hole with two balls.

After the doubtful situation has arisen and before taking further action, the *competitor* must announce to his *marker* or *fellow-competitor* that he intends to play two balls and which ball he wishes to count if the *Rules* permit.

The *competitor* must report the facts of the situation to the *Committee* before returning his score card. If he fails to do so, **he is disqualified.**

> **NOTE**
>
> If the *competitor* takes further action before dealing with the doubtful situation, Rule 3-3 is not applicable. The score with the original ball counts or, if the original ball is not one of the balls being played, the score with the first ball put into play counts, even if the *Rules* do not allow the procedure adopted for that ball. However, the *competitor* incurs no penalty for having played a second ball, and any *penalty strokes* incurred solely by playing that ball do not count in his score.

3-3 b Determination of Score for Hole

(i)   If the ball that the *competitor* selected in advance to count has been played in accordance with the *Rules*, the score with that ball is the *competitor's* score for the hole. Otherwise, the score with the other ball counts if the *Rules* allow the procedure adopted for that ball.

(ii)   If the *competitor* fails to announce in advance his decision to complete the hole with two balls, or which ball he wishes to count, the score with the original ball counts, provided it has been played in accordance with the *Rules*. If the original ball is not one of the balls being played, the first ball put into play counts, provided it has been played in accordance with the *Rules*. Otherwise, the score with the other ball counts if the *Rules* allow the procedure adopted for that ball.

NOTE 1
If a *competitor* plays a second ball under Rule 3-3, the *strokes* made after this Rule has been invoked with the ball ruled not to count and *penalty strokes* incurred solely by playing that ball are disregarded.
NOTE 2
A second ball played under Rule 3-3 is not a *provisional ball* under Rule 27-2.

3-4   Refusal to Comply with a Rule
If a *competitor* refuses to comply with a *Rule* affecting the rights of another *competitor*, he is disqualified.

3-5   General Penalty
The penalty for a breach of a *Rule* in stroke play is two strokes except when otherwise provided.

► RULE 4
CLUBS

DEFINITIONS
All defined terms are in *italics* and are listed in the Definitions section – see pages 13–23.

A player in doubt as to the conformity of a club should consult the *R&A*.

A manufacturer should submit to the *R&A* a sample of a club to be manufactured for a ruling as to whether the club conforms with the *Rules*. The sample becomes the property of the *R&A* for reference purposes. If a manufacturer fails to submit a sample or, having submitted a sample, fails to await a ruling before manufacturing and/or marketing the club, the manufacturer assumes the risk of a ruling that the club does not conform with the *Rules*.

4-1   Form and Make of Clubs
4-1 a   General
The player's clubs must conform with this Rule and the provisions, specifications and interpretations set forth in Appendix II.

NOTE
The *Committee* may require, in the conditions of a competition (Rule 33-1), that any driver the player carries must have a clubhead, identified by model and loft, that is named on the current List of Conforming Driver Heads issued by the *R&A*.

NON-CONFORMING CLUB CARRIED BUT NOT USED

4-1 b Wear and Alteration

A club that conforms with the *Rules* when new is deemed to conform after wear
through normal use. Any part of a club that has been purposely altered is regarded as
new and must, in its altered state, conform with the *Rules*.

4-2 Playing Characteristics Changed and Foreign Material

4-2 a Playing Characteristics Changed

During a *stipulated round*, the playing characteristics of a club must not be purposely
changed by adjustment or by any other means.

4-2 b Foreign Material

Foreign material must not be applied to the club face for the purpose of influencing
the movement of the ball.

---

* PENALTY

**For carrying, but not making stroke with, club or clubs in breach of Rule
4-1 or 4-2:**

Match play – At the conclusion of the hole at which the breach is discovered,
the state of the match is adjusted by deducting one hole for each hole at which
a breach occurred; maximum deduction per round – Two holes.

Stroke play – Two strokes for each hole at which any breach occurred;
maximum penalty per round – Four strokes.

Match or stroke play – In the event of a breach between the play of two holes,
the penalty applies to the next hole.

33

Bogey and par competitions – See Note 1 to Rule 32-1a.

Stableford competitions – See Note 1 to Rule 32-1b.

* Any club or clubs carried in breach of Rule 4-1 or 4-2 must be declared out of play by the player to his opponent in match play or his *marker* or a *fellow-competitor* in stroke play immediately upon discovery that a breach has occurred. If the player fails to do so, he is disqualified.

For making stroke with club in breach of Rule 4-1 or 4-2: Disqualification.

4-3   Damaged Clubs: Repair and Replacement

4-3 a   Damage in Normal Course of Play

If, during a *stipulated round*, a player's club is damaged in the normal course of play, he may:

(i)   use the club in its damaged state for the remainder of the *stipulated round*; or

(ii)   without unduly delaying play, repair it or have it repaired; or

(iii)   as an additional option available only if the club is unfit for play, replace the damaged club with any club. The replacement of a club must not unduly delay play and must not be made by borrowing any club selected for play by any other person playing on the *course*.

PENALTY

For breach of Rule 4-3a:

See Penalty Statement for Rule 4-4a or b, and Rule 4-4c.

CLUB UNFIT FOR PLAY

If a player's club is damaged in the normal course of play (e.g. in playing a stroke or accidentally dropping it), the player may, without unduly delaying play, repair it or have it repaired or, if the club is unfit for play, replace the damaged club with any club. However, he may not borrow a club being used by anyone playing on the course.

When a club is damaged other than in the normal course of play, rendering it non-conforming or changing its playing characteristics, it may not be used during the remainder of the round.

At the 2008 WGC-CA Championship at Doral, after missing an eight-foot putt for par at the 14th, and when walking to the 15th tee, Ian Poulter's putter smacked against a cart path, knocking loose a weight bar on the back of it. As his putter was not damaged in the normal course of play, Poulter was not allowed to use the putter again during his round. Poulter spent the rest of the round putting with his wedge.

"It was one of those things," he said. "Dropped my putter on the path, probably a little bit of frustration. I guess concrete and metal don't really mix too well."

BREACH OF FOURTEEN-CLUB RULE IN MATCH PLAY

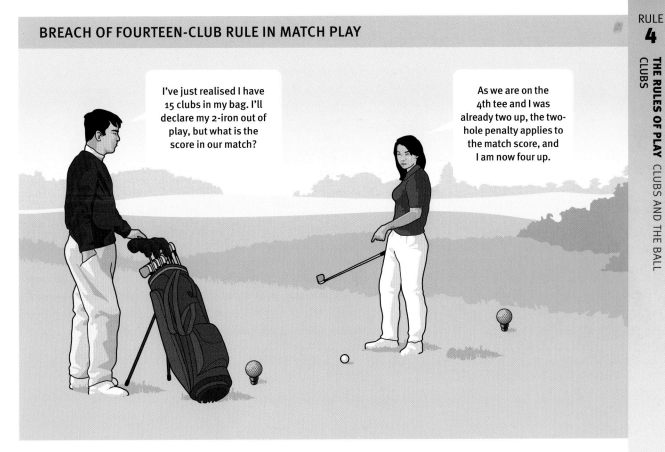

NOTE

A club is unfit for play if it is substantially damaged, e.g. the shaft is dented, significantly bent or breaks into pieces; the clubhead becomes loose, detached or significantly deformed; or the grip becomes loose. A club is not unfit for play solely because the club's lie or loft has been altered, or the clubhead is scratched.

4-3 b Damage Other Than in Normal Course of Play

If, during a *stipulated round*, a player's club is damaged other than in the normal course of play rendering it non-conforming or changing its playing characteristics, the club must not subsequently be used or replaced during the round.

4-3 c Damage Prior to Round

A player may use a club damaged prior to a round, provided the club, in its damaged state, conforms with the *Rules*.

Damage to a club that occurred prior to a round may be repaired during the round, provided the playing characteristics are not changed and play is not unduly delayed.

PENALTY

For breach of Rule 4-3b or c:

Disqualification.

(Undue delay – see Rule 6-7)

4-4 Maximum of Fourteen Clubs

4-4 a Selection and Addition of Clubs

The player must not start a *stipulated round* with more than fourteen clubs. He is limited to the clubs thus selected for that round except that, if he started with fewer than fourteen clubs, he may add any number, provided his total number does not exceed fourteen.

The addition of a club or clubs must not unduly delay play (Rule 6-7) and the player must not add or borrow any club selected for play by any other person playing on the *course*.

4-4 b Partners May Share Clubs

Partners may share clubs, provided that the total number of clubs carried by the *partners* so sharing does not exceed fourteen.

PENALTY
For breach of Rule 4-4a or b, regardless of number of excess clubs carried:
Match play – At the conclusion of the hole at which the breach is discovered, the state of the match is adjusted by deducting one hole for each hole at which a breach occurred; maximum deduction per round – Two holes.
Stroke play – Two strokes for each hole at which any breach occurred; maximum penalty per round – Four strokes.
Bogey and par competitions – See Note 1 to Rule 32-1a.
Stableford competitions – See Note 1 to Rule 32-1b.

4-4 c Excess Club Declared Out of Play

Any club or clubs carried or used in breach of Rule 4-3a(iii) or Rule 4-4 must be declared out of play by the player to his opponent in match play or his *marker* or a *fellow-competitor* in stroke play immediately upon discovery that a breach has occurred. The player must not use the club or clubs for the remainder of the *stipulated round*.

PENALTY
For breach of Rule 4-4c:
Disqualification.

▶ RULE 4

INCIDENTS

In the 2001 Open Championship at Royal Lytham & St Annes, Ian Woosnam played his tee shot at the par-3 1st hole to six inches. Having started the final round as joint leader, he then tapped in for what appeared to be a birdie two – a fantastic start.

Standing on the 2nd tee, Woosnam's caddie, Miles Byrne, turned to Woosnam and said, "You're going to go ballistic. We have 15 clubs." On the practice ground Woosnam had been testing two drivers and, rushing from the practice ground to the 1st tee, he had not counted his clubs to ensure that he had no more than the stipulated 14. So, under Rule 4-4, Ian Woosnam incurred a two-stroke penalty at the 1st hole and his birdie two became a bogey four. "I felt like I'd been kicked in the teeth," he said afterwards.

It can only be guessed how the penalty affected Woosnam's game. We do know, however, that Woosnam finished in a tie for third place on a score of 278. If he had

Ian Woosnam is informed by the Referee in his game, John Paramor (Chief Referee, European Tour), that the penalty for carrying 15 clubs is two strokes. A player is only permitted to carry a maximum of 14 clubs under Rule 4-4a.

finished on 276 he would have achieved second place on his own and be £220,000 the richer, and he would have qualified for the European team for the 34th Ryder Cup.

During the third round of the 2008 HSBC Champions in Shanghai, Anthony Kim was disqualified for making a stroke with a club that had been damaged other than in the normal course of play.

After teeing off on the 7th hole, the player was walking with his driver in hand and hit the toe of the club on a sprinkler head. When he used the driver on the next tee, he only hit the ball 150 yards, and out of bounds. When he hit his provisional very poorly, he realised that there was something wrong with the club and consulted with Andy McFee, Senior Referee on the European Tour. The Referee explained to Kim that he had no way of knowing if the club had been damaged, but he said to the player, "If you tell me that the club has been damaged and that is how you did it, it is a disqualification."

Rule 4-3b provides that if, during a round, a player's club is damaged other than in the normal course of

play, and this changes its playing characteristics, the club must not subsequently be used or replaced during the round.

The term "normal course of play" envisages making a stroke, practice swing or practice stroke, and also includes acts such as removing or replacing a club in a bag, leaning on a club or accidentally dropping a club. However, Decisions 4-3/1 and 4-3/9 confirm that acts such as throwing a club, intentionally hitting something with a club (other than during a stroke, practice swing or practice stroke), and hitting or tapping a club on the ground are not considered to be in the normal course of play.

When Kim confirmed that the club had definitely been altered, and that this must have occurred when he hit the club on the sprinkler head, McFee had no option but to disqualify the player for his breach of the Rule.

Another Rule 4 incident occurred at the 2006 Ryder Cup during Tiger Woods' singles match against Robert Karlsson. At the 7th hole Woods' caddie, Steve Williams,

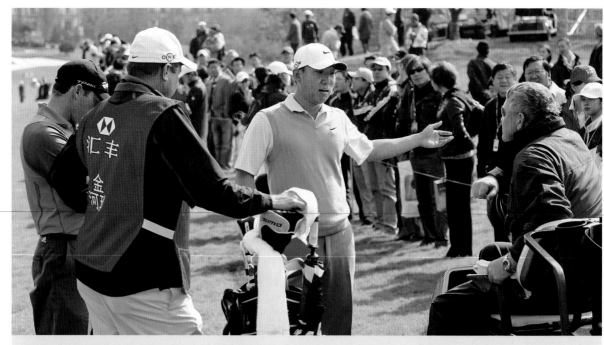

Anthony Kim explains that he believes his club has been damaged and its playing characteristics changed as a result. Unfortunately for Kim, the fact that he had used the club in its damaged state resulted in his disqualification (Rule 4-3b).

slipped on a rock while trying to dip his towel in a water hazard near the green. As a result, the 9-iron he was holding slipped out of his hand and dropped into the depths of the water.

A club that has become damaged in the normal course of play and, as a result, has become unfit for play, can be replaced during the round, provided the replacement does not delay play and the replacement club is not borrowed from any other person playing the course (Rule 4-3a). The term "damaged in the normal course of play" includes a club that has been damaged as a result of being dropped (Decision 4-3/1).

However, in Woods' case, the club had not actually been damaged at all and, therefore, Rule 4-3a was not

applicable. The club was, in fact, lost and Decision 4-3/10 confirms that, if a player starts the round with 14 clubs and then manages to lose one of his clubs, he is not entitled to replace that club.

If Woods had decided that the club was too important to leave in the water, he could have tried to retrieve it or have someone attempt to retrieve it for him, but he would have been required to continue play without delay. The five-minute search period that applies to a ball that cannot be found does not apply to a club. Woods continued play with his remaining 13 clubs and his 9-iron was returned to him when playing the 15th hole after a diver had retrieved it.

▶ RULE 4
FREQUENTLY ASKED QUESTION

Q Can a player play with both right-handed and left-handed clubs?

A The Rules of Golf do not restrict a player in his choice of clubs in terms of whether they are left-handed or right-handed. The player may select up to 14 clubs (the maximum permitted under Rule 4-4) and they can

consist of right- and left-handed clubs. For example, some players prefer to play right-handed, but will putt left-handed, and so carry a left-handed putter. This is permitted by the Rules provided the total number of clubs selected does not exceed 14 and all clubs conform to the Rules.

Tiger Woods looks on in dismay as his 9-iron slips out of the grasp of his caddie and into the water at the 7th hole at the K Club. The club was returned to him on the 15th hole.

► RULE 5
THE BALL

5-1 General

The ball the player plays must conform to the requirements specified in Appendix III.

DEFINITIONS
All defined terms are in *italics* and are listed in the Definitions section – see pages 13–23.

NOTE

The *Committee* may require, in the conditions of a competition (Rule 33-1), that the ball the player plays must be named on the current List of Conforming Golf Balls issued by the *R&A*.

5-2 Foreign Material

Foreign material must not be applied to a ball for the purpose of changing its playing characteristics.

PENALTY

For breach of Rule 5-1 or 5-2:
Disqualification.

5-3 Ball Unfit for Play

A ball is unfit for play if it is visibly cut, cracked or out of shape. A ball is not unfit for play solely because mud or other materials adhere to it, its surface is scratched or scraped or its paint is damaged or discoloured.

If a player has reason to believe his ball has become unfit for play during play of the hole being played, he may lift the ball, without penalty, to determine whether it is unfit.

Before lifting the ball, the player must announce his intention to his opponent in match play or his *marker* or a *fellow-competitor* in stroke play and mark the position of the ball. He may then lift and examine it, provided that he gives his opponent, *marker* or *fellow-competitor* an opportunity to examine the ball and observe the lifting and replacement. The ball must not be cleaned when lifted under Rule 5-3.

If the player fails to comply with all or any part of this procedure, or if he lifts the ball without having reason to believe that it has become unfit to play during play of the hole being played, **he incurs a penalty of one stroke**.

If it is determined that the ball has become unfit for play during play of the hole being played, the player may *substitute* another ball, placing it on the spot where the original ball lay. Otherwise, the original ball must be replaced. If a player *substitutes* a ball when not permitted and makes a *stroke* at the wrongly *substituted ball*, **he incurs the general penalty for a breach of Rule 5-3**, but there is no additional penalty under this Rule or Rule 15-2.

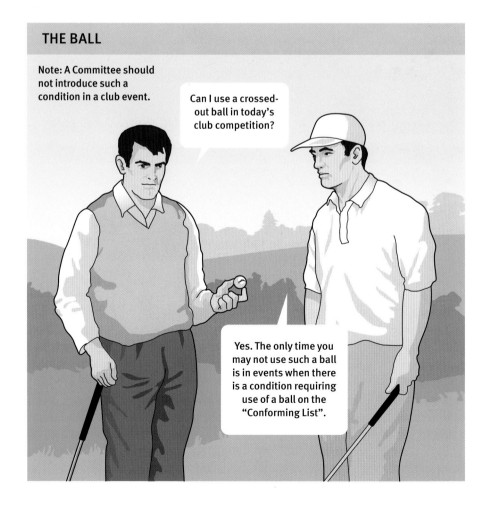

THE BALL

Note: A Committee should not introduce such a condition in a club event.

Can I use a crossed-out ball in today's club competition?

Yes. The only time you may not use such a ball is in events when there is a condition requiring use of a ball on the "Conforming List".

BALL UNFIT FOR PLAY

If a ball breaks into pieces as a result of a *stroke*, the *stroke* is cancelled and the player must play a ball, without penalty, as nearly as possible at the spot from which the original ball was played (see Rule 20-5).

---

* PENALTY
For breach of Rule 5-3:
Match play – Loss of hole;
Stroke play – Two strokes.
* If a player incurs the general penalty for a breach of Rule 5-3, there is no additional penalty under this Rule.

NOTE 1
If the opponent, *marker* or *fellow-competitor* wishes to dispute a claim of unfitness, he must do so before the player plays another ball.
NOTE 2
If the original lie of a ball to be placed or replaced has been altered, see Rule 20–3b.
(Cleaning ball lifted from putting green or under any other Rule – see Rule 21)

▶ RULE 5

INCIDENT

At most top-level professional events, the Committee introduces a condition of competition known as the "One Ball Condition" (Appendix I, Part C, 1c). This condition prevents a player from changing brands and models of golf balls during a stipulated round, and is intended to prevent a player from seeking to gain an advantage by using balls with different performance characteristics on different holes – for example, a hard ball on longer holes and a soft ball on shorter holes. In addition, a condition is introduced that requires players to play a ball that is named on the List of Conforming Golf Balls (Appendix I, Part C, 1b). This List contains all the balls that have been tested and found to conform to the Rules of Golf.

At the Second Stage of the 2008 PGA Tour Qualifying Tournament, during play of the 12th hole of his first round, JP Hayes realised that he was playing a different type of ball than the one he started the round with (same brand, but different type). He called for a ruling, and it was determined that he had breached the One Ball Condition, incurring a two-stroke penalty on that hole.

Later in the evening, Hayes was thinking about how the ball came to be in his bag, causing this incident to happen, and it then occurred to him that the ball might have been a prototype ball. He phoned the officials and the next morning it was determined, after reviewing the ball, that it was not listed on the List of Conforming Golf Balls. This meant that Hayes was disqualified from the event, and lost his tour card for 2009.

Hayes admits to being overly pedantic about his equipment and he commented, "I go through my bag every night. I want to know what's in there. It's almost therapeutic for me." But this time, Hayes missed one ball. The prototype should have been easy to spot because, while it bore the manufacturer's brand name, there was no label on the "seam" to identify the model.

When asked about calling the penalty on himself and then taking it another step and volunteering information that got him disqualified, Hayes said, "I would say everybody out here (on the PGA Tour) would have done the same thing."

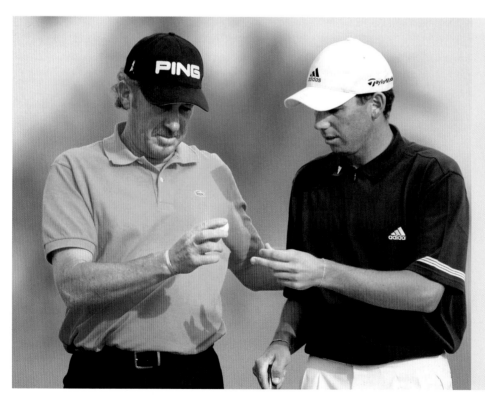

The player must give his opponent, marker or fellow-competitor an opportunity to inspect a ball that he believes is unfit for play. In some cases, a Referee may be asked to participate in this process.

► RULE 5
FREQUENTLY ASKED QUESTIONS

Q Can I use an "x-out", "refurbished" or "practice" ball to play a round of golf?

A "X-out' is the common name used for a golf ball that a manufacturer considers to be imperfect (usually for aesthetic reasons only: for example, paint or printing errors) and, therefore, has crossed out the brand name. A "refurbished" golf ball is a second-hand ball that has been cleaned and stamped as "refurbished".

In the absence of strong evidence to suggest that an "x-out" or "refurbished" ball does not conform to the Rules, it is permissible for such a ball to be used. However, in a competition where the Committee has adopted the condition that the ball the player uses must be named on the List of Conforming Golf Balls (see Note to Rule 5-1), such a ball may not be used, even if the ball in question (without the "x"s or without the "refurbished" stamp) does appear on the List.

In most cases, "practice" balls are simply listed conforming golf balls that have been stamped "PRACTICE" (for example, just like a ball with a golf club's logo). Such balls may be used even where the Committee has adopted the condition that the ball the player uses must be named on the List of Conforming Golf Balls.

Q May a player borrow golf balls from an opponent or fellow-competitor if he runs out of golf balls during the round?

A The Rules of Golf do not prevent a player from borrowing a golf ball from another player on the course. The Rules only limit the borrowing of clubs and not golf balls.

Q What is the status of a ball that is not included on the List of Conforming Golf Balls?

A Ball types or models that do not appear on the current List of Conforming Golf Balls fall into the following three categories:

1. models that have never been submitted for testing by the manufacturer,

2. models that have appeared on a previous List, but have not been re-submitted for inclusion on the current List, and

3. models that have been tested and found not to conform to the Rules and specifications set forth in Appendix III.

Balls in categories 1 and 2 are presumed to conform, unless there is strong evidence to suggest that they do not. All models in category 3 are deemed to be non-conforming.

► RULE 6
THE PLAYER

DEFINITIONS
All defined terms are in *italics* and are listed in the Definitions section – see pages 13–23.

6-1 Rules
The player and his *caddie* are responsible for knowing the *Rules*. During a *stipulated round*, for any breach of a *Rule* by his *caddie*, the player incurs the applicable penalty.

6-2 Handicap
6-2 a Match Play
Before starting a match in a handicap competition, the players should determine from one another their respective handicaps. If a player begins a match having declared a handicap higher than that to which he is entitled and this affects the number of strokes given or received, **he is disqualified**; otherwise, the player must play off the declared handicap.

6-2 b Stroke Play

In any round of a handicap competition, the *competitor* must ensure that his handicap is recorded on his score card before it is returned to the *Committee*. If no handicap is recorded on his score card before it is returned (Rule 6-6b), or if the recorded handicap is higher than that to which he is entitled and this affects the number of strokes received, **he is disqualified** from the handicap competition; otherwise, the score stands.

> **NOTE**
> It is the player's responsibility to know the holes at which handicap strokes are to be given or received.

6-3 Time of Starting and Groups

6-3 a Time of Starting

The player must start at the time established by the *Committee*.

6-3 b Groups

In stroke play, the *competitor* must remain throughout the round in the group arranged by the *Committee,* unless the *Committee* authorises or ratifies a change.

> **PENALTY**
> **For breach of Rule 6-3:**
> Disqualification
> (Best-ball and four-ball play – see Rules 30-3a and 31-2)

> **NOTE**
> The *Committee* may provide, in the conditions of a competition (Rule 33-1), that if the player arrives at his starting point, ready to play, within five minutes after his starting time, in the absence of circumstances that warrant waiving the penalty of disqualification as provided in Rule 33-7, the penalty for failure to start on time is **loss of the first hole in match play or two strokes at the first hole in stroke play** instead of disqualification.

6-4 Caddie

The player may be assisted by a *caddie,* but he is limited to only one *caddie* at any one time.

> **PENALTY**
> **For breach of Rule 6-4:**
> **Match play** – At the conclusion of the hole at which the breach is discovered, the state of the match is adjusted by deducting one hole for each hole at which a breach occurred; maximum deduction per round – Two holes.
> **Stroke play** – Two strokes for each hole at which any breach occurred; maximum penalty per round – Four strokes.
> **Match or stroke play** – In the event of a breach between the play of two holes, the penalty applies to the next hole. A player having more than one *caddie* in breach of this Rule must immediately upon discovery that a breach has occurred ensure that he has no more than one *caddie* at any one time during the remainder of the *stipulated round*. Otherwise, the player is disqualified.

Bogey and par competitions – See Note 1 to Rule 32-1a.
Stableford competitions – See Note 1 to Rule 32-1b.

NOTE

The *Committee* may, in the conditions of a competition (Rule 33-1), prohibit the use of *caddies* or restrict a player in his choice of *caddie*.

6-5   Ball

The responsibility for playing the proper ball rests with the player. Each player should put an identification mark on his ball.

6-6   Scoring in Stroke Play

6-6 a   Recording Scores

After each hole the *marker* should check the score with the *competitor* and record it. On completion of the round the *marker* must sign the score card and hand it to the *competitor*. If more than one *marker* records the scores, each must sign for the part for which he is responsible.

6-6 b   Signing and Returning Score Card

After completion of the round, the *competitor* should check his score for each hole and settle any doubtful points with the *Committee*.

He must ensure that the *marker* or markers have signed the score card, sign the score card himself and return it to the *Committee* as soon as possible.

PENALTY

For breach of Rule 6-6b:

Disqualification.

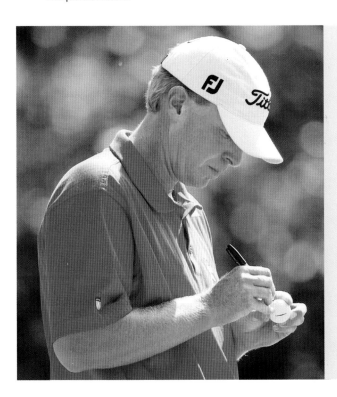

Steve Stricker puts an identification mark on his ball, as the responsibility for playing the proper ball rests with the player.

6-6 c   Alteration of Score Card

No alteration may be made on a score card after the *competitor* has returned it to the *Committee*.

6-6 d   Wrong Score for Hole

The *competitor* is responsible for the correctness of the score recorded for each hole on his score card. If he returns a score for any hole lower than actually taken, **he is disqualified**. If he returns a score for any hole higher than actually taken, the score as returned stands.

NOTE 1

The *Committee* is responsible for the addition of scores and application of the handicap recorded on the score card – see Rule 33-5.

NOTE 2

In *four-ball* stroke play, see also Rule 31-3 and 31-7a.

6-7   Undue Delay; Slow Play

The player must play without undue delay and in accordance with any pace of play guidelines that the *Committee* may establish. Between completion of a hole and playing from the next *teeing ground*, the player must not unduly delay play.

UNDUE DELAY: ENTERING CLUBHOUSE

COMPETITION **SPRING STROKE PLAY**   DATE **14 . 6 . 09**

PLAYER **D. BROWN**   HANDICAP **10**   Game No **21**

Hole	Yards	Par	Stroke Index	Score	W=+ L=- H=0 POINTS	Mar Score	Hole	Yards	Par	Stroke Index	Score	W=+ L=- H=0 POINTS	Mar Score
1	312	4	17	5		6	10	369	4	12	̶6̶5	c	
2	446	4	1	4		4	11	433	4	2	3		
3	310	4	13	4		3	12	361	4	14	4		
4	370	4	9	5	b	5	13	415	4	6	5		
5	478	5	3	6			14	155	3	16	6		
̶6̶7	429	4	11	4			15	338	4	8	5		
̶7̶6	385	4	5	3			16	316	4	10	4		
8	178	3	7	4			17	191	3	4	5		
9	354	4	15	6			18	508	5	18	7		
OUT	3262			41			IN	3086	35		44		
							OUT	3262	36		41		
							TOTAL	6348	71		85		
							HANDICAP				10		
							NETT				75	d	

a

Markers Signature **D. B.**   e & f

Players Signature **Bill White**

Competitor's Responsibilities:

1 To record the correct handicap somewhere on the score card before it is returned to the Committee.
2 To check the gross score recorded for each hole is correct.
3 To ensure that the marker has signed the card and to countersign the card himself before it is returned to the Committee.

Committee Responsibilities:

1 Issue to each competitor a score card containing the date and the competitor's name.
2 To add the scores for each hole and apply the handicap recorded on the card.

Points to Note:

(a) Hole numbers may be altered if hole scores have been recorded in the wrong boxes.
(b) A marker need not keep a record of his own score, however it is recommended.
(c) There is nothing in the Rules that requires an alteration to be initialled.
(d) The competitor is responsible only for the correctness of the score recorded for each hole. If the competitor records a wrong total score or net score, the Committee must correct the error, without penalty to the competitor. In this instance, the Committee have added the scores for each hole and applied the handicap.
(e) There is no penalty if a marker signs the competitor's score card in the space provided for the competitor's signature, and the competitor then signs in the space provided for the marker's signature.
(f) The initialling of the score card by the competitor is sufficient for the purpose of countersignature.

DISCONTINUANCE OF PLAY

Stroke play

Match play

PENALTY

For breach of Rule 6-7:

Match play – Loss of hole;

Stroke play – Two strokes.

Bogey and par competitions – See Note 2 to Rule 32-1a.

Stableford competitions – See Note 2 to Rule 32-1b.

For subsequent offence – Disqualification.

NOTE 1

If the player unduly delays play between holes, he is delaying the play of the next hole and, except for bogey, par and Stableford competitions (see Rule 32), the penalty applies to that hole.

NOTE 2

For the purpose of preventing slow play, the *Committee* may, in the conditions of a competition (Rule 33-1), establish pace of play guidelines including maximum periods of time allowed to complete a *stipulated round*, a hole or a *stroke*. In stroke play only, the *Committee* may, in such a condition, modify the penalty for a breach of this Rule as follows:

First offence – One stroke;

Second offence – Two strokes.

For subsequent offence – Disqualification.

6-8 Discontinuance of Play; Resumption of Play

6-8 a When Permitted

The player must not discontinue play unless:

(i) the *Committee* has suspended play;

(ii) he believes there is danger from lightning;

(iii) he is seeking a decision from the *Committee* on a doubtful or disputed point (see Rules 2-5 and 34-3); or

(iv) there is some other good reason such as sudden illness.

Bad weather is not of itself a good reason for discontinuing play.

If the player discontinues play without specific permission from the *Committee*, he must report to the *Committee* as soon as practicable. If he does so and the *Committee* considers his reason satisfactory, there is no penalty. Otherwise, **the player is disqualified.**

Exception

In match play: Players discontinuing match play by agreement are not subject to disqualification, unless by so doing the competition is delayed.

NOTE

Leaving the *course* does not of itself constitute discontinuance of play.

6-8 b   Procedure When Play Suspended by Committee

When play is suspended by the *Committee*, if the players in a match or group are between the play of two holes, they must not resume play until the *Committee* has ordered a resumption of play. If they have started play of a hole, they may discontinue play immediately or continue play of the hole, provided they do so without delay. If the players choose to continue play of the hole, they are permitted to discontinue play before completing it. In any case, play must be discontinued after the hole is completed.

The players must resume play when the *Committee* has ordered a resumption of play.

PENALTY

For breach of Rule 6-8b:

Disqualification.

NOTE

The *Committee* may provide, in the conditions of a competition (Rule 33-1), that in potentially dangerous situations play must be discontinued immediately following a suspension of play by the *Committee*. If a player fails to discontinue play immediately, **he is disqualified,** unless circumstances warrant waiving the penalty as provided in Rule 33-7.

6-8 c   Lifting Ball When Play Discontinued

When a player discontinues play of a hole under Rule 6-8a, he may lift his ball, without penalty, only if the *Committee* has suspended play or there is a good reason to lift it. Before lifting the ball the player must mark its position. If the player discontinues play and lifts his ball without specific permission from the *Committee*, he must, when reporting to the *Committee* (Rule 6-8a), report the lifting of the ball.

If the player lifts the ball without a good reason to do so, fails to mark the position of the ball before lifting it or fails to report the lifting of the ball, **he incurs a penalty of one stroke.**

6-8 d   Procedure When Play Resumed

Play must be resumed from where it was discontinued, even if resumption occurs on a subsequent day. The player must, either before or when play is resumed, proceed as follows:

(i)   if the player has lifted the ball, he must, provided he was entitled to lift it under Rule 6-8c, place the original or a *substituted* ball on the spot from which the original ball was lifted. Otherwise, the original ball must be replaced;

(ii)   if the player has not lifted his ball, he may, provided he was entitled to lift it under Rule 6-8c, lift, clean and replace the ball, or *substitute* a ball, on the spot from which the original ball was lifted. Before lifting the ball he must mark its position; or

(iii) if the player's ball or ball-marker is moved (including by wind or water) while play is discontinued, a ball or ball-marker must be placed on the spot from which the original ball or ball-marker was moved.

NOTE

If the spot where the ball is to be placed is impossible to determine, it must be estimated and the ball placed on the estimated spot. The provisions of Rule 20-3c do not apply.

---

* PENALTY

For breach of Rule 6-8d:

Match play – Loss of hole;

Stroke play – Two strokes.

* If a player incurs the general penalty for a breach of Rule 6-8d, there is no additional penalty under Rule 6-8c.

▶ RULE 6

INCIDENTS

As the ultimate testament to a player's performance on the course in a stroke play competition, the score card must never contain a score lower than actually taken and it must be signed by the competitor, attested by the marker and returned as soon as possible to the Committee. Failure to meet any of these criteria results in disqualification.

Roberto De Vicenzo signed for a higher score than he actually made at the 1968 Masters Tournament, which did not disqualify him but it prevented the Argentinian from forcing a play-off with Bob Goalby.

Playing in front of Goalby on Sunday, De Vicenzo, the reigning Open Champion, sank a five-foot birdie putt on the 17th hole for a three. A bogey at the 18th gave him an 11-under total of 277. Goalby managed a five-footer for par at the 18th for a 66 and another 277.

However, De Vicenzo's fellow-competitor and marker, Tommy Aaron, had mistakenly given De Vicenzo a four at

the 17th rather than the three. De Vicenzo, who had not noticed the mistake at the time, signed and returned the score card, then rushed away from the scorer's table for press interviews. A little later, Aaron noticed the mistake and brought it to the attention of tournament officials.

Augusta National founder Bob Jones searched for a way around the ensuing ruling but none could be found. Once the score card was signed and returned, the decision under the Rules was straightforward: the higher score must stand. Goalby was the Masters Champion.

An hour later, De Vicenzo told the media, "It's my fault. Tommy feels like I feel, very bad. I think the Rule is hard." The day's drama was compounded by the fact that it was De Vincenzo's 45th birthday.

One of the most unfortunate Rules incidents of recent times was the disqualification of Jesper Parnevik and Mark Roe from The 2003 Open at Royal St George's.

A disconsolate Roberto de Vicenzo (left) thinks about "what might have been" after signing for a higher score than he actually took at the 1968 Masters. The winner, Bob Goalby, awaits the presentation of the coveted green jacket.

Parnevik and Roe were handed their own score cards on the 1st tee by the starter in accordance with custom and practice at The Open and consistent with the practice on the PGA European Tour. Unfortunately, the players failed to exchange score cards. This resulted in each player writing the other's score on his own card. After completing their rounds, the players checked the scores they had recorded, signed the score cards, returned them and left the recorder's area.

Rule 6-6d in the Rules of Golf provides that a player is responsible for the correctness of the score recorded for each hole on his score card. If he returns a score for a hole that is lower than actually taken, he is disqualified. At that time, Decision 6-6d/4 stipulated that, if players fail to exchange cards and this results in each player having recorded and signed for at least one score for a hole that is lower than actually taken, both players are disqualified. Therefore, the Committee had no option but to apply the Rule and disqualify Parnevik and Roe.

It was disappointing that such an incident should arise during the third round of The Open, especially for Mark Roe who had played so well that day and would have been playing in one of the final groups on the Sunday.

The R&A stated that the many views expressed by the golfing public on the outcome of the case would form part of The R&A's ongoing review of the Rules of Golf. In 2006, Decision 6-6d/4 was amended to provide that, in the circumstances where the players fail to exchange score cards and, as a result, return score cards that mismatch players' printed names with reported scores, this should be deemed an administrative error on the part of the players that the Committee should simply correct by striking out the printed names and entering the name of the player whose scores are recorded on the card.

Jesper Parnevik and Mark Roe shake hands at the end of their third round at The 2003 Open at Royal St George's. Subsequently, they learned that they had both been disqualified under Rule 6-6d, for inadvertently recording scores on their fellow-competitor's card.

► RULE 6

FREQUENTLY ASKED QUESTIONS

Q Must a player enter his handicap in the box provided on the score card?

A Although under Rule 6-2b a competitor must ensure that his handicap is recorded on his score card before it is returned to the Committee, it does not stipulate where the handicap must be recorded; as long as it appears somewhere on the card, the competitor has fulfilled his duty. Consequently, a competitor cannot be disqualified for failure to record his handicap in the "official" box provided on the score card.

Q Can a player be disqualified for an omission or error in entering his score into a computer?

A The Rules of Golf do not require a competitor to enter scores into a computer. Therefore, a competitor may not be penalised or disqualified under the Rules of Golf if the scores entered into the computer are incorrect, or indeed if he fails to enter these scores. The Committee could, however, impose a disciplinary penalty (for example, ineligibility to enter the next Club competition) under its Club regulations for failure to enter scores into a computer.

Q Can a player be disqualified for not initialling any alterations made on his score card?

A A Committee cannot require that alterations made on score cards be initialled. Consequently, a player should not be disqualified for failure to do so.

► RULE 7

PRACTICE

DEFINITIONS
All defined terms are in *italics* and are listed in the Definitions section – see pages 13–23.

7-1   Before or Between Rounds

7-1 a   Match Play

On any day of a match play competition, a player may practise on the competition *course* before a round.

7-1 b   Stroke Play

Before a round or play-off on any day of a stroke play competition, a *competitor* must not practise on the competition *course* or test the surface of any *putting green* on the *course* by rolling a ball or roughening or scraping the surface.

When two or more rounds of a stroke play competition are to be played over consecutive days, a *competitor* must not practise between those rounds on any competition *course* remaining to be played, or test the surface of any *putting green* on such *course* by rolling a ball or roughening or scraping the surface.

Exception

Practice putting or chipping on or near the first *teeing ground* before starting a round or play-off is permitted.

PENALTY
For breach of Rule 7-1b:
Disqualification.

NOTE

The *Committee* may, in the conditions of a competition (Rule 33-1), prohibit practice on the competition *course* on any day of a match play competition or permit practice on the competition *course* or part of the *course* (Rule 33-2c) on any day of or between rounds of a stroke play competition.

7-2   During Round

A player must not make a practice *stroke* during play of a hole.

Between the play of two holes a player must not make a practice *stroke*, except that he may practise putting or chipping on or near:

a.   the *putting green* of the hole last played,

b.   any practice *putting green*, or

c.   the *teeing ground* of the next hole to be played in the round,

provided a practice *stroke* is not made from a *hazard* and does not unduly delay play (Rule 6-7).

Strokes made in continuing the play of a hole, the result of which has been decided, are not practice *strokes*.

Exception

When play has been suspended by the *Committee*, a player may, prior to resumption of play, practise (a) as provided in this Rule, (b) anywhere other than on the competition *course* and (c) as otherwise permitted by the *Committee*.

PRACTICE DURING A ROUND

Practice putting and chipping on or near
the tee of the next hole to be played is
permitted as long as play is not delayed.

PENALTY

For breach of Rule 7-2:

Match play – Loss of hole;

Stroke play – Two strokes.

In the event of a breach between the play of two holes, the penalty applies to the next hole.

NOTE 1

A practice swing is not a practice *stroke* and may be taken at any place, provided the player does not breach the *Rules*.

NOTE 2

The *Committee* may, in the conditions of a competition (Rule 33-1), prohibit:

a. practice on or near the *putting green* of the hole last played, and

b. rolling a ball on the *putting green* of the hole last played.

► RULE 7

INCIDENT

After the suspension of play during the fourth round of the 2001 Players Championship at Sawgrass, both the penultimate group and the final group were required to resume play from the 10th tee. Tiger Woods, playing in the final group, was aware that the group in front would resume play first and that he would have additional time to arrive at the 10th tee.

Officials, concerned that Woods may have continued to hit practice shots on the practice range after the signal for a resumption of play had been sounded, advised Woods that such action would be in breach of Rule 7-2. Play was resumed without incident and Woods went on to win The Players Championship by one stroke from Vijay Singh.

► RULE 7

FREQUENTLY ASKED QUESTION

Q May a player practise on the competition course?

A Before a match, a player may practise on the competition course, unless prohibited by the Committee in the conditions of competition.

In stroke play, a competitor is not permitted to practise on the competition course before the competition, or test the surface of any putting green, unless permitted to do so by the Committee in the conditions of competition – see Note to Rule 7-1.

In match or stroke play, during the round, a player is not permitted to play a practice stroke either during the play of a hole or between play of two holes, except that, between the play of two holes, the player may practise putting or chipping on or near:

• the putting green of the hole last played,

• any practice putting green, or

• the teeing ground of the next hole to be played.

You should check the conditions of competition to see if the Committee has laid down any restrictions on practising during a round.

► RULE 8

ADVICE; INDICATING LINE OF PLAY

8-1 Advice

During a *stipulated round*, a player must not:

a.   give *advice* to anyone in the competition playing on the *course* other than his *partner*, or

b.   ask for *advice* from anyone other than his *partner* or either of their *caddies*.

DEFINITIONS
All defined terms are in *italics* and are listed in the Definitions section – see pages 13–23.

8-2 Indicating Line of Play

8-2 a Other Than on Putting Green

Except on the *putting green*, a player may have the *line of play* indicated to him by anyone, but no one may be positioned by the player on or close to the line or an extension of the line beyond the *hole* while the *stroke* is being made. Any mark placed by the player or with his knowledge to indicate the line must be removed before the *stroke* is made.

Exception

Flagstick attended or held up – see Rule 17-1.

8-2 b On the Putting Green

When the player's ball is on the *putting green*, the player, his *partner* or either of their *caddies* may, before but not during the *stroke*, point out a line for putting, but in so doing the *putting green* must not be touched. A mark must not be placed anywhere to indicate a line for putting.

ADVICE

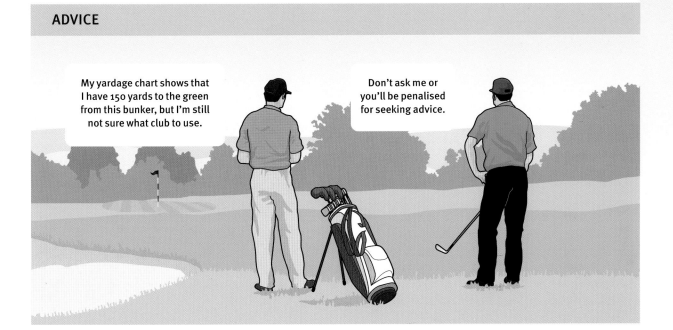

My yardage chart shows that I have 150 yards to the green from this bunker, but I'm still not sure what club to use.

Don't ask me or you'll be penalised for seeking advice.

INDICATING LINE OF PLAY

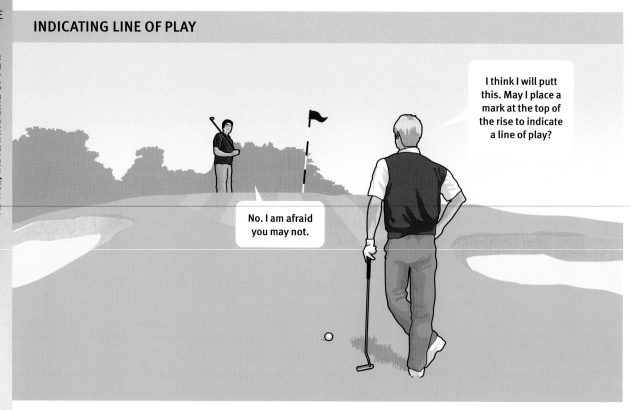

PENALTY

For breach of Rule:

Match play – Loss of hole;

Stroke play – Two strokes.

NOTE

The *Committee* may, in the conditions of a team competition (Rule 33-1), permit each team to appoint one person who may give *advice* (including pointing out a line for putting) to members of that team. The *Committee* may establish conditions relating to the appointment and permitted conduct of that person, who must be identified to the *Committee* before giving *advice*.

► RULE 8

INCIDENT

During the third round of the 1991 PGA Championship, while advising John Daly about the break of a putt on Crooked Stick's 11th green, Daly's caddie, Jeff "Squeeky" Medlen, accidentally touched the green with the flagstick.

As ninth alternate, Daly had been included in the Championship field when Nick Price withdrew to be present at the birth of his child and three alternates ahead of Daly declined for various reasons. The unknown Arkansan had taken the outright lead for the title after posting a 69 and 67 for the first and second rounds respectively. Playing with Bruce Lietzke on Saturday, Daly was on his way to a third round 69. At the 11th, Medlen used his hand to point out the line of Daly's first putt. In his other hand, Medlen held the flagstick and inadvertently allowed it to touch the green.

The potential breach of the Rules was televised to millions and, fortunately, videotaped for review. Alerted almost immediately to what had taken place, Rules officials met Daly at the end of the round to discuss the matter and make a decision before Daly returned his score card.

Daly, Medlen, Lietzke and Rules officials reviewed the videotape. The tape showed Medlen holding the

removed flagstick and allowing it to touch the putting green about three feet to the right of the hole while indicating the line of putt with his other hand. Rule 8-2 states that, while a line for putting may be pointed out, the green shall not be touched in doing so.

After speaking with all involved and watching the tape, officials were satisfied that no penalty was incurred. Daly returned his third round card with a score of 69. The following day, he won the PGA Championship by three shots.

► RULE 8

FREQUENTLY ASKED QUESTION

Q Can a player place a club on the ground to aid in his alignment?

A Yes, provided the club is removed before playing the stroke. Otherwise, a breach of Rule 8-2a would occur.

► RULE 9

INFORMATION AS TO STROKES TAKEN

9-1 General
The number of *strokes* a player has taken includes any *penalty strokes* incurred.

DEFINITIONS
All defined terms are in *italics* and are listed in the Definitions section – see pages 13–23.

9-2 Match Play
9-2 a Information as to Strokes Taken
An opponent is entitled to ascertain from the player, during the play of a hole, the number of *strokes* he has taken and, after play of a hole, the number of *strokes* taken on the hole just completed.

9-2 b Wrong Information
A player must not give wrong information to his opponent. If a player gives wrong information, **he loses the hole.**
A player is deemed to have given wrong information if he:
(i)   fails to inform his opponent as soon as practicable that he has incurred a penalty, unless (a) he was obviously proceeding under a *Rule* involving a penalty and this was observed by his opponent, or (b) he corrects the mistake before his opponent makes his next *stroke*; or
(ii)   gives incorrect information during play of a hole regarding the number of *strokes* taken and does not correct the mistake before his opponent makes his next *stroke*; or
(iii)   gives incorrect information regarding the number of *strokes* taken to complete a hole and this affects the opponent's understanding of the result of the hole, unless he corrects the mistake before any player makes a *stroke* from the next *teeing ground* or, in the case of the last hole of the match, before all players leave the *putting green*.

INFORMATION AS TO STROKES TAKEN

A player has given wrong information even if it is due to the failure to include a penalty that he did not know he had incurred. It is the player's responsibility to know the *Rules*.

9-3 Stroke Play

A *competitor* who has incurred a penalty should inform his *marker* as soon as practicable.

▶ RULE 10

ORDER OF PLAY

DEFINITIONS
All defined terms are in *italics* and are listed in the Definitions section – see pages 13–23.

10-1 Match Play

10-1 a When Starting Play of Hole

The *side* that has the *honour* at the first *teeing ground* is determined by the order of the draw. In the absence of a draw, the *honour* should be decided by lot.

The *side* that wins a hole takes the *honour* at the next *teeing ground*. If a hole has been halved, the *side* that had the *honour* at the previous *teeing ground* retains it.

10-1 b During Play of Hole

After both players have started play of the hole, the ball farther from the *hole* is played first. If the balls are equidistant from the *hole* or their positions relative to the *hole* are not determinable, the ball to be played first should be decided by lot.

Exception

Rule 30-3b (*best-ball* and *four-ball* match play).

> **NOTE**
>
> When it becomes known that the original ball is not to be played as it lies and the player is required to play a ball as nearly as possible at the spot from which the original ball was last played (see Rule 20-5), the order of play is determined by the spot from which the previous *stroke* was made. When a ball may be played from a spot other than where the previous *stroke* was made, the order of play is determined by the position where the original ball came to rest.

10-1 c Playing Out of Turn

If a player plays when his opponent should have played, there is no penalty, but the opponent may immediately require the player to cancel the *stroke* so made and, in correct order, play a ball as nearly as possible at the spot from which the original ball was last played (see Rule 20-5).

10-2 Stroke Play

10-2 a When Starting Play of Hole

The *competitor* who has the *honour* at the first *teeing ground* is determined by the order of the draw. In the absence of a draw, the *honour* should be decided by lot.

ORDER OF PLAY

Should I have played first as I am off the putting green?

No. Even though you are off the putting green, I am farther away from the hole and so it was still my turn to play first.

The *competitor* with the lowest score at a hole takes the *honour* at the next *teeing ground*. The *competitor* with the second lowest score plays next and so on. If two or more *competitors* have the same score at a hole, they play from the next *teeing ground* in the same order as at the previous *teeing ground*.

Exception

Rule 32-1 (handicap bogey, par and Stableford competitions).

10-2 b During Play of Hole

After the *competitors* have started play of the hole, the ball farthest from the *hole* is played first. If two or more balls are equidistant from the *hole* or their positions relative to the *hole* are not determinable, the ball to be played first should be decided by lot.

Exceptions

Rules 22 (ball assisting or interfering with play) and 31-4 (*four-ball* stroke play).

> **NOTE**
>
> When it becomes known that the original ball is not to be played as it lies and the *competitor* is required to play a ball as nearly as possible at the spot from which the original ball was last played (see Rule 20-5), the order of play is determined by the spot from which the previous *stroke* was made. When a ball may be played from a spot other than where the previous *stroke* was made, the order of play is determined by the position where the original ball came to rest.

10-2 c Playing Out of Turn

If a *competitor* plays out of turn, there is no penalty and the ball is played as it lies. If, however, the *Committee* determines that *competitors* have agreed to play out of turn to give one of them an advantage, **they are disqualified**.
(Making stroke while another ball in motion after stroke from putting green – see Rule 16-1f)
(Incorrect order of play in threesome and foursome stroke play – see Rule 29-3)

10-3 Provisional Ball or Another Ball from Teeing Ground

If a player plays a *provisional ball* or another ball from the *teeing ground*, he must do so after his opponent or *fellow-competitor* has made his first *stroke*. If more than one player elects to play a *provisional ball* or is required to play another ball from the *teeing ground*, the original order of play must be retained. If a player plays a *provisional ball* or another ball out of turn, Rule 10-1c or 10-2c applies.

▸ RULE 10
INCIDENT

On the second day of the 2003 Walker Cup at Ganton, the Great Britain & Ireland pairing of Gary Wolstenholme and Oliver Wilson were up against Trip Kuehne and Bill Haas of the USA in the morning foursomes.

Kuehne played first from the 2nd tee, hitting a long but wayward drive into some gorse bushes, then Wolstenholme followed with a shorter drive into a fairway bunker. When the players arrived at their balls, a search for the USA ball was ongoing. Before the end of the five-minute search period, Wilson played out of the bunker for Great Britain & Ireland and then Wolstenholme played the ball on to the green.

At this point, the USA side queried whether the home team had played out of turn as Wolstenholme may have played from closer to the hole than the point where the USA's lost ball could have been. It was ruled that, as the USA ball could not be found, its position for establishing the correct order of play had to be estimated and the match Referee decided that, on the basis of this estimation, the Great Britain & Ireland ball had been farther from the hole and therefore had not been played out of turn.

It was recognised at the time that the Rules would benefit from greater clarification in this type of situation and the Note to Rule 10-1b now provides that, when it becomes known that the original ball is not to be played as it lies (for example, if it is not found within five minutes) and the player is required to play a ball as near as possible to the spot where the original ball was last played, the order of play is determined by the spot from where the original ball was last played. Therefore, in the Walker Cup case, at the point where the USA ball became lost it would have been their turn to play as they were required to play again from the teeing ground.

Bob Lewis, the USA 2003 Walker Cup captain, queries with the Referee walking with the match whether the Great Britain & Ireland team had played out of turn and in breach of Rule 10-1b.

► RULE 10
FREQUENTLY ASKED QUESTION

Q In a handicap stroke play competition, how is the honour determined?
A At the 1st hole, the honour is determined by the order of the draw. Thereafter, the honour is determined according to the lowest gross score at each individual hole. For handicap Stableford competitions, see page 161.

► RULE 11

TEEING GROUND

DEFINITIONS
All defined terms are in *italics* and are listed in the Definitions section – see pages 13–23.

11-1   Teeing

When a player is putting a ball into play from the *teeing ground*, it must be played from within the *teeing ground* and from the surface of the ground or from a conforming *tee* in or on the surface of the ground.

For the purposes of this Rule, the surface of the ground includes an irregularity of surface (whether or not created by the player) and sand or other natural substance (whether or not placed by the player).

If a player makes a *stroke* at a ball on a non-conforming *tee*, or at a ball teed in a manner not permitted by this Rule, **he is disqualified.**

A player may stand outside the *teeing ground* to play a ball within it.

11-2   Tee-Markers

Before a player makes his first *stroke* with any ball on the *teeing ground* of the hole being played, the tee-markers are deemed to be fixed. In these circumstances, if the player moves or allows to be moved a tee-marker for the purpose of avoiding interference with his *stance*, the area of his intended swing or his *line of play*, **he incurs the penalty for a breach of Rule 13-2.**

11-3   Ball Falling off Tee

If a ball, when not *in play*, falls off a *tee* or is knocked off a *tee* by the player in *addressing* it, it may be re-teed, without penalty. However, if a *stroke* is made at the

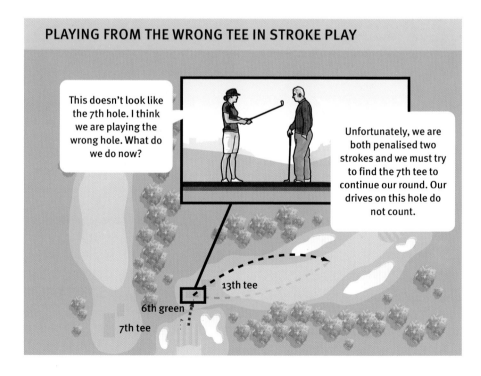

PLAYING FROM THE WRONG TEE IN STROKE PLAY

This doesn't look like the 7th hole. I think we are playing the wrong hole. What do we do now?

Unfortunately, we are both penalised two strokes and we must try to find the 7th tee to continue our round. Our drives on this hole do not count.

13th tee

6th green

7th tee

ball in these circumstances, whether the ball is moving or not, the *stroke* counts, but there is no penalty.

11-4 Playing from Outside Teeing Ground

11-4 a Match Play

If a player, when starting a hole, plays a ball from outside the *teeing ground*, there is no penalty, but the opponent may immediately require the player to cancel the *stroke* and play a ball from within the *teeing ground*.

11-4 b Stroke Play

If a *competitor*, when starting a hole, plays a ball from outside the *teeing ground*, **he incurs a penalty of two strokes** and must then play a ball from within the *teeing ground*.

If the *competitor* makes a *stroke* from the next *teeing ground* without first correcting his mistake or, in the case of the last hole of the round, leaves the *putting green* without first declaring his intention to correct his mistake, **he is disqualified.**

The *stroke* from outside the *teeing ground* and any subsequent *strokes* by the *competitor* on the hole prior to his correction of the mistake do not count in his score.

11-5 Playing from Wrong Teeing Ground

The provisions of Rule 11-4 apply.

► RULE 11

INCIDENT

At the 1990 US Open Championship, the drama and competitive tension at Medinah Country Club had been intense all week. Hale Irwin had summoned a wave of talent reflective of his 33 professional victories, which included two previous US Open victories in 1974 and 1979. Indeed, he had holed a 45-foot birdie putt on the 72nd hole of play to force an 18-hole play-off with Mike Donald whose only PGA Tour victory had come the previous year in Williamsburg, Virginia.

The players walked off the 17th green of the play-off round with Donald leading by one. On the 18th tee Mike Donald teed up in front of the markers. The walking Referee noticed, whereupon Donald was asked to re-tee the ball.

Rule 11, as it applies to stroke play, is exact. A player incurs a penalty of two strokes if he plays from outside the teeing ground, and must then play a ball from within the teeing ground. Had Donald's mistake been observed a few moments later, after he had played from ahead of the markers, the resulting two-stroke penalty would have reversed that state of the play-off and given Irwin a one-stroke lead.

Hale Irwin jumps for joy after holing the winning putt at the 91st hole of the 1990 US Open Championship.

The Referee's intervention prevented the breach, but Donald's bogey at the 90th hole resulted in both men scoring 74 in the play-off round. In accordance with the conditions of competition, and for the first time in its history, the US Open then moved to sudden death to determine the winner.

On the first sudden-death hole, the 91st hole of the championship, Irwin holed an eight-foot birdie putt to become the US Open's oldest winner.

▶ RULE 11

FREQUENTLY ASKED QUESTION

Q What do you do if you play from the wrong teeing ground?
A In stroke play, you must correct the mistake and play a ball from the correct teeing ground, incurring a penalty of two strokes. The stroke made from the wrong teeing ground, and any subsequent strokes made on the wrong hole, do not count in your score.

In match play, there is no penalty and you continue with the ball played from the wrong teeing ground, unless your opponent immediately requires you to cancel the stroke and play a ball from within the correct teeing ground.

▶ RULE 12

SEARCHING FOR AND IDENTIFYING BALL

DEFINITIONS
All defined terms are in *italics* and are listed in the Definitions section – see pages 13–23.

12-1 Searching for Ball; Seeing Ball

In searching for his ball anywhere on the *course*, the player may touch or bend long grass, rushes, bushes, whins, heather or the like, but only to the extent necessary to find and identify it, provided that this does not improve the lie of the ball, the area of his intended *stance* or swing or his *line of play*.

A player is not necessarily entitled to see his ball when making a *stroke*.

In a *hazard*, if a ball is believed to be covered by *loose impediments* or sand, the player may remove by probing or raking with a club or otherwise, as many *loose impediments* or as much sand as will enable him to see a part of the ball. If an excess is removed, there is no penalty and the ball must be re-covered so that only a part of it is visible. If the ball is *moved* during the removal, there is no penalty; the ball must be replaced and, if necessary, re-covered. As to removal of *loose impediments* outside a *hazard*, see Rule 23-1.

If a ball lying in or on an *obstruction* or in an *abnormal ground condition* is accidentally *moved* during search, there is no penalty; the ball must be replaced, unless the player elects to proceed under Rule 24-1b, 24-2b or 25-1b as applicable. If the player replaces the ball, he may still proceed under Rule 24-1b, 24-2b or 25-1b if applicable.

If a ball is believed to be lying in water in a *water hazard*, the player may probe for it with a club or otherwise. If the ball is *moved* in probing, it must be replaced, unless the player elects to proceed under Rule 26-1. There is no penalty for causing the ball to

SEARCHING FOR A BALL IN A BUNKER

If a player's ball is buried in a bunker, he may search for it by probing the sand with his fingers or he may use a rake or a club. If the ball is moved, there is no penalty but it must be replaced and, if necessary, re-covered so that only part of it is visible.

move, provided the movement of the ball was directly attributable to the specific act of probing. Otherwise, **the player incurs a *penalty stroke*** under Rule 18-2a.

PENALTY
For breach of Rule 12-1:
Match play – Loss of hole;
Stroke play – Two strokes.

12-2 Identifying Ball

The responsibility for playing the proper ball rests with the player. Each player should put an identification mark on his ball.

If a player has reason to believe a ball at rest is his and it is necessary to lift the ball in order to identify it, he may lift the ball, without penalty, in order to do so.

Before lifting the ball, the player must announce his intention to his opponent in match play or his *marker* or a *fellow-competitor* in stroke play and mark the position of the ball. He may then lift the ball and identify it, provided that he gives his opponent, *marker* or *fellow-competitor* an opportunity to observe the lifting and replacement. The ball must not be cleaned beyond the extent necessary for identification when lifted under Rule 12-2.

If the ball is the player's ball and he fails to comply with all or any part of this procedure, or he lifts his ball in order to identify it when not necessary to do so, **he incurs a penalty of one stroke.** If the lifted ball is the player's ball, he must replace it. If he fails to do so, **he incurs the general penalty for a breach of Rule 12-2,** but there is no additional penalty under this Rule.

NOTE
If the original lie of a ball to be placed or replaced has been altered, see Rule 20-3b.

65

IDENTIFYING A BALL IN A BUNKER

A player may lift a ball in order to identify it, even if the ball lies in a bunker or water hazard. The position of the ball must be marked before it is lifted and the player must tell his opponent, fellow-competitor or marker what he intends doing before he lifts the ball. The ball must not be cleaned beyond what is necessary to identify it.

* PENALTY

For breach of Rule 12-2:

Match play – Loss of hole;

Stroke play – Two strokes.

* If a player incurs the general penalty for a breach of Rule 12-2, there is no additional penalty under this Rule.

► RULE 12

INCIDENT

While playing in the 2003 Dubai Desert Classic at the Emirates Golf Club, Alastair Forsyth's ball lodged in a tree at a spot where it could not be reached. When the player initially arrived at the ball, he was able to see that the ball was the make and number that he was playing with and he called for a ruling in order to clarify his relief options.

When the Rules official arrived at the scene, Forsyth pointed out the ball in the tree. However, by this time the ball had moved its position slightly and the markings were no longer visible. The official questioned whether

Forsyth actually knew that the ball was his, but the Scotsman, with the support of his fellow-competitors, was able to advise the official that when he had first reached the ball it had been identifiable.

Satisfied with this, the official went on to explain to Forsyth that, if he deemed the ball unplayable, one of his options would be to drop a ball, under penalty of one stroke, within two club-lengths of the point on the ground immediately below the place where the ball lay in the tree, as provided in Decision 28/11. The player decided to exercise this option.

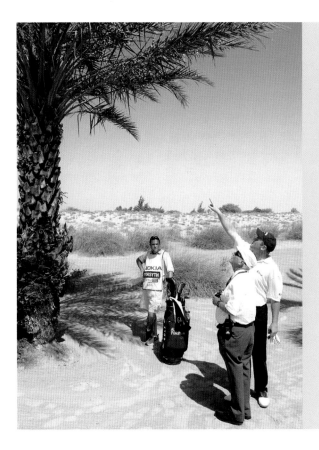

Golf balls can be very difficult to identify. At the 2003 Dubai Desert Classic, Alastair Forsyth's ball lodged in a palm tree. It subsequently moved slightly before the Rules official had reached the scene, and then it could not be readily identified.

► RULE 12

FREQUENTLY ASKED QUESTION

Q Is it permissible to put an identification mark on a ball, in the form of a line that completely encircles the ball?
A Yes. It is recommended that each player puts a personal identification mark on his ball. This can take any form, including a line encircling the ball, which the player may then use to help with alignment.

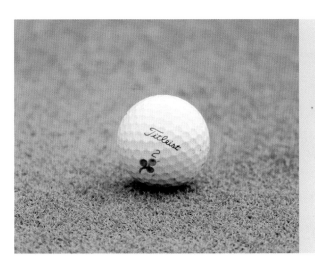

The responsibility for playing the proper golf ball rests with the player. Darren Clarke puts a shamrock on each of his golf balls as an identification mark.

▶ RULE 13

BALL PLAYED AS IT LIES

DEFINITIONS
All defined terms are in *italics* and are listed in the Definitions section – see pages 13–23.

13-1 General

The ball must be played as it lies, except as otherwise provided in the *Rules*.
(Ball at rest moved – see Rule 18)

13-2 Improving Lie, Area of Intended Stance or Swing, or Line of Play

A player must not improve or allow to be improved:

*   the position or lie of his ball,
*   the area of his intended *stance* or swing,
*   his *line of play* or a reasonable extension of that line beyond the *hole*, or
*   the area in which he is to drop or place a ball,

by any of the following actions:

*   pressing a club on the ground,
*   moving, bending or breaking anything growing or fixed (including immovable *obstructions* and objects defining *out of bounds*),
*   creating or eliminating irregularities of surface,
*   removing or pressing down sand, loose soil, replaced divots or other cut turf placed in position, or
*   removing dew, frost or water.

However, the player incurs no penalty if the action occurs:

*   in grounding the club lightly when *addressing the ball*,
*   in fairly taking his *stance*,

IMPROVING AREA OF INTENDED SWING OR LINE OF PLAY

A player must not break an interfering branch or remove sand that is off the putting green but on the line of play.

- in making a *stroke* or the backward movement of his club for a *stroke* and the *stroke* is made,
- in creating or eliminating irregularities of surface within the *teeing ground* (Rule 11-1) or in removing dew, frost or water from the *teeing ground*, or
- on the *putting green* in removing sand and loose soil or in repairing damage (Rule 16-1).

Exception
Ball in hazard – see Rule 13-4.

13-3 Building Stance
A player is entitled to place his feet firmly in taking his *stance*, but he must not build a *stance*.

13-4 Ball in Hazard; Prohibited Actions
Except as provided in the *Rules*, before making a *stroke* at a ball that is in a *hazard* (whether a *bunker* or a *water hazard*) or that, having been lifted from a *hazard*, may be dropped or placed in the *hazard*, the player must not:

a. Test the condition of the *hazard* or any similar *hazard*;

b. Touch the ground in the *hazard* or water in the *water hazard* with his hand or a club; or

c. Touch or move a *loose impediment* lying in or touching the *hazard*.

CREATING OR ELIMINATING IRREGULARITIES OF SURFACE

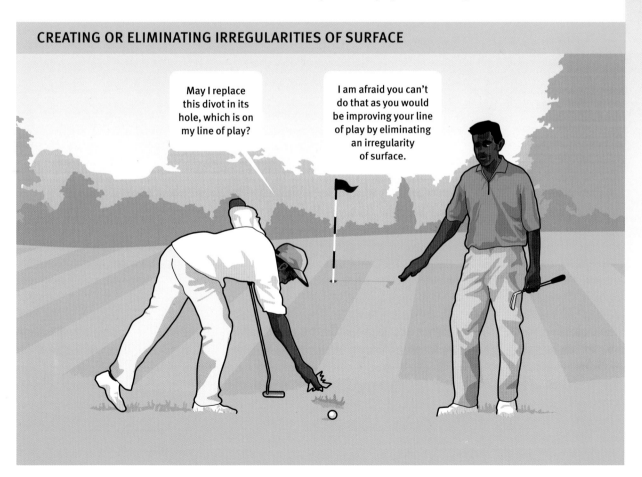

May I replace this divot in its hole, which is on my line of play?

I am afraid you can't do that as you would be improving your line of play by eliminating an irregularity of surface.

PLACING CLUBS IN HAZARD

The player may place his clubs in the hazard provided he does not test the condition of the hazard or improve the lie of the ball.

TOUCHING HAZARD TO PREVENT FALLING

The player may use a club to enter or leave a hazard provided he does not test the condition of the hazard or improve the lie of the ball.

Exceptions

1   Provided nothing is done that constitutes testing the condition of the *hazard* or improves the lie of the ball, there is no penalty if the player (a) touches the ground or *loose impediments* in any *hazard* or water in a *water hazard* as a result of or to prevent falling, in removing an *obstruction*, in measuring or in marking the position of, retrieving, lifting, placing or replacing a ball under any *Rule* or (b) places his clubs in a *hazard*.

2   After making the *stroke*, if the ball is still in the *hazard* or has been lifted from the *hazard* and may be dropped or placed in the *hazard*, the player may smooth sand or soil in the *hazard*, provided nothing is done to breach Rule 13-2 with respect to his next *stroke*. If the ball is outside the *hazard* after the *stroke*, the player may smooth sand or soil in the *hazard* without restriction.

3   If the player makes a *stroke* from a *hazard* and the ball comes to rest in another *hazard*, Rule 13-4a does not apply to any subsequent actions taken in the *hazard* from which the *stroke* was made.

NOTE

At any time, including at *address* or in the backward movement for the *stroke*, the player may touch, with a club or otherwise, any *obstruction*, any construction declared by the *Committee* to be an integral part of the *course* or any grass, bush, tree or other growing thing.

PENALTY
For breach of Rule:
Match play – Loss of hole;
Stroke play – Two strokes.
(Searching for ball – see Rule 12-1)
(Relief for ball in water hazard – see Rule 26)

BALL IN A BUNKER

Before making a stroke at a ball that is in a bunker the player must not:

... touch the ground with his club;

... touch a loose impediment with his club at address or on his backswing;

... remove loose impediments;

... or smooth sand.

GROUNDING CLUB ON BRIDGE IN WATER HAZARD

Yes. In a hazard, a player may touch an obstruction, such as a bridge, at any time.

Is it OK to ground my club on this bridge?

▸ RULE 13

INCIDENTS

In the third round of a US Tour event at Torrey Pines near San Diego in 1987, when playing from underneath the branches of a tree, Craig Stadler unwittingly breached Rule 13-3 when he knelt on a towel to keep his trousers dry. Rule 13-3 states that a player is entitled to place his feet firmly in taking a stance but he must not build a stance. Prior to the incident, Decision 13-3/2 had been published stating that the act of kneeling on a towel in such circumstances was deemed to be building a stance.

A television viewer watching the incident recorded coverage of the earlier rounds and brought the incident to the attention of Tournament officials during the final round of the competition. Unfortunately, because Stadler had returned his score card for the third round containing a score for a hole lower than actually taken, he was disqualified under Rule 6-6d.

However, in 1995 Stadler had the satisfaction of returning to Torrey Pines to assist in cutting down the tree that was now dying of a fungus infection. He also recreated his stroke for the assembled media.

During play of the second round of the 2008 BMW Championship at the Bellerive Country Club in St. Louis, Martin Laird's shot to a par 3 made a pitch-mark in the fringe, off the putting green. His fellow-competitor, Bart Bryant, played after Laird, his ball coming to rest off the putting green with the pitch-mark on his line of play.

Laird asked Bryant, "Is this [the pitch-mark] on your line?" Bryant replied, "Yes", and Laird repaired the pitch-mark before Bryant played. Bryant then pitched the ball over the pitch-mark. Bryant was obviously concerned about what had happened and, in the scoring area, he told the Committee about the situation and asked if a penalty had been incurred.

Rule 16-1c provides that a player may repair damage to the putting green caused by the impact of a ball, whether or not his ball lies on the putting green. However, in this case the pitch-mark was on the fringe, not on the putting green.

Rule 13-2 provides that a player must not improve, or allow to be improved, his line of play by creating or eliminating irregularities of surface. The repair of a ball mark is considered to be an elimination of an irregularity. Consequently, the Committee ruled that Bryant had allowed his line of play to be improved by Laird, and thus had incurred a two-stroke penalty under Rule 13-2. The fact that Bryant chipped the ball over the repaired pitch-mark did not alter the fact that the line of play had been improved in breach of the Rule.

There was some better news for Bryant when, four holes into his third round, he made a hole-in-one.

Craig Stadler takes great pleasure in cutting down the tree at Torrey Pines that was the scene of a Rules incident that resulted in his disqualification at an event there in 1987.

Rule 13-4c provides that a player cannot touch or move a loose impediment lying in a hazard prior to the stroke. The "stroke" begins only once the player has begun the forward movement of the club (see the Definition of "stroke"). Michelle Wie infringed this Rule when she touched some loose moss in a bunker when making her backswing at the 2006 Women's British Open.

England's Ross Fisher won the 2007 KLM Open at the Kennemer Golf and Country Club, but not before he had to endure an investigation into a Rules incident at the conclusion of his fourth round.

Fisher and Rules officials returned to the 12th hole, where the player had moved a bramble runner thinking that it was a loose impediment, only to find that it was still attached and growing. Fisher advised the officials that he had left the runner alone on realising that it was attached. However, as it is not permissible for a player to improve the lie of his ball, the area of his intended stance or swing, his line of play or the area in which a ball is to be dropped, by moving anything that is growing, the officials had to determine whether the initial movement had created an improvement in the player's circumstances. This would have brought with it a two-stroke penalty under Rule 13-2, resulting in the player being relegated to second place.

A player is entitled to move a branch or the like to the extent necessary to determine whether it is loose or attached. If the object is found to be loose, it may be removed. If the object is not loose, the player incurs no penalty provided the object has not become loose because of his actions and it can be restored to its original position prior to the next stroke being made (where failure to do so would result in the player having created an improvement to his situation (Decision 13-2/26)).

In Fisher's case, although he did not return the object to its original position, with the help of video footage the officials were able to determine that the movement of the bramble runner had not resulted in an improvement to the player's lie, stance, swing or line of play, and no breach of the Rules had occurred.

The incident was remarkably similar to a ruling at the 1992 Dutch Open, when Mike McLean of England, who thought he had won the tournament, was taken from the final green to review video footage of his moving of a bramble earlier in the fourth round. However, in this case, McLean was assessed a two-stroke penalty as his actions had clearly improved his lie.

► RULE 13

FREQUENTLY ASKED QUESTIONS

Q If you do not get your ball out of a bunker, can you rake the bunker before your next shot?
A Yes. Provided in doing so nothing is done to breach Rule 13-2 with respect to the next stroke. That is, by smoothing the sand, the player cannot improve the new lie of the ball, the area of his intended stance or swing, or his line of play for the next stroke.

Q Can I place my clubs or a rake in the hazard while I play my stroke out of the hazard?
A Yes. The action of placing clubs – even a bag of clubs – or the rake in a hazard is not considered testing the condition of the hazard. However, the player must be careful that he does nothing that constitutes testing the condition of the hazard or improves the lie of the ball – see Exception 1 to Rule 13-4.

► RULE 14

STRIKING THE BALL

DEFINITIONS
All defined terms are in *italics* and are listed in the Definitions section – see pages 13–23.

14-1 Ball to be Fairly Struck At
The ball must be fairly struck at with the head of the club and must not be pushed, scraped or spooned.

14-2 Assistance
In making a *stroke*, a player must not:
a.   Accept physical assistance or protection from the elements; or

BALL TO BE FAIRLY STRUCK AT WITH CLUBHEAD

A player may strike the ball with the back or toe of the clubhead.

Paul Broadhurst's caddie holds onto Broadhurst's trousers during a practice round for the 2006 Open Championship, to prevent the player falling into the bunker. Broadhurst would have incurred a two-stroke penalty if this had happened in the actual Championship, for allowing someone to give him physical assistance while making a stroke.

b. Allow his *caddie*, his *partner* or his *partner's caddie* to position himself on or close to an extension of the *line of play* or the *line of putt* behind the ball.

PENALTY
For breach of Rule 14-1 or 14-2:
Match play – Loss of hole;
Stroke play – Two strokes.

14-3 Artificial Devices, Unusual Equipment and Unusual Use of Equipment

The *R&A* reserves the right, at any time, to change the Rules relating to artificial devices, unusual *equipment* and the unusual use of *equipment* and to make or change the interpretations relating to these Rules.

A player in doubt as to whether use of an item would constitute a breach of Rule 14-3 should consult the *R&A*.

A manufacturer should submit to the *R&A* a sample of an item to be manufactured for a ruling as to whether its use during a *stipulated round* would cause a player to be in breach of Rule 14-3. The sample becomes the property of the *R&A* for reference purposes. If a manufacturer fails to submit a sample or, having submitted a sample, fails to await a ruling before manufacturing and/or marketing the item, the manufacturer assumes the risk of a ruling that use of the item would be contrary to the *Rules*.

Except as provided in the *Rules*, during a *stipulated round* the player must not use any artificial device or unusual *equipment*, or use any *equipment* in an unusual manner:

a. That might assist him in making a *stroke* or in his play; or

b. For the purpose of gauging or measuring distance or conditions that might affect his play; or

CADDIE POSITIONED ON EXTENSION OF LINE OF PLAY BEHIND BALL

c.   That might assist him in gripping the club, except that:
  (i)   plain gloves may be worn;
  (ii) resin, powder and drying or moisturising agents may be used; and
  (iii) a towel or handkerchief may be wrapped around the grip.

Exceptions

1   A player is not in breach of this Rule if (a) the *equipment* or device is designed for or has the effect of alleviating a medical condition, (b) the player has a legitimate medical reason to use the *equipment* or device, and (c) the *Committee* is satisfied that its use does not give the player any undue advantage over other players.

2   A player is not in breach of this Rule if he uses *equipment* in a traditionally accepted manner.

PENALTY
For breach of Rule 14-3:
Disqualification.

NOTE
The *Committee* may make a Local Rule allowing players to use devices that measure or gauge distance only.

14-4 Striking the Ball More Than Once
If a player's club strikes the ball more than once in the course of a *stroke*, the player must count the *stroke* and **add a *penalty stroke*,** making two *strokes* in all.

14-5 Playing Moving Ball
A player must not make a *stroke* at his ball while it is moving.

Exceptions

- Ball falling off *tee* – Rule 11-3
- Striking the ball more than once – Rule 14-4
- Ball moving in water – Rule 14-6

When the ball begins to *move* only after the player has begun the *stroke* or the backward movement of his club for the *stroke*, he incurs no penalty under this Rule for playing a moving ball, but he is not exempt from any penalty under the following Rules:

- Ball at rest *moved* by player – Rule 18-2a
- Ball at rest moving after *address* – Rule 18-2b

(Ball purposely deflected or stopped by player, partner or caddie – see Rule 1-2)

14-6 Ball Moving in Water

When a ball is moving in water in a *water hazard*, the player may, without penalty, make a *stroke*, but he must not delay making his *stroke* in order to allow the wind or current to improve the position of the ball. A ball moving in water in a *water hazard* may be lifted if the player elects to invoke Rule 26.

PENALTY
For breach of Rule 14-5 or 14-6:
Match play – Loss of hole;
Stroke play – Two strokes.

▶ RULE 14

INCIDENTS

During the final round of the 2007 Volvo China Open, a Rules official halted eventual winner, Markus Brier, just before he attempted a birdie putt on the 9th green. The reason for the official's intervention was that he was concerned that the player's caddie was standing on, or close to, an extension of the line of putt behind the ball and that, had the stroke been made, the player would have been in breach of Rule 14-2b, which prevents such action.

It is questionable whether Brier's caddie was actually in a position that would have resulted in a breach of the Rule, but from where the official was standing there was sufficient doubt that he felt it best to eliminate any possibility of a penalty by interjecting and asking the caddie to move farther away from the line. The interruption did not seem to distract Brier unduly as he holed his putt for birdie.

While the Rules allow a caddie to stand on an extension of the line behind the ball and align the player prior to a stroke being made, the caddie is not permitted to remain in position while the stroke is being executed. Therefore, if the caddie has taken up such a

position, he must move off to the side before the stroke is made to avoid the player incurring a loss-of-hole penalty in match play or a two-stroke penalty in stroke play. This applies to all strokes, not just strokes from the putting green.

Jeong Jang's misdemeanour occurred during the third round of the 2006 US Women's Open, when she attempted to hit the ball out of thick rough just off the 18th fairway. Immediately on making the stroke, television commentators remarked that it looked as though the player had hit the ball twice during the course of the stroke. According to Rule 14-4, a player cannot hit a ball more than once during a stroke, and if it happens the player counts one stroke but must add a one-stroke penalty.

In Jang's case the evidence that she had indeed hit the ball twice was not conclusive, so her swing sequence was reviewed several times on television replays. The initial ruling by the walking officials was that they did not feel Jang had struck her ball twice on the same swing. Nor did Jang and her caddie believe she had struck the

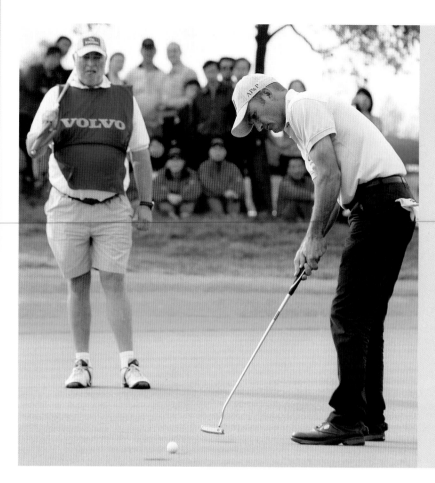

Markus Brier holes a putt *en route* to winning the 2007 Volvo China Open, as his caddie stands near by. A player's caddie must not stand on, or close to, an extension of the line of play or line of putt behind the ball when the stroke is being made.

ball twice, even though her caddie had asked her immediately after her swing whether she had done so. However, some doubt remained and, on a sophisticated plasma screen provided by NBC, further replays were cued up for review by USGA officials. The video was run again and again before it was determined conclusively that the Korean had definitely hit her ball twice. Jang

was alerted that she would have a penalty of one stroke. Thus, she was given a seven on the 18th hole of her third round.

At no point did USGA Rules officials believe Jang had tried to mislead anyone. It was obvious that she believed that she had hit the ball once, although repeated replays proved that the one-stroke penalty was deserved.

► RULE 14

FREQUENTLY ASKED QUESTION

Q Am I permitted to use the following during a stipulated round?:

(a) a distance-measuring device, for example, a range-finder or GPS;

(b) a compass; and

(c) a pair of binoculars?

A (a) No. Rule 14-3 provides that "during a stipulated round the player shall not use any artificial device or unusual equipment ... for the purpose of gauging or

measuring distance or conditions which might affect his play". However, the Committee may, in the Local Rules, permit such distance-measuring devices – see Appendix I, Part B, 9 for the Specimen Local Rule.

(b) No. Using a compass would be contrary to Rule 14-3.

(c) Yes. Binoculars that have no range-finder attachments or markings are not artificial devices in terms of Rule 14-3.

► RULE 15
SUBSTITUTED BALL; WRONG BALL

DEFINITIONS
All defined terms are in *italics*
and are listed in the Definitions
section – see pages 13–23.

15-1 General
A player must hole out with the ball played from the *teeing ground*, unless the ball
is *lost* or *out of bounds* or the player *substitutes* another ball, whether or not
substitution is permitted (see Rule 15-2). If a player plays a *wrong ball*, see Rule 15-3.

15-2 Substituted Ball
A player may *substitute* a ball when proceeding under a *Rule* that permits the player to
play, drop or place another ball in completing the play of a hole. The *substituted ball*
becomes the *ball in play*.

    If a player *substitutes* a ball when not permitted to do so under the *Rules*, that
substituted ball is not a *wrong ball*; it becomes the *ball in play*. If the mistake is
not corrected as provided in Rule 20-6 and the player makes a *stroke* at a wrongly
substituted ball, **he loses the hole in match play or incurs a penalty of two strokes in
stroke play under the applicable Rule** and, in stroke play, must play out the hole with
the *substituted ball*.

PLAYING A SUBSTITUTED BALL

I lifted my ball
from the putting
green to clean it, but
I have just noticed
that I have played
the other ball I had
in my pocket.

Unfortunately, you
have substituted a ball
when not permitted to do so.
It is now the ball in play and
you incur a two-stroke
penalty. If we had been
playing a match you would
have lost the hole.

PLAYING A WRONG BALL IN STROKE PLAY

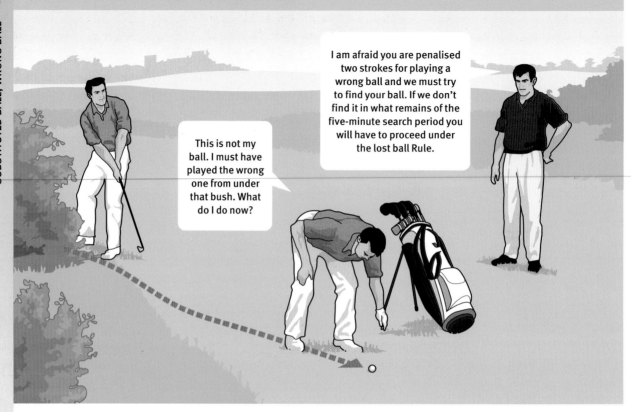

Exception

If a player incurs a penalty for making a *stroke* from a wrong place, there is no additional penalty for substituting a ball when not permitted.

(Playing from wrong place – see Rule 20-7)

15-3 Wrong Ball

15-3 a Match Play

If a player makes a *stroke* at a *wrong ball*, **he loses the hole**.

If the *wrong ball* belongs to another player, its owner must place a ball on the spot from which the *wrong ball* was first played.

If the player and opponent exchange balls during the play of a hole, the first to make a *stroke* at a *wrong ball* **loses the hole**; when this cannot be determined, the hole must be played out with the balls exchanged.

Exception

There is no penalty if a player makes a *stroke* at a *wrong ball* that is moving in water in a *water hazard*. Any *strokes* made at a *wrong ball* moving in water in a *water hazard* do not count in the player's score. The player must correct his mistake by playing the correct ball or by proceeding under the *Rules*.

15-3 b Stroke Play

If a *competitor* makes a *stroke* or *strokes* at a *wrong ball*, **he incurs a penalty of two strokes**.

The *competitor* must correct his mistake by playing the correct ball or by proceeding under the *Rules*. If he fails to correct his mistake before making a *stroke* on the next *teeing ground* or, in the case of the last hole of the round, fails to declare his intention to correct his mistake before leaving the *putting green*, **he is disqualified**.

Strokes made by a *competitor* with a *wrong ball* do not count in his score. If the *wrong ball* belongs to another *competitor*, its owner must place a ball on the spot from which the *wrong ball* was first played.

Exception

There is no penalty if a *competitor* makes a *stroke* at a *wrong ball* that is moving in water in a *water hazard*. Any *strokes* made at a *wrong ball* moving in water in a *water hazard* do not count in the *competitor's* score.

(Lie of ball to be placed or replaced altered – see Rule 20-3b)

(Spot not determinable – see Rule 20-3c)

▶ RULE 15

INCIDENTS

At the 2001 Compass Group English Open at Forest of Arden, playing the 17th hole in the last round, Raymond Russell marked the position of his ball on the putting green and threw it to his caddie to clean as usual. He failed to catch the ball and it went into the lake at the side of the green. On being told that if he substituted a ball in order to finish the hole he would be penalised two strokes under Rule 15-2, his caddie took off his shoes and socks and lowered himself into the lake to try to find the ball in the murky water. After a short while, and with players on the fairway waiting to play their approach shots to the green, it was clear that the ball would not be found and, so, Russell had to substitute a ball and incurred a two-stroke penalty.

A similar incident occurred at the 4th hole of the last round of The Players' Championship in 2004 at Sawgrass. Ian Poulter picked up his ball on the putting green, after marking its position, but he lost his grip on it and the ball went into the nearby lake. He would have incurred a two-stroke penalty, however, Kam Bhambra, his fitness coach, was watching and stripped down to his boxer shorts, jumped into the water and retrieved Poulter's ball. "It was the first ball I found," he said. "I was a bit worried about alligators, but duty called." Poulter parred the hole after avoiding the two-stroke penalty. This saved him from dropping 20 places on the leaderboard, which would have resulted in a loss of $20,000 in prize money.

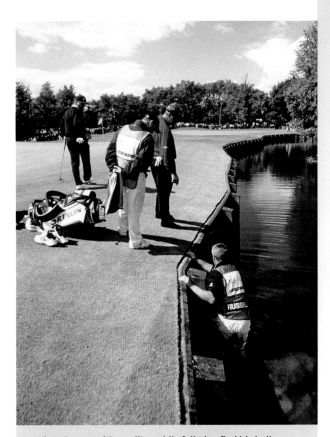

When Raymond Russell's caddie failed to find his ball, which had accidentally rolled into the lake at Forest of Arden, Russell received a two-stroke penalty as he had to substitute another ball to enable him to complete the hole.

▶ RULE 15

FREQUENTLY ASKED QUESTION

Q Must a player announce to his opponent(s) or fellow-competitor(s) that he intends to change his ball between the play of two holes?

A Although such an announcement would be courteous, and could help avoid any possible confusion, a player is not required by the Rules to inform anyone what type of ball he intends to play at a hole.

▶ RULE 16

THE PUTTING GREEN

DEFINITIONS
All defined terms are in *italics* and are listed in the Definitions section – see pages 13–23.

16-1 General

16-1 a Touching Line of Putt

The *line of putt* must not be touched except:

(i) the player may remove *loose impediments*, provided he does not press anything down;

(ii) the player may place the club in front of the ball when *addressing* it, provided he does not press anything down;

(iii) in measuring – Rule 18-6;

(iv) in lifting or replacing the ball – Rule 16-1b;

TOUCHING THE LINE OF PUTT: EXAMPLES OF WHEN PERMITTED

addressing the ball

removing a loose impediment

repairing a ball mark

repairing an old hole plug

CLEANING BALL AND REPAIRING DAMAGE

A player may clean a ball by rubbing it on the green, provided he doesn't test the green's surface. However, such a method of cleaning a ball is not recommended – Decision 16-1d/5.

A player may not repair spike damage if it might subsequently assist him.

(v) in pressing down a ball-marker;

(vi) in repairing old *hole* plugs or ball marks on the *putting green* – Rule 16-1c; and

(vii) in removing movable *obstructions* – Rule 24-1.

(Indicating line for putting on putting green – see Rule 8-2b)

16-1 b Lifting and Cleaning Ball

A ball on the *putting green* may be lifted and, if desired, cleaned. The position of the ball must be marked before it is lifted and the ball must be replaced (see Rule 20-1).

16-1 c Repair of Hole Plugs, Ball Marks and Other Damage

The player may repair an old *hole* plug or damage to the *putting green* caused by the impact of a ball, whether or not the player's ball lies on the *putting green*. If a ball or ball-marker is accidentally *moved* in the process of the repair, the ball or ball-marker must be replaced. There is no penalty, provided the movement of the ball or ball-marker is directly attributable to the specific act of repairing an old *hole* plug or damage to the *putting green* caused by the impact of a ball. Otherwise, Rule 18 applies.

Any other damage to the *putting green* must not be repaired if it might assist the player in his subsequent play of the hole.

16-1 d Testing Surface

During the *stipulated round*, a player must not test the surface of any *putting green* by rolling a ball or roughening or scraping the surface.

Exception

Between the play of two holes, a player may test the surface of any practice *putting green* and the *putting green* of the hole last played, unless the *Committee* has prohibited such action (see Note 2 to Rule 7-2).

STANDING ON THE LINE OF PUTT

There is no penalty for standing on the line of putt if it is done inadvertently or to avoid standing on another player's line of putt.

16-1 e Standing Astride or on Line of Putt

The player must not make a *stroke* on the *putting green* from a *stance* astride, or with either foot touching, the *line of putt* or an extension of that line behind the ball.

Exception

There is no penalty if the *stance* is inadvertently taken on or astride the *line of putt* (or an extension of that line behind the ball) or is taken to avoid standing on another player's *line of putt* or prospective *line of putt*.

REMOVING LOOSE IMPEDIMENTS FROM THE LINE OF PUTT

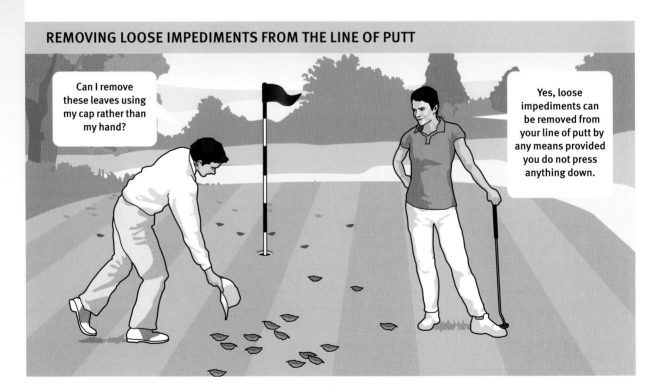

Can I remove these leaves using my cap rather than my hand?

Yes, loose impediments can be removed from your line of putt by any means provided you do not press anything down.

BALL OVERHANGING HOLE

16-1 f Making Stroke While Another Ball in Motion

The player must not make a *stroke* while another ball is in motion after a *stroke* from the *putting green*, except that if a player does so, there is no penalty if it was his turn to play.

(Lifting ball assisting or interfering with play while another ball in motion – see Rule 22)

PENALTY
For breach of Rule 16-1:
Match play – Loss of hole;
Stroke play – Two strokes.
(Position of caddie or partner – see Rule 14-2)
(Wrong putting green – see Rule 25-3)

16-2 Ball Overhanging Hole

When any part of the ball overhangs the lip of the *hole*, the player is allowed enough time to reach the *hole* without unreasonable delay and an additional ten seconds to determine whether the ball is at rest. If by then the ball has not fallen into the *hole*, it is deemed to be at rest. If the ball subsequently falls into the *hole*, the player is deemed to have *holed* out with his last *stroke*, and **must add a *penalty stroke*** to his score for the hole; otherwise, there is no penalty under this Rule.

(Undue delay – see Rule 6-7)

85

▶ RULE 16

INCIDENTS

An uncharacteristically unsettled summer caused havoc at golf events in the UK in 2008, with the S4C Wales Ladies Championship of Europe being no exception. The Championship, played at Machynys Peninsula Golf and Country Club, was reduced to 54 holes when play had to be abandoned on the Saturday during the third round, due to unplayable conditions.

During the second round of the Championship, although the course remained playable, the winds had been so strong that the flagsticks were being blown out of the holes, resulting in the edges of some of the holes becoming damaged.

In such a situation, the provisions of Decision 16-1a/6 provide that, if the hole is damaged (other than by a ball mark), but the proper dimensions of the hole (4¼ inches/ 108 mm in diameter) have not been changed materially, the player should continue play without repairing the hole. In such circumstances, if the player touches the hole prior to putting, she would be in breach of Rule 16-1a for touching the line of putt.

If the proper dimensions of the hole have been materially altered, the player should ask the Committee to have the hole repaired. If a member of the Committee is not readily available, the player may repair the damage herself, without penalty.

This meant officials had a busy day trying to restore holes to their proper dimensions. In fact, in order to reduce the instances of flagsticks being blown out of the holes, officials took the unusual, but entirely reasonable, step of using rubber bands to attach the flags closely to the flagsticks in order to minimise the effect of the wind on the flagsticks.

At the 2004 Shell Houston Open, Thomas Levet's ball came to rest overhanging the edge of the hole after the player had putted it from just off the green at a par-3. Having walked promptly to the hole, the Frenchman began to count down the seconds on the fingers of his hands. Levet knew that Rule 16-2 allowed him to wait ten seconds to see if the ball would drop into the

Richie Ramsay's caddie looks on forlornly having infringed Rule 16-1 during the 2006 US Amateur Championship.

hole. Should the ball drop into the hole within the ten-second period, then he would have scored a birdie two. However, should the ball fall into the hole after the ten-second period had elapsed, Levet would have to add a penalty stroke to his score, giving him a three.

Just a moment after Levet had counted off the fingers on both hands, his ball toppled into the hole. It then became a question of whether his personal ten-second countdown had been accurate and whether television pictures might be able to establish if, in fact, Levet had counted too quickly. Luckily for Levet, Rules officials were able to review footage of the incident, which demonstrated clearly that his own count had been too quick and that the ball had fallen into the hole well within the ten-second period provided for in Rule 16-2. The fortunate Frenchman had therefore scored a two.

However, had the television evidence not been available and had there not been a more accurate timing taken by any witnesses to the incident, Levet's own count would have had to be taken as accurate, resulting in a one-stroke penalty.

In 2006, on the way to becoming the first Scotsman since 1898 to win the US Amateur Championship, Richie Ramsay had more than his fair share of Rules difficulties. The first issue arose at the 17th hole during his quarter-final match with Californian Rickie Fowler, when Ramsay's caddie, a 17-year-old high-school student Thomas Buller, attempted to point out where he thought Ramsay should hit his 20-foot birdie putt. In so doing, Buller touched his player's line of putt, in breach of Rule 16-1.

Rule 6-1 provides that, for any breach of a Rule by his caddie, the player incurs the applicable penalty and, consequently, a loss-of-hole penalty was applied to Ramsay. The young caddie must have been very relieved when the Scotsman managed to win the match at the third extra hole.

▶ RULE 16

FREQUENTLY ASKED QUESTIONS

Q What are the Rules concerning the location of the hole on the putting green?
A The location of the hole on the putting green is not a matter covered under the Rules of Golf. However, when setting such locations, various specific points should be considered.

There must be sufficient putting surface between the hole and the front and the sides of the green to accommodate the required shot. For example, if the hole requires a long iron or wood shot to the green, the hole should be placed deeper in the green and farther from its sides than would be the case if the hole requires a short pitch shot.

It is recommended that the hole should be positioned at least four paces from any edge of the green. In addition, an area of 2–3 feet (0.6–0.9 metres) in radius around the hole should be as nearly level as possible. Every effort should be made to ensure that holes are not positioned within three paces of a very severe slope or ridge or of a recently used hole. In general, there should be a balanced selection of hole positions for the entire course with respect to left, right, central, front and back positions. Six quite difficult, six moderately difficult and

six relatively easy positions are recommended. One should also try to keep a balance of using the left and right of the green: for example, on the first nine, there should be four hole positions to the left, four to the right and one in the centre. The second nine should be similar.

Finally, in order to observe the Rules of Golf, the greenkeeper who cuts the hole must make sure that any hole-liner does not exceed 4¼ inches (108 mm) in outer diameter, and if possible any liner must be sunk at least 1 inch (25.4 mm) below the putting green surface.

Additional guidance regarding hole positions is contained in The R&A's *Guidance on Running a Competition* publication (available via The R&A website, www.randa.org).

Q May a player clean his ball by rubbing it on the putting green?
A Yes, provided the act is not for the purpose of testing the surface of the putting green (Rule 16-1d). It is recommended that a ball be cleaned in other ways to eliminate any question as to the player's intentions.

► RULE 17

THE FLAGSTICK

DEFINITIONS
All defined terms are in *italics* and are listed in the Definitions section – see pages 13–23.

17-1 Flagstick Attended, Removed or Held Up

Before making a *stroke* from anywhere on the *course*, the player may have the *flagstick* attended, removed or held up to indicate the position of the *hole*.

If the *flagstick* is not attended, removed or held up before the player makes a *stroke*, it must not be attended, removed or held up during the *stroke* or while the player's ball is in motion if doing so might influence the movement of the ball.

NOTE 1

If the *flagstick* is in the *hole* and anyone stands near it while a *stroke* is being made, he is deemed to be attending the *flagstick*.

NOTE 2

If, prior to the *stroke*, the *flagstick* is attended, removed or held up by anyone with the player's knowledge and he makes no objection, the player is deemed to have authorised it.

ADJUSTMENT OF FLAGSTICK: PLAYER'S BALL OFF GREEN

BALL STRIKING ATTENDED FLAGSTICK IN STROKE PLAY

NOTE 3

If anyone attends or holds up the *flagstick* while a *stroke* is being made, he is deemed to be attending the *flagstick* until the ball comes to rest.

(Moving attended, removed or held up flagstick while ball in motion – see Rule 24-1.)

17-2 Unauthorised Attendance

If an opponent or his *caddie* in match play or a *fellow-competitor* or his *caddie* in stroke play, without the player's authority or prior knowledge, attends, removes or holds up the *flagstick* during the *stroke* or while the ball is in motion, and the act might influence the movement of the ball, the opponent or *fellow-competitor* incurs the applicable penalty.

---

* PENALTY

For breach of Rule 17-1 or 17-2:

Match play – Loss of hole;

Stroke play – Two strokes.

* In stroke play, if a breach of Rule 17-2 occurs and the *competitor's* ball subsequently strikes the *flagstick*, the person attending or holding it or anything carried by him, the *competitor* incurs no penalty. The ball is played as it lies except that, if the *stroke* was made on the *putting green*, the *stroke* is cancelled and the ball must be replaced and replayed.

17-3 Ball Striking Flagstick or Attendant

The player's ball must not strike:

a. The *flagstick* when it is attended, removed or held up;

b. The person attending or holding up the *flagstick* or anything carried by him; or

c. The *flagstick* in the *hole*, unattended, when the *stroke* has been made on the *putting green*.

Exception

When the *flagstick* is attended, removed or held up without the player's authority – see Rule 17-2.

PENALTY

For breach of Rule 17-3:

Match play – Loss of hole;

Stroke play – Two strokes and the ball must be played as it lies.

17-4 Ball Resting Against Flagstick

When a player's ball rests against the *flagstick* in the *hole* and the ball is not *holed*, the player or another person authorised by him may move or remove the *flagstick*, and if the ball falls into the *hole*, the player is deemed to have *holed* out with his last *stroke*; otherwise, the ball, if *moved*, must be placed on the lip of the *hole*, without penalty.

▶ RULE 17

INCIDENTS

During the 2000 Open at St. Andrews, Jack Nicklaus hit his approach to the 2nd green well left. His ball ended up on the 16th-hole portion of this dual green, with a bunker between himself and the hole. He floated up a perfect wedge shot that almost went in the hole. The Referee accompanying the group was unsighted by the bunker and assumed that Nicklaus had played his shot from the fairway beyond the green.

As they walked to the next tee Nicklaus admitted that he was unsure if his ball was on the green or not and the Referee reminded him that if he had played from the green he should have had the flagstick attended.

"I had a 40-yard pitch shot over a bunker," said Nicklaus after the round. "You don't think much about having the pin attended. I've never done that before. It never entered my mind."

Another very uncommon incident in professional golf occurred with Phillip Price during the 2004 Dubai Desert Classic. Having played his second shot just on to the green at the par-5 3rd hole, his caddie was about to attend the flagstick prior to the Welshman putting. At this point, Price asked his caddie to take a look at the line of putt from behind his ball.

After conferring on the line, Price and his caddie forgot to have the flagstick attended and the player putted from the green with the flagstick in the hole, which, of itself, is not a breach of the Rules. Unfortunately, Price's putt was perfect and the ball rolled into the hole. Rule 17-3c provides that the player's ball must not strike the flagstick in the hole when a stroke has been made from the putting green and the resultant two-stroke penalty meant that Price's eagle three became a par 5.

In the 2007 Arnold Palmer Invitational, Boo Weekley found himself incurring a two-stroke penalty after trying to save his fellow-competitor, Tom Johnson, from a

penalty during their third round. At the par-3 2nd hole, Johnson hit his tee shot on to the right side of the green, 85 feet from the hole. Because of the steep slope on the green and the back-left hole location, he determined that the best way to get the ball close to the hole was to chip from the green, which is permitted, and try to land it in the back fringe so the ball could run down to the hole. However, as Johnson later said, "I spaced out and forgot to tell my caddie to attend the pin." Johnson played the perfect shot and the ball was rolling down slowly towards the hole when Weekley noticed that the ball might strike the flagstick in the hole. He therefore ran over and pulled the flagstick out.

Someone in the gallery mentioned what he had seen to a Rules official, and the matter was raised with the players in the scoring area before they returned their score cards. "They asked me if I had authorised Boo to pull the pin," Johnson said. "And I didn't." This meant that Weekley had removed the flagstick without authorisation while a ball was in motion. As the act could have influenced the movement of Johnson's ball, Weekley was subject to a penalty of two strokes under Rule 17-2.

Weekley, whose 67 was turned into a 69, was reported as having said, "Thanks, I learned something" to the Rules officials. Johnson said, "I just put my arm around him and told him he handles adversity better than anyone I've ever played with."

► RULE 17

FREQUENTLY ASKED QUESTIONS

Q May the player have the flagstick attended even if his ball is not on the putting green?

A Yes. Rule 17-1 states that, before making a stroke from anywhere on the course, the player may have the flagstick attended, removed or held up.

Q May a player putt with one hand while holding the flagstick with the other?

A Yes, provided the flagstick has been removed from the hole and the ball therefore does not strike it. If the ball were to strike the flagstick, a breach of Rule 17-3a would occur. The player must not lean on the flagstick in order to steady himself whilst he putts, as that would be contrary to Rule 14-3, resulting in a penalty of disqualification.

► RULE 18

BALL AT REST MOVED

DEFINITIONS
All defined terms are in *italics* and are listed in the Definitions section – see pages 13–23.

18-1 By Outside Agency

If a ball at rest is *moved* by an *outside agency*, there is no penalty and the ball must be replaced.

> **NOTE**
> It is a question of fact whether a ball has been *moved* by an *outside agency*. In order to apply this Rule, it must be known or virtually certain that an *outside agency* has *moved* the ball. In the absence of such knowledge or certainty, the player must play the ball as it lies or, if the ball is not found, proceed under Rule 27-1.
> (Player's ball at rest moved by another ball – see Rule 18-5)

18-2 By Player, Partner, Caddie or Equipment
18-2 a General

When a player's ball is *in play*, if:

(i) the player, his *partner* or either of their *caddies* lifts or *moves* it, touches it purposely (except with a club in the act of *addressing* it) or causes it to *move* except as permitted by a *Rule*, or

(ii) *equipment* of the player or his *partner* causes the ball to *move*, **the player incurs a penalty of one stroke.** If the ball is *moved*, it must be replaced unless the movement of the ball occurs after the player has begun the *stroke* or the backward movement of the club for the *stroke* and the *stroke* is made.

Under the *Rules* there is no penalty if a player accidentally causes his ball to *move* in the following circumstances:

- In searching for a ball in a *hazard* covered by *loose impediments* or sand, for a ball in an *obstruction* or *abnormal ground condition* or for a ball believed to be in water in a *water hazard* – Rule 12-1

By Outside Agency – no penalty and replace ball (Rule 18-1).

By Player, Partner, Caddie or Equipment – one-stroke penalty and replace ball (Rule 18-2a).

After Address – one-stroke penalty and replace ball (Rule 18-2b).

By Opponent, Caddie or Equipment Not During Search – opponent incurs one-stroke penalty and replace ball (Rule 18-3b).

By Opponent, Caddie or Equipment During Search – no penalty and replace ball (Rule 18-3a).

By Another Ball – replace moved ball (Rule 18-5).

By Fellow-Competitor, Caddie or Equipment – no penalty and replace ball (Rule 18-4).

In Measuring – no penalty and replace ball (Rule 18-6).

- In repairing a *hole* plug or ball mark – Rule 16-1c
- In measuring – Rule 18-6
- In lifting a ball under a *Rule* – Rule 20-1
- In placing or replacing a ball under a *Rule* – Rule 20-3a
- In removing a *loose impediment* on the *putting green* – Rule 23-1
- In removing movable *obstructions* – Rule 24-1

18-2 b Ball Moving After Address

If a player's *ball in play moves* after he has *addressed* it (other than as a result of a *stroke*), the player is deemed to have *moved* the ball and **incurs a penalty of one stroke.** The ball must be replaced, unless the movement of the ball occurs after the player has begun the *stroke* or the backward movement of the club for the *stroke* and the *stroke* is made.

18-3 By Opponent, Caddie or Equipment in Match Play
18-3 a During Search

If, during search for a player's ball, an opponent, his *caddie* or his *equipment moves* the ball, touches it or causes it to *move*, there is no penalty. If the ball is *moved*, it must be replaced.

18-3 b Other Than During Search

If, other than during search for a player's ball, an opponent, his *caddie* or his *equipment moves* the ball, touches it purposely or causes it to *move*, except as otherwise provided in the *Rules*, **the opponent incurs a penalty of one stroke.** If the ball is *moved*, it must be replaced.
(Playing a wrong ball – see Rule 15-3)
(Ball moved in measuring – see Rule 18-6)

18-4 By Fellow-Competitor, Caddie or Equipment in Stroke Play

If a *fellow-competitor*, his *caddie* or his *equipment moves* the player's ball, touches it or causes it to *move*, there is no penalty. If the ball is *moved*, it must be replaced.
(Playing a wrong ball – see Rule 15-3)

18-5 By Another Ball

If a *ball in play* and at rest is *moved* by another ball in motion after a *stroke*, the *moved* ball must be replaced.

18-6 Ball Moved in Measuring

If a ball or ball-marker is *moved* in measuring while proceeding under or in determining the application of a *Rule*, the ball or ball-marker must be replaced. There is no penalty, provided the movement of the ball or ball-marker is directly attributable to the specific act of measuring. Otherwise, the provisions of Rules 18-2a, 18-3b or 18-4 apply.

* PENALTY
For breach of Rule:
Match play – Loss of hole;
Stroke play – Two strokes.
* If a player who is required to replace a ball fails to do so, or if he makes a *stroke* at a ball *substituted* under Rule 18 when such *substitution* is not

permitted, he incurs the general penalty for breach of Rule 18, but there is no additional penalty under this Rule.

NOTE 1
If a ball to be replaced under this Rule is not immediately recoverable, another ball may be *substituted*.

NOTE 2
If the original lie of a ball to be placed or replaced has been altered, see Rule 20-3b.

NOTE 3
If it is impossible to determine the spot on which a ball is to be placed, see Rule 20-3c.

► RULE 18

INCIDENTS

At the 71st hole of the Ballantine's Championship in Korea in 2008, eventual runner-up Jeev Milkha Singh hit his tee shot into the rough and his ball was driven over by a golf cart. When the player and a Rules official arrived at the scene, there was evidence of a tyre mark over the ball, and it looked like the ball had been pushed down into the ground.

As the golf cart was not connected to the player in any way, it had the status of an outside agency under the Rules. Normally when a ball at rest is moved by an outside agency, it is replaced without penalty (Rule 18-1). However, in this case, no one had seen the lie of the ball before it was moved and the original lie had also been altered.

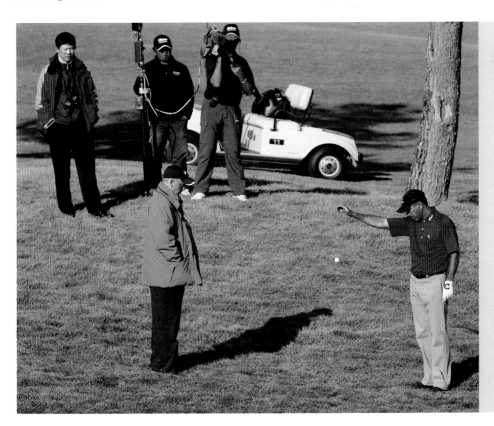

Jeev Milkha Singh drops his ball back into play after it had been driven over by a golf cart.

In such a case there are, potentially, two Rules that can apply. As the exact spot where the ball lay in the rough was not known, Rule 20-3c(i) provides that the player should drop the ball as near as possible to the place where it lay. However, Rule 20-3b(i) provides that, if the original lie of a ball to be replaced has been altered, except in a hazard, the ball must be placed in the nearest lie most similar to the original lie that is not more than one club-length from the original lie, not nearer the hole and not in a hazard.

Thankfully, Decision 20-3b/5 in the *Decisions on the Rules of Golf* clears up this potential conflict by providing that, if the player does not know the original lie of the ball, then you cannot begin to try to find the nearest most similar lie. As neither Singh nor anyone else knew how the ball was lying before the cart ran over it, Rule 20-3b could not be applied and, therefore, the player was required to drop the ball at the estimated position under Rule 20-3c.

Rule 18 was again infringed when a misunderstanding between Chris DiMarco and a Rules official at the 2006 HSBC Champions Tournament led to an unusual situation in which a score card was altered after it had been returned. On the first day, DiMarco was on the 8th green and had just grounded his putter behind the ball to tap in a short putt, when his ball moved. At that point, DiMarco called for a Rules official, and they agreed that, as the player had not completed his stance, and therefore had not addressed the ball, he was not automatically deemed to have caused the ball to move. The question then became whether the grounding of the club had caused the ball to move, in which case DiMarco would incur a one-stroke penalty under Rule 18-2a and the ball would be replaced.

Because the Rules official had misconstrued DiMarco's comments on how close his putter was to the ball when it was grounded, he ruled that the ball had moved of its own volition and DiMarco was advised to play the ball from its new position without penalty. However, on reviewing the incident on television later, it became clear to the Committee that the proximity of DiMarco's club to the ball when it was grounded was such that the weight of evidence was strongly in favour of the player's actions having caused the ball to move and that he should have been penalised.

By this point, DiMarco had returned his score card without a penalty included, but as the failure to include the penalty was due to the Rules official's instruction,

based on a misunderstanding of the player's comments, it would have been unfair to disqualify the player for returning a score lower than actually taken. In such a case, Decision 34-3/1 allows for the correction of an incorrect decision, and in this case that meant adding a penalty stroke to the player's score for the hole. Although under Rule 18-2a the ball should have been replaced, it was too late to correct that error and no penalty was applied for the ball having been played from the wrong position in view of the Rules official's advice.

Decision 34-3/1 provides a necessary exception to the basic principle under Rule 6-6c – no alteration can be made on a score card once it is returned to the Committee by a competitor.

A Rules official was called during the final round of the 2006 BMW Championship at Wentworth and a discussion ensued about whether Angel Cabrera's actions of taking a practice swing had caused his ball to move or whether the ball had moved of its own volition. Cabrera had touched the ground with a practice swing quite near his ball, which was precariously balanced on a slight slope in the rough, and a few seconds later the ball had rolled off its spot and come to rest in another place.

If it was determined that the player had caused the ball to move, he would have been required to replace the ball under penalty of one stroke (Rule 18-2a). If the player had not caused the ball to move, there would be no penalty and the ball would be played from its new position.

In some cases, it may never be possible to say with absolute certainty what, in fact, has caused the ball to move. Decision 18-2a/30 provides that such decisions need to be made on the balance of the weight of evidence. On this basis, as the ball had been at rest for a considerable period of time prior to Cabrera making the practice swing and the movement of the ball had occurred so quickly after the practice swing had been made, it was ruled that the Argentine's actions had caused the ball to move and he incurred a one-stroke penalty under Rule 18-2a and replaced the ball.

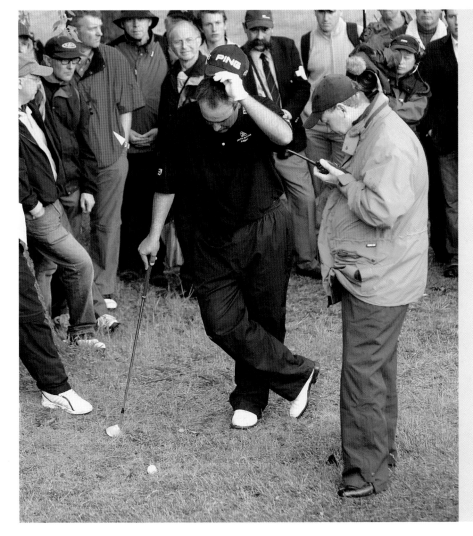

Angel Cabrera and a Rules official await a decision on his ball, which had rolled down the slight slope. Under Rule 18-2, if a ball is moved, it must be replaced unless the movement of the ball occurs after the player has begun the stroke.

▸ RULE 18
FREQUENTLY ASKED QUESTIONS

Q A player places his ball on a tee within the teeing ground and, in taking a practice swing, he accidentally moves his ball. Does he incur a penalty?

A The ball was not in play, as he has not yet made a stroke at it. The player has simply moved his ball with a practice swing and he must retrieve the ball, or put another ball on the tee, and carry on.

A ball is only in play at a hole after the player has made a stroke at it, and a player is only considered to have made a stroke when he swings the club back down towards the ball – the forward movement of the club – with the intention of striking the ball. As the player was taking a practice swing, he had no intention of

striking the ball, he has not made a stroke, hence, the ball was not in play. See the definitions of "ball in play" and "stroke".

Q A player's ball is lying on the fairway and, in taking a practice swing, he accidentally moves the ball. Does he incur a penalty?

A The player did not make a stroke, as he had no intention of making a stroke (see the definition of "stroke"); however, the ball was in play and the player has moved his ball (which was at rest). The player incurs a penalty of one stroke and must replace the ball (Rule 18-2a).

► RULE 19

BALL IN MOTION DEFLECTED OR STOPPED

DEFINITIONS
All defined terms are in *italics* and are listed in the Definitions section – see pages 13–23.

19-1 By Outside Agency

If a player's ball in motion is accidentally deflected or stopped by any *outside agency*, it is a *rub of the green*, there is no penalty and the ball must be played as it lies except:

a. If a player's ball in motion after a *stroke* other than on the *putting green* comes to rest in or on any moving or animate *outside agency*, the ball must *through the green* or in a *hazard* be dropped, or on the *putting green* be placed, as near as possible to the spot directly under the place where the ball came to rest in or on the *outside agency*, but not nearer the *hole*, and

b. If a player's ball in motion after a *stroke* on the *putting green* is deflected or stopped by, or comes to rest in or on, any moving or animate *outside agency* except a worm, insect or the like, the *stroke* is cancelled. The ball must be replaced and replayed.

If the ball is not immediately recoverable, another ball may be *substituted*.

Exception

Ball striking person attending or holding up *flagstick* or anything carried by him – see Rule 17-3b.

> **NOTE**
>
> If the *referee* or the *Committee* determines that a player's ball has been purposely deflected or stopped by an *outside agency*, Rule 1-4 applies to the player. If the *outside agency* is a *fellow-competitor* or his *caddie*, Rule 1-2 applies to the *fellow-competitor*.
>
> (Player's ball deflected or stopped by another ball – see Rule 19-5)

19-2 By Player, Partner, Caddie or Equipment

If a player's ball is accidentally deflected or stopped by himself, his *partner* or either of their *caddies* or *equipment*, **the player incurs a penalty of one stroke**. The ball must be played as it lies, except when it comes to rest in or on the player's, his *partner's* or either of their *caddies'* clothes or *equipment*, in which case the ball must *through the green* or in a *hazard* be dropped, or on the *putting green* be placed, as near as possible to the spot directly under the place where the ball came to rest in or on the article, but not nearer the *hole*.

Exceptions

1   Ball striking person attending or holding up *flagstick* or anything carried by him – see Rule 17-3b.

2   Dropped ball – see Rule 20-2a.

(Ball purposely deflected or stopped by player, partner or caddie – see Rule 1-2)

BALL IN MOTION DEFLECTED OR STOPPED

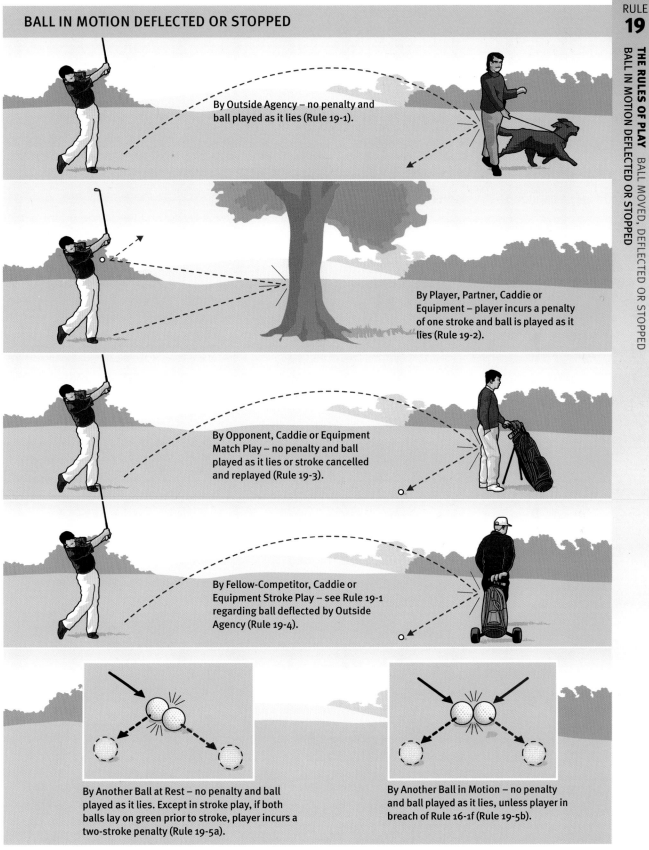

By Outside Agency – no penalty and ball played as it lies (Rule 19-1).

By Player, Partner, Caddie or Equipment – player incurs a penalty of one stroke and ball is played as it lies (Rule 19-2).

By Opponent, Caddie or Equipment Match Play – no penalty and ball played as it lies or stroke cancelled and replayed (Rule 19-3).

By Fellow-Competitor, Caddie or Equipment Stroke Play – see Rule 19-1 regarding ball deflected by Outside Agency (Rule 19-4).

By Another Ball at Rest – no penalty and ball played as it lies. Except in stroke play, if both balls lay on green prior to stroke, player incurs a two-stroke penalty (Rule 19-5a).

By Another Ball in Motion – no penalty and ball played as it lies, unless player in breach of Rule 16-1f (Rule 19-5b).

19-3 By Opponent, Caddie or Equipment in Match Play

If a player's ball is accidentally deflected or stopped by an opponent, his *caddie* or his *equipment*, there is no penalty. The player may, before another *stroke* is made by either *side*, cancel the *stroke* and play a ball, without penalty, as nearly as possible at the spot from which the original ball was last played (Rule 20-5) or he may play the ball as it lies. However, if the player elects not to cancel the *stroke* and the ball has come to rest in or on the opponent's or his *caddie's* clothes or *equipment*, the ball must *through the green* or in a *hazard* be dropped, or on the *putting green* be placed, as near as possible to the spot directly under the place where the ball came to rest in or on the article, but not nearer the *hole*.

Exception

Ball striking person attending or holding up *flagstick* or anything carried by him – see Rule 17-3b.
(Ball purposely deflected or stopped by opponent or caddie – see Rule 1-2)

19-4 By Fellow-Competitor, Caddie or Equipment in Stroke Play

See Rule 19-1 regarding ball deflected by *outside agency*.

Exception

Ball striking person attending or holding up *flagstick* or anything carried by him – see Rule 17-3b.

19-5 By Another Ball
19-5 a At Rest

If a player's ball in motion after a *stroke* is deflected or stopped by a *ball in play* and at rest, the player must play his ball as it lies. In match play, there is no penalty. In stroke play, there is no penalty unless both balls lay on the *putting green* prior to the *stroke*, in which case **the player incurs a penalty of two strokes.**

19-5 b In Motion

If a player's ball in motion after a *stroke* is deflected or stopped by another ball in motion after a *stroke*, the player must play his ball as it lies. There is no penalty, unless the player was in breach of Rule 16-1f, in which case **he incurs the penalty for breach of that Rule.**

Exception

If the player's ball is in motion after a *stroke* on the *putting green* and the other ball in motion is an *outside agency* – see Rule 19-1b.

PENALTY
For breach of Rule:
Match play – Loss of hole;
Stroke play – Two strokes.

► RULE 19

INCIDENTS

Tiger Woods found himself in a situation involving Rule 19 at the 1st hole in the second round of the 2006 PGA Championship. Woods' drive went left towards the gallery lining the fairway. It bounced near a fairway bunker, was deflected by a spectator and came to rest near the rope line restricting the gallery. A Rules official in the area immediately asked for information – including whether or not the ball was purposefully or accidentally deflected – from spectators and marshals who were present. No one was of the opinion that the ball had been purposefully deflected and, therefore, it was correctly played as it lay.

It later came to light through the use of television replays that there had, in fact, been a deliberate deflection by one of the spectators, who had raised a hand and swatted the ball back towards the fairway, although the ball had deflected only far enough to come to rest in thick rough. Had this information been available to the officials at the time, under the Note to Rule 19-1 they could have taken the view that, without the deflection, the ball would have come to rest beyond the gallery in the area and, in equity (Rule 1-4), Woods would have been required to drop his ball at the spot where it was estimated that it would have come to rest without the deliberate spectator intervention.

In the course of the 2003 Masters Tournament, Jeff Maggert accidentally deflected his own ball in an attempt to play from the fairway bunker at the 3rd hole. Maggert was playing in the final group on the final day when his drive at the par-4 finished in one of four bunkers at the left of the landing zone. The ball was far enough behind the forward lip of the bunker for him to judge that he could play a full approach to the putting green. However, once struck, the ball smashed into the lip, ricocheted backwards and hit him. The Rules official walking with the group informed Maggert that a two-stroke penalty had been incurred and the ball had to be played as it lay (Rule 19-2b).

However, further to the introduction of the new Rules on 1 January 2008, if the same incident were to occur now the result would be a penalty of one stroke. This is due to the fact that the penalty for a player's ball in motion being accidentally deflected or stopped by

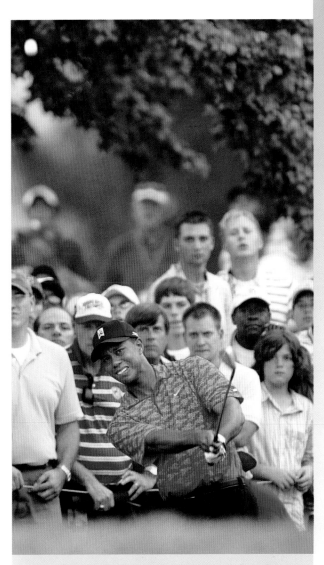

Tiger Woods' ball was deemed to have been deflected unintentionally when it went into the gallery lining the fairway at the 2006 PGA Championship, so Rule 19-1 was not invoked. However, subsequent camera evidence spotted that the ball had been deliberately deflected by a spectator.

himself, his partner or either of their caddies or equipment has been reduced from loss of hole in match play and two strokes in stroke play to one stroke in both forms of play.

Jeff Maggert's assault on the 2003 Masters was derailed at the 3rd hole in the final round when his ball struck the lip of a bunker and ricocheted back and hit him. He was given a two-stroke penalty. The penalty was amended in January 2008 and is now one-stroke, in both match play and stroke play.

▸ RULE 19

FREQUENTLY ASKED QUESTIONS

Q What do I do if my ball strikes a tee marker or a direction post?

A If a ball strikes a tee marker, water hazard post, direction post or similar, it is simply a rub of the green and the ball must be played as it lies, without penalty (Rule 19-1).

Q What penalty do I incur if I strike my ball and it hits my golf bag as a result?

A In match play or stroke play, the player incurs a penalty of one stroke for a breach and must play the ball as it lies, without penalty (Rule 19-2).

▶ RULE 20

LIFTING, DROPPING AND PLACING; PLAYING FROM WRONG PLACE

20-1 Lifting and Marking

A ball to be lifted under the *Rules* may be lifted by the player, his *partner* or another person authorised by the player. In any such case, the player is responsible for any breach of the *Rules*.

The position of the ball must be marked before it is lifted under a *Rule* that requires it to be replaced. If it is not marked, **the player incurs a penalty of one stroke** and the ball must be replaced. If it is not replaced, **the player incurs the general penalty for breach of this Rule** but there is no additional penalty under Rule 20-1.

If a ball or ball-marker is accidentally *moved* in the process of lifting the ball under a *Rule* or marking its position, the ball or ball-marker must be replaced. There is no penalty, provided the movement of the ball or ball-marker is directly attributable to the specific act of marking the position of or lifting the ball. Otherwise, **the player incurs a penalty of one stroke** under this Rule or Rule 18-2a.

DEFINITIONS
All defined terms are in *italics* and are listed in the Definitions section – see pages 13–23.

PROCEDURE FOR LIFTING BALL

Although I want your ball lifted because it is interfering with my play, why are you marking it?

Because when a ball is lifted anywhere on the course and it has to be replaced, its position must be marked.

Exception

If a player incurs a penalty for failing to act in accordance with Rule 5-3 or 12-2, there is no additional penalty under Rule 20-1.

> **NOTE**
>
> The position of a ball to be lifted should be marked by placing a ball-marker, a small coin or other similar object immediately behind the ball. If the ball-marker interferes with the play, *stance* or *stroke* of another player, it should be placed one or more clubhead-lengths to one side.

20-2 Dropping and Re-Dropping

20-2 a By Whom and How

A ball to be dropped under the *Rules* must be dropped by the player himself. He must stand erect, hold the ball at shoulder height and arm's length and drop it. If a ball is dropped by any other person or in any other manner and the error is not corrected as provided in Rule 20-6, **the player incurs a penalty of one stroke.**

If the ball, when dropped, touches any person or the *equipment* of any player before or after it strikes a part of the *course* and before it comes to rest, the ball must be re-dropped, without penalty. There is no limit to the number of times a ball must be re-dropped in these circumstances.

(Taking action to influence position or movement of ball – see Rule 1-2)

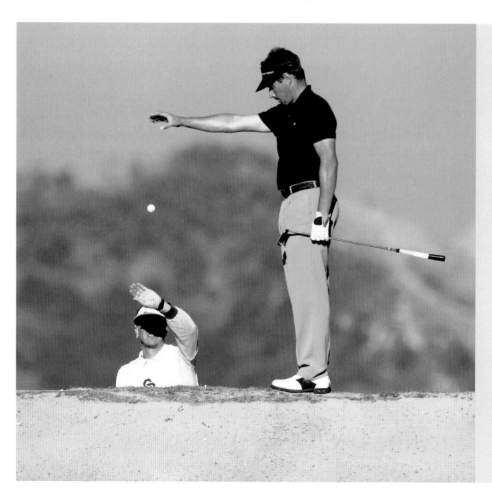

The player shall stand up straight, hold the ball at shoulder height and arm's length, and drop it.

WHEN TO RE-DROP BALL

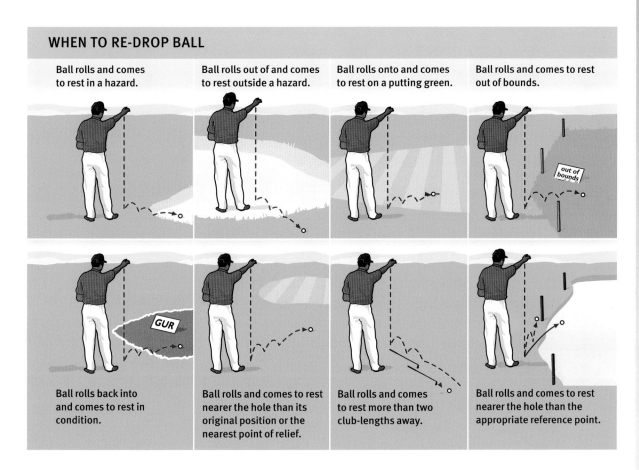

| Ball rolls and comes to rest in a hazard. | Ball rolls out of and comes to rest outside a hazard. | Ball rolls onto and comes to rest on a putting green. | Ball rolls and comes to rest out of bounds. |

| Ball rolls back into and comes to rest in condition. | Ball rolls and comes to rest nearer the hole than its original position or the nearest point of relief. | Ball rolls and comes to rest more than two club-lengths away. | Ball rolls and comes to rest nearer the hole than the appropriate reference point. |

20-2 b Where to Drop

When a ball is to be dropped as near as possible to a specific spot, it must be dropped not nearer the *hole* than the specific spot which, if it is not precisely known to the player, must be estimated.

A ball when dropped must first strike a part of the *course* where the applicable *Rule* requires it to be dropped. If it is not so dropped, Rules 20-6 and 20-7 apply.

20-2 c When to Re-Drop

A dropped ball must be re-dropped, without penalty, if it:

(i)   rolls into and comes to rest in a *hazard*;

(ii) rolls out of and comes to rest outside a *hazard*;

(iii) rolls onto and comes to rest on a *putting green*;

(iv) rolls and comes to rest *out of bounds*;

(v)   rolls to and comes to rest in a position where there is interference by the condition from which relief was taken under Rule 24-2b (immovable obstruction), Rule 25-1 (abnormal ground conditions), Rule 25-3 (wrong putting green) or a Local Rule (Rule 33-8a), or rolls back into the pitch-mark from which it was lifted under Rule 25-2 (embedded ball);

(vi) rolls and comes to rest more than two club-lengths from where it first struck a part of the *course*; or

(vii) rolls and comes to rest nearer the *hole* than:

    (a) its original position or estimated position (see Rule 20-2b) unless otherwise permitted by the *Rules*; or

(b)   the *nearest point of relief* or maximum available relief (Rule 24-2, 25-1 or 25-3); or

(c)   the point where the original ball last crossed the margin of the *water hazard* or *lateral water hazard* (Rule 26-1).

If the ball when re-dropped rolls into any position listed above, it must be placed as near as possible to the spot where it first struck a part of the *course* when re-dropped.

NOTE 1

If a ball when dropped or re-dropped comes to rest and subsequently *moves*, the ball must be played as it lies, unless the provisions of any other *Rule* apply.

NOTE 2

If a ball to be re-dropped or placed under this Rule is not immediately recoverable, another ball may be *substituted*.

(Use of dropping zone – see Appendix I; Part B; section 8)

20-3 Placing and Replacing

20-3 a By Whom and Where

A ball to be placed under the *Rules* must be placed by the player or his *partner*. If a ball is to be replaced, the player, his *partner* or the person who lifted or *moved* it must place it on the spot from which it was lifted or *moved*. If the ball is placed or replaced by any other person and the error is not corrected as provided in Rule 20-6, **the player incurs a penalty of one stroke**. In any such case, the player is responsible for any other breach of the *Rules* that occurs as a result of the placing or replacing of the ball.

If a ball or ball-marker is accidentally *moved* in the process of placing or replacing the ball, the ball or ball-marker must be replaced. There is no penalty, provided the movement of the ball or ball-marker is directly attributable to the specific act of

LIE OF BALL ALTERED

LIE OF BALL ALTERED

placing or replacing the ball or removing the ball-marker. Otherwise, **the player incurs a penalty of one stroke** under Rule 18-2a or 20-1.

If a ball to be replaced is placed other than on the spot from which it was lifted or *moved* and the error is not corrected as provided in Rule 20-6, **the player incurs the general penalty, loss of hole in match play or two strokes in stroke play, for a breach of the applicable *Rule*.**

20-3 b Lie of Ball to be Placed or Replaced Altered

If the original lie of a ball to be placed or replaced has been altered:

(i)   except in a *hazard*, the ball must be placed in the nearest lie most similar to the original lie that is not more than one club-length from the original lie, not nearer the *hole* and not in a *hazard*;

(ii) in a *water hazard*, the ball must be placed in accordance with Clause (i) above, except that the ball must be placed in the *water hazard*;

(iii) in a *bunker*, the original lie must be re-created as nearly as possible and the ball must be placed in that lie.

20-3 c Spot Not Determinable

If it is impossible to determine the spot where the ball is to be placed or replaced:

(i)   *through the green*, the ball must be dropped as near as possible to the place where it lay but not in a *hazard* or on a *putting green*;

(ii) in a *hazard*, the ball must be dropped in the *hazard* as near as possible to the place where it lay;

(iii) on the *putting green*, the ball must be placed as near as possible to the place where it lay but not in a *hazard*.

Exception

When resuming play (Rule 6-8d), if the spot where the ball is to be placed is impossible to determine, it must be estimated and the ball placed on the estimated spot.

20-3 d Ball Fails to Come to Rest on Spot

If a ball when placed fails to come to rest on the spot on which it was placed, there is no penalty and the ball must be replaced. If it still fails to come to rest on that spot:

(i)   except in a *hazard*, it must be placed at the nearest spot where it can be placed at rest that is not nearer the *hole* and not in a *hazard*;

(ii)   in a *hazard*, it must be placed in the *hazard* at the nearest spot where it can be placed at rest that is not nearer the *hole*.

If a ball when placed comes to rest on the spot on which it is placed, and it subsequently *moves*, there is no penalty and the ball must be played as it lies, unless the provisions of any other *Rule* apply.

PENALTY

For breach of Rule 20-1, 20-2 or 20-3:

Match play – Loss of hole;

Stroke play – Two strokes.

20-4 When Ball Dropped or Placed is in Play

If the player's *ball in play* has been lifted, it is again in play when dropped or placed.

   A *substituted ball* becomes the *ball in play* when it has been dropped or placed.

(Ball incorrectly substituted – see Rule 15-2)

(Lifting ball incorrectly substituted, dropped or placed – see Rule 20-6)

20-5 Making Next Stroke from Where Previous Stroke Made

When a player elects or is required to make his next *stroke* from where a previous *stroke* was made, he must proceed as follows:

(a)   **On the Teeing Ground:** The ball to be played must be played from within the *teeing ground*. It may be played from anywhere within the *teeing ground* and may be teed.

(b)   **Through the Green:** The ball to be played must be dropped and when dropped must first strike a part of the *course through the green*.

(c)   **In a Hazard:** The ball to be played must be dropped and when dropped must first strike a part of the *course* in the *hazard*.

(d)   **On the Putting Green:** The ball to be played must be placed on the *putting green*.

PENALTY

For breach of Rule 20-5:

Match play – Loss of hole;

Stroke play – Two strokes.

20-6 Lifting Ball Incorrectly Substituted, Dropped or Placed

A ball incorrectly *substituted*, dropped or placed in a wrong place or otherwise not in accordance with the *Rules* but not played may be lifted, without penalty, and the player must then proceed correctly.

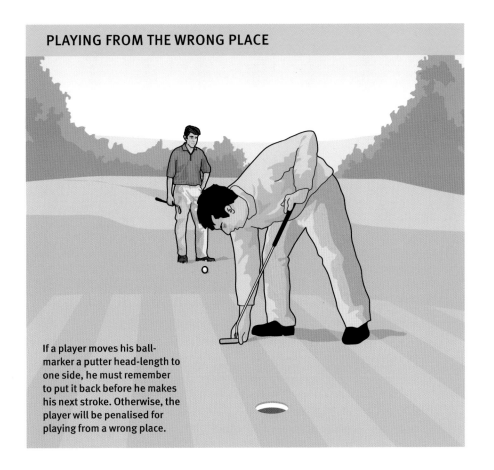

PLAYING FROM THE WRONG PLACE

If a player moves his ball-marker a putter head-length to one side, he must remember to put it back before he makes his next stroke. Otherwise, the player will be penalised for playing from a wrong place.

20-7 Playing from Wrong Place

20-7 a General

A player has played from a wrong place if he makes a *stroke* at his *ball in play*:

(i)   on a part of the *course* where the *Rules* do not permit a *stroke* to be played or a ball to be dropped or placed; or

(ii) when the *Rules* require a dropped ball to be re-dropped or a *moved* ball to be replaced.

> NOTE
>
> For a ball played from outside the *teeing ground* or from a wrong *teeing ground* – see Rule 11-4.

20-7 b Match Play

If a player makes a *stroke* from a wrong place, **he loses the hole.**

20-7 c Stroke Play

If a *competitor* makes a *stroke* from a wrong place, **he incurs a penalty of two strokes under the applicable *Rule*.** He must play out the hole with the ball played from the wrong place, without correcting his error, provided he has not committed a serious breach (see Note 1).

If a *competitor* becomes aware that he has played from a wrong place and believes that he may have committed a serious breach, he must, before making a *stroke* on the next *teeing ground*, play out the hole with a second ball played in accordance with the

Rules. If the hole being played is the last hole of the round, he must declare, before leaving the *putting green*, that he will play out the hole with a second ball played in accordance with the *Rules*.

If the *competitor* has played a second ball, he must report the facts to the *Committee* before returning his score card; if he fails to do so, **he is disqualified**. The *Committee* must determine whether the *competitor* has committed a serious breach of the applicable *Rule*. If he has, the score with the second ball counts and **the *competitor* must add two *penalty strokes*** to his score with that ball. If the *competitor* has committed a serious breach and has failed to correct it as outlined above, **he is disqualified**.

NOTE 1

A *competitor* is deemed to have committed a serious breach of the applicable *Rule* if the *Committee* considers he has gained a significant advantage as a result of playing from a wrong place.

NOTE 2

If a *competitor* plays a second ball under Rule 20-7c and it is ruled not to count, *strokes* made with that ball and *penalty strokes* incurred solely by playing that ball are disregarded. If the second ball is ruled to count, the *stroke* made from the wrong place and any *strokes* subsequently taken with the original ball including *penalty strokes* incurred solely by playing that ball are disregarded.

NOTE 3

If a player incurs a penalty for making a *stroke* from a wrong place, there is no additional penalty for *substituting* a ball when not permitted.

▶ RULE 20
INCIDENTS

Dropping the ball (under Rule 20) is one of the most fundamental and frequently used procedures in the Rules of Golf, and an excellent demonstration of the application of this Rule was seen during the closing holes of the 2004 MCI Heritage at Harbour Town Golf Links.

Ted Purdy was leading the tournament, but was acutely aware of a low total posted by eventual play-off winner Stewart Cink. At the 13th hole, Purdy's ball came to rest on a drain cover (an immovable obstruction) in the fairway, from which he was entitled to free relief. Purdy clearly knew the procedure under the relevant Rule (Rule 24-2) and decided to proceed without the assistance of an official. However, when he came to drop his ball within one club-length of the nearest point of relief, he did so with his hand well below shoulder height when the ball was released.

Rule 20-2a provides that a player, when dropping a ball, must stand erect, hold the ball at shoulder height and arm's length and drop it. If a player makes a stroke at a ball dropped in an incorrect manner, he is subject to a penalty of one stroke. However, if the error is realised prior to a stroke being made, it can be corrected without penalty by lifting the ball and dropping it correctly.

In Purdy's case, he was lucky that a Rules official was watching his procedure and intervened before the player made a stroke. It is the Rules official's duty to prevent a breach if he can do so. He advised Purdy of his error and had the player lift the ball and drop it properly, thus saving him a penalty stroke.

Less fortunate was Retief Goosen in the first round of the 2006 South African Airways Open. As he stood on the 17th tee, he was eight under par and could not have imagined what was about to happen on the 543-yard par 5. Having struck a wayward tee shot, he then hit a poor provisional ball from the tee. Because he was unable to find his first ball within the five-minute search period, his provisional ball, which had been found in a bush, became the ball in play.

The South African elected to deem the provisional ball unplayable and (under Rule 28c) dropped within two club-lengths of the spot where the ball lay. The ball when dropped rolled outside the two club-length dropping area, but did not roll more than two club-lengths from where it had first struck the course and did not roll closer to the hole than the ball's original position. As the ball had not rolled into any of the positions requiring a re-drop under Rule 20-2c, the ball was in play.

Inexplicably, Goosen thought he had to re-drop because the ball had rolled outside the area measured under Rule 28c. He therefore lifted the ball, dropped it again and played from the new spot. As a result, he incurred the general penalty of two strokes under Rule 18 for lifting a ball without authority and failing to replace it. He later told officials that he knew the Rule but had just had a "brain freeze".

With a lost ball, an unplayable drop and two-stroke penalty, Goosen finished with an 11 on the 17th hole, although he still managed to birdie the final hole of the round to post a three-under-par 69.

During the final round of the 2008 US Open at Torrey Pines, Brandt Snedeker marked and lifted his ball on the 9th green and, as he was crouching with the intention of replacing the ball, the ball slipped out of his hand and moved his ball-marker.

Rule 20-3a provides that, if a ball-marker is accidentally moved in the process of replacing the ball, the ball or ball-marker must be replaced and there is no penalty, provided the movement of the ball-marker is directly attributable to the specific act of replacing the ball. However, if the movement of the ball-marker is not in the specific act of replacing the ball, the player incurs a penalty of one stroke and must replace the ball or ball-marker.

Decision 20-1/15 provides that, in order for the movement of the ball-marker to be considered directly attributable to the specific act of replacing the ball, the movement has to occur when the ball was actually placed in front of the ball-marker such that the player's hand or the placement of the ball caused the ball-marker to move. The Decision goes on to say that any accidental movement of the ball-marker that occurs before the specific act, such as dropping the ball, regardless of the height from which it was dropped, is not considered directly attributable to the specific act of replacing the ball.

Consequently, as Snedeker had dropped his ball prior to the specific act of replacing it, he was penalised one stroke for the accidental movement of his ball-marker, and was required to replace his ball on the original spot from which it was lifted.

► RULE 20
FREQUENTLY ASKED QUESTIONS

Q Must a player use a small coin or similar object to mark the position of his ball before lifting it?
A The Note to Rule 20-1 states in part that the position of the ball should be marked by placing a ball-marker, small coin or other small object immediately behind the ball. When the word "should" is used in the Rules of Golf it is a recommendation only and failure to comply does not result in a penalty – see the section entitled "How to Use the Rule Book" on page 5. The intention is to emphasise that use of a ball-marker or other small object (such as a coin) is considered to be the best way to mark a ball.

Q Is the person who lifted the player's ball the only person who may replace it?
A No. Up to a maximum of three different people may replace a ball, depending on the circumstances, that is the player, his partner or the person who lifted it. For example, in a four-ball match, if a player were to authorise his caddie to lift his ball, the caddie, the player or the player's partner could replace it. However, if the player lifts the ball himself, only the player or his partner may replace it – see Rule 20-3a.

► RULE 21

CLEANING BALL

A ball on the *putting green* may be cleaned when lifted under Rule 16-1b. Elsewhere, a ball may be cleaned when lifted, except when it has been lifted:

a.   To determine if it is unfit for play (Rule 5-3);

b.   For identification (Rule 12-2), in which case it may be cleaned only to the extent necessary for identification; or

c.   Because it is assisting or interfering with play (Rule 22).

If a player cleans his ball during play of a hole except as provided in this Rule, **he incurs a penalty of one stroke** and the ball, if lifted, must be replaced.

If a player who is required to replace a ball fails to do so, **he incurs the general penalty under the applicable Rule**, but there is no additional penalty under Rule 21.

Exception

If a player incurs a penalty for failing to act in accordance with Rule 5-3, 12-2 or 22, there is no additional penalty under Rule 21.

► RULE 21

FREQUENTLY ASKED QUESTION

Q A player is asked to lift his ball because it is interfering with the play of a fellow-competitor (Rule 22-2) and puts it in his pocket. Is he deemed to have cleaned it?
A Whether the ball is cleaned is a question of fact. The action of putting the ball into a pocket can result in the ball being cleaned and any doubt should be resolved against the player. In both match play and stroke play, the player would incur a one-stroke penalty if it were considered that he has cleaned his ball.

► RULE 22

BALL ASSISTING OR INTERFERING WITH PLAY

22-1 Ball Assisting Play

Except when a ball is in motion, if a player considers that a ball might assist any other player, he may:

a.   Lift the ball if it is his ball; or

b.   Have any other ball lifted.

A ball lifted under this Rule must be replaced (see Rule 20-3). The ball must not be cleaned unless it lies on the *putting green* (see Rule 21).

BALL INTERFERING WITH OR ASSISTING PLAY

In stroke play, a player required to lift his ball may play first rather than lift the ball.

In stroke play, if the *Committee* determines that *competitors* have agreed not to lift a ball that might assist any *competitor*, **they are disqualified.**

22-2 Ball Interfering with Play

Except when a ball is in motion, if a player considers that another ball might interfere with his play, he may have it lifted.

A ball lifted under this Rule must be replaced (see Rule 20-3). The ball must not be cleaned, unless it lies on the *putting green* (see Rule 21).

In stroke play, a player required to lift his ball may play first rather than lift the ball.

NOTE

Except on the *putting green*, a player may not lift his ball solely because he considers that it might interfere with the play of another player. If a player lifts his ball without being asked to do so, **he incurs a penalty of one stroke** for a breach of Rule 18-2a, but there is no additional penalty under Rule 22.

PENALTY
For breach of Rule:
Match play – Loss of hole;
Stroke play – Two strokes.

▶ RULE 22

INCIDENT

Because golf is played on the largest playing field of any sport, it's rare for one ball to touch another.

However, Jesper Parnevik and Scott Hoch found themselves in such a predicament just off the 6th green at Pinehurst No.2 during the 1999 US Open. Fortunately, the procedure in such a situation is concise.

Rule 22 allows any player to lift his ball if he believes it will assist another player, or have any ball lifted that might interfere with his play or assist any other player. Except on the putting green, a ball lifted under this Rule may not be cleaned.

Hoch and Parnevik both played just to the left side of the green at this 222-yard par 3. Upon arriving at the green, they found that the balls were touching one another and lay about three inches off the fringe in the Bermuda grass rough. Both balls were held slightly off the ground by the stiff nature of the grass. Because Hoch's ball was closer to the hole, it was necessary that it be lifted in order for Parnevik to play his shot.

When Hoch lifted his ball, Parnevik's moved an inch closer to the hole. Under a Rules official's watchful eye, Parnevik attempted to replace his ball in its original location. However, the supporting nature of the Bermuda grass could not be reintroduced and Parnevik's ball sunk a little deeper into the rough than its original position. Under the Rules, it does not matter if the movement is vertical or horizontal. The ball could not be replaced in its original position so that it would remain at rest.

Rule 20-3d covers such a situation by stating that if a ball, when placed or replaced, fails to come to rest on that spot it must be replaced. If it again fails to remain at rest, it must be placed at the nearest spot where it can be placed at rest, which is not nearer the hole and not in a hazard.

Therefore, Parnevik found another spot that was nearest to the original position where the ball would remain at rest. He chipped on to the green and in doing so altered Hoch's lie.

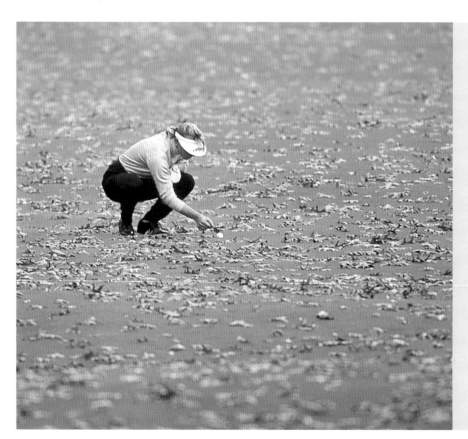

A player is entitled to remove any loose impediment without penalty, except when both the loose impediment and the ball lie in or touch the same hazard.

In this case, Hoch was entitled to the lie that his shot gave him. Since his lie had been altered, he found the nearest lie most similar to and within one club-length of his original lie and placed his ball at that spot. Then he chipped the ball in for a birdie two.

▶ RULE 22

FREQUENTLY ASKED QUESTION

Q What is the procedure when one ball lies close to another in a bunker?
A When two balls lie very close together in a bunker and one ball is interfering with the play of the other, the player whose turn it is to play first can have the other ball lifted (Rule 22). The position of the ball must be marked before it is lifted and it must not be cleaned.

If the lie of the ball that has been lifted is altered by the play of the other ball, the player is required to re-create his original lie and replace the ball. The original lie may be re-created using hands, a rake, club, or whatever. In stroke play, a player required to lift his ball that may interfere with another, may play first rather than lift the ball, to save time – see Decision 20-3b/1.

▶ RULE 23

LOOSE IMPEDIMENTS

23-1 Relief

Except when both the *loose impediment* and the ball lie in or touch the same *hazard*, any *loose impediment* may be removed without penalty.

If the ball lies anywhere other than on the *putting green* and the removal of a *loose impediment* by the player causes the ball to *move*, Rule 18-2a applies.

On the *putting green*, if the ball or ball-marker is accidentally *moved* in the process of the player removing a *loose impediment*, the ball or ball-marker must be replaced. There is no penalty, provided the movement of the ball or ball-marker is directly attributable to the removal of the *loose impediment*. Otherwise, if the player causes the ball to *move*, **he incurs a penalty of one stroke** under Rule 18-2a.

When a ball is in motion, a *loose impediment* that might influence the movement of the ball must not be removed.

DEFINITIONS
All defined terms are in *italics* and are listed in the Definitions section – see pages 13–23.

> **NOTE**
> If the ball lies in a *hazard*, the player must not touch or move any *loose impediment* lying in or touching the same *hazard* – see Rule 13-4c.

PENALTY
For breach of Rule:
Match play – Loss of hole;
Stroke play – Two strokes.
(Searching for ball in hazard – see Rule 12-1)
(Touching line of putt – see Rule 16-1a)

▸ RULE 23

INCIDENT

The Rules of Golf permitted Tiger Woods to gain assistance from his substantial gallery in moving a loose impediment during the 1999 Phoenix Open.

During the final round, Woods' drive from the 13th tee travelled 360 yards before finishing in the desert just off the left side of the fairway. The ball stopped about two feet directly behind a boulder that was roughly four feet wide, two feet high and two feet thick. The rock was too heavy for Woods to move by himself, and his ball was too close to it to play over or around. Without moving the rock, his best option would have been to play sideways on to the fairway.

With 225 yards to the putting green, Woods was not inclined to pitch out without first knowing what his options were with regard to the rock.

A PGA Tour Rules official appeared at the scene. With a glimmer of a smile, Woods kicked the rock and asked, "… It's not a pebble but is it a loose impediment?"

The definition within the Rules of Golf states that loose impediments are natural objects that are not fixed or growing, not solidly embedded and do not adhere to the ball. There is no reference to size or weight.

Decision 23-1/2 states that stones of any size are loose impediments and may be removed, as long as they are not solidly embedded and their removal does not unduly delay play.

The official replied, "It's readily movable if you have people who can move it real quick."

"Really?" Woods responded to the revelation quietly.

Then the official added in an enquiring tone, "But it kind of looks embedded to me."

"It's embedded?" Woods asked as they both stepped back to look.

The official decided the stone was just lying on the desert floor and was not solidly embedded. He also knew that Decision 23-1/3 specifically permits spectators, caddies, fellow-competitors – essentially anyone – to assist in the removing of a large loose impediment.

Several men rolled the stone out of Woods' line of play as others watched and cheered. Following the removal, Woods shook each man's hand and then played his shot directly toward the green, where it finished in the bunker to the right of the green.

Loose impediments are natural objects that come in all shapes and sizes. At the 1999 Phoenix Open, Tiger Woods learned that a player can receive assistance in removing a large loose impediment. Details of this incident can be reviewed above.

► RULE 23

FREQUENTLY ASKED QUESTIONS

Q Can I use my putter, hand, cap or towel to remove loose impediments?
A Yes. Loose impediments may be removed by any means. In removing loose impediments on the line of putt, the player must not press anything down.

Q Can I remove stones from bunkers?
A Stones are, by definition, loose impediments. Generally, it is not permitted to remove a loose impediment that lies in the same hazard as your ball (Rule 13-4c); however, a Committee can introduce a Local Rule stating that stones in bunkers are movable obstructions (Appendix I, Part B, 5).

► RULE 24

OBSTRUCTIONS

24-1 Movable Obstruction

A player may take relief, without penalty, from a movable *obstruction* as follows:

a. If the ball does not lie in or on the *obstruction*, the *obstruction* may be removed. If the ball *moves*, it must be replaced, and there is no penalty, provided that the movement of the ball is directly attributable to the removal of the *obstruction*. Otherwise, Rule 18-2a applies.

DEFINITIONS
All defined terms are in *italics* and are listed in the Definitions section – see pages 13–23.

BALL ON MOVABLE OBSTRUCTION

I'll just place a mark next to the ball before I remove the towel so I know roughly where my ball lay. Then I can lift my ball and the towel and drop the ball as near as possible to where it lay, but not nearer the hole.

BALL AGAINST RAKE ROLLS INTO BUNKER WHEN RAKE REMOVED

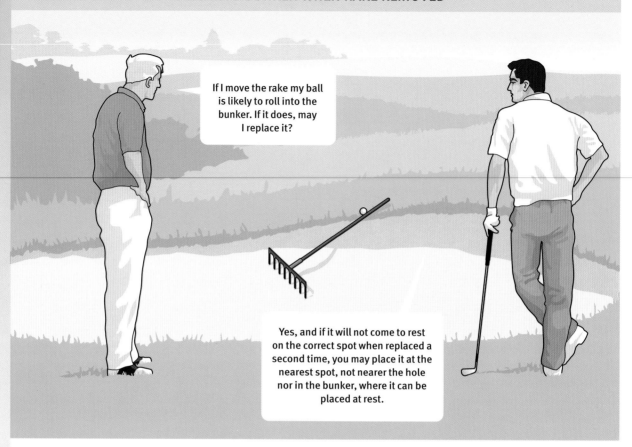

b.   If the ball lies in or on the *obstruction*, the ball may be lifted and the *obstruction* removed. The ball must *through the green* or in a *hazard* be dropped, or on the *putting green* be placed, as near as possible to the spot directly under the place where the ball lay in or on the *obstruction*, but not nearer the *hole*.
The ball may be cleaned when lifted under this Rule.

   When a ball is in motion, an *obstruction* that might influence the movement of the ball, other than *equipment* of any player or the *flagstick* when attended, removed or held up, must not be moved.
(Exerting influence on ball – see Rule 1-2)

NOTE
If a ball to be dropped or placed under this Rule is not immediately recoverable, another ball may be *substituted*.

24-2 Immovable Obstruction
24-2 a Interference
Interference by an immovable *obstruction* occurs when a ball lies in or on the *obstruction*, or when the *obstruction* interferes with the player's *stance* or the area of his intended swing. If the player's ball lies on the *putting green*, interference also occurs if an immovable *obstruction* on the *putting green* intervenes on his *line of putt*. Otherwise, intervention on the *line of play* is not, of itself, interference under this Rule.

24-2 b Relief

Except when the ball is in a *water hazard* or a *lateral water hazard*, a player may take relief from interference by an immovable *obstruction* as follows:

(i) **Through the Green:** If the ball lies *through the green*, the player must lift the ball and drop it, without penalty, within one club-length of and not nearer the *hole* than the *nearest point of relief*. The *nearest point of relief* must not be in a *hazard* or on a *putting green*. When the ball is dropped within one club-length of the *nearest point of relief*, the ball must first strike a part of the *course* at a spot that avoids interference by the immovable *obstruction* and is not in a *hazard* and not on a *putting green*.

(ii) **In a Bunker:** If the ball is in a *bunker*, the player must lift the ball and drop it either:

(a) Without penalty, in accordance with Clause (i) above, except that the *nearest point of relief* must be in the *bunker* and the ball must be dropped in the *bunker*; or

FLAGSTICK REMOVED WHEN BALL IN MOTION

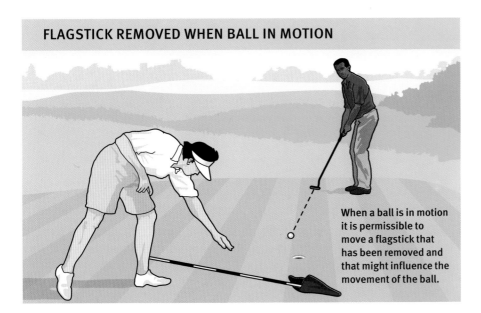

When a ball is in motion it is permissible to move a flagstick that has been removed and that might influence the movement of the ball.

BALL BEHIND IMMOVABLE OBSTRUCTION

I have found my ball and it is playable but this shelter is in my way. Am I entitled to any free relief?

No, because the shelter does not interfere with your stance or the area of your intended swing.

ROADS AND PATHS

Am I entitled to relief without penalty from this road?

Yes. The road is an immovable obstruction, but your nearest point of relief will be in the bushes. You can, of course, play it as it lies.

DIRECTION OF PLAY

DETERMINING THE NEAREST POINT OF RELIEF FROM IMMOVABLE OBSTRUCTION

No. You are entitled to relief but your nearest point of relief must be in the bunker and the ball must be dropped in the bunker. Alternatively, you may drop out of the bunker under penalty of one stroke, keeping the point where the ball lay directly between the hole and the spot on which the ball is dropped.

I have interference from these steps, which are an immovable obstruction. The nearest point of relief appears to be outside the bunker, is that correct?

(b) Under penalty of one stroke, outside the *bunker* keeping the point where the ball lay directly between the *hole* and the spot on which the ball is dropped, with no limit to how far behind the *bunker* the ball may be dropped.

(iii) On the Putting Green: If the ball lies on the *putting green*, the player must lift the ball and place it, without penalty, at the *nearest point of relief* that is not in a *hazard*. The *nearest point of relief* may be off the *putting green*.

(iv) On the Teeing Ground: If the ball lies on the *teeing ground*, the player must lift the ball and drop it, without penalty, in accordance with Clause (i) above.

The ball may be cleaned when lifted under this Rule.

RELIEF FOR SIDEWAYS STROKE

(Ball rolling to a position where there is interference by the condition from which relief was taken – see Rule 20-2c(v))

Exception

A player may not take relief under this Rule if (a) it is clearly unreasonable for him to make a *stroke* because of interference by anything other than an immovable *obstruction* or (b) interference by an immovable *obstruction* would occur only through use of an unnecessarily abnormal *stance*, swing or direction of play.

> **NOTE 1**
> If a ball is in a *water hazard* (including a *lateral water hazard*), the player may not take relief from interference by an immovable *obstruction*. The player must play the ball as it lies or proceed under Rule 26-1.
> **NOTE 2**
> If a ball to be dropped or placed under this Rule is not immediately recoverable, another ball may be *substituted*.
> **NOTE 3**
> The *Committee* may make a Local Rule stating that the player must determine the *nearest point of relief* without crossing over, through or under the *obstruction*.

24-3 Ball in Obstruction Not Found

It is a question of fact whether a ball that has not been found after having been struck toward an *obstruction* is in the *obstruction*. In order to apply this Rule, it must be known or virtually certain that the ball is in the *obstruction*. In the absence of such knowledge or certainty, the player must proceed under Rule 27-1.

RELIEF FROM OBSTRUCTION GIVES RELIEF FOR LINE OF PLAY

Now I've dropped the ball I'm in a far better position. Can I go for the green?

Yes. After dropping the ball the Rules permit you to play in any direction you wish. Also, the Rules don't distinguish between fairway and rough and it is your good fortune that the bush no longer hinders your shot to the green.

After David Frost was denied relief from the road to the left of the 2nd hole at Carnoustie he played his ball on to the road and then took relief under Rule 24-2 – see incident on pages 124–125.

24-3 a Ball in Movable Obstruction Not Found

If it is known or virtually certain that a ball that has not been found is in a movable *obstruction*, the player may *substitute* another ball and take relief, without penalty, under this Rule. If he elects to do so, he must remove the *obstruction* and *through the green* or in a *hazard* drop a ball, or on the *putting green* place a ball, as near as possible to the spot directly under the place where the ball last crossed the outermost limits of the movable *obstruction*, but not nearer the hole.

24-3 b Ball in Immovable Obstruction Not Found

If it is known or virtually certain that a ball that has not been found is in an immovable *obstruction*, the player may take relief under this Rule. If he elects to do so, the spot

NO RELIEF WITHOUT PENALTY IN WATER HAZARD

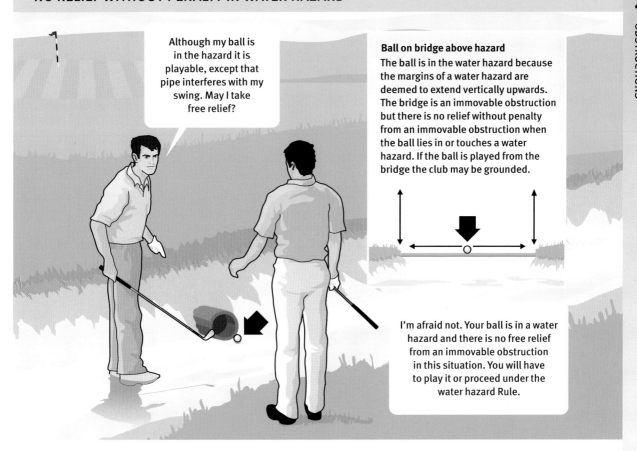

Although my ball is in the hazard it is playable, except that pipe interferes with my swing. May I take free relief?

Ball on bridge above hazard
The ball is in the water hazard because the margins of a water hazard are deemed to extend vertically upwards. The bridge is an immovable obstruction but there is no relief without penalty from an immovable obstruction when the ball lies in or touches a water hazard. If the ball is played from the bridge the club may be grounded.

I'm afraid not. Your ball is in a water hazard and there is no free relief from an immovable obstruction in this situation. You will have to play it or proceed under the water hazard Rule.

STILE IN BOUNDARY FENCE

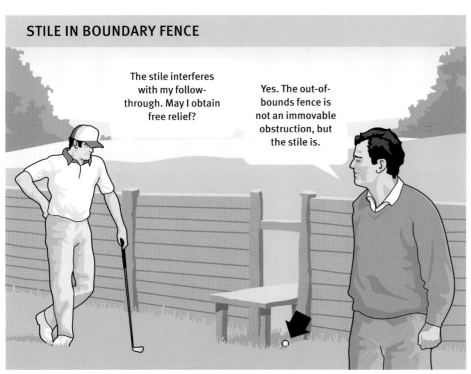

The stile interferes with my follow-through. May I obtain free relief?

Yes. The out-of-bounds fence is not an immovable obstruction, but the stile is.

where the ball last crossed the outermost limits of the *obstruction* must be determined and, for the purpose of applying this Rule, the ball is deemed to lie at this spot and the player must proceed as follows:

(i) Through the Green: If the ball last crossed the outermost limits of the immovable *obstruction* at a spot *through the green*, the player may *substitute* another ball, without penalty, and take relief as prescribed in Rule 24-2b(i).

(ii) In a Bunker: If the ball last crossed the outermost limits of the immovable *obstruction* at a spot in a *bunker*, the player may *substitute* another ball, without penalty, and take relief as prescribed in Rule 24-2b(ii).

(iii) In a Water Hazard (including a Lateral Water Hazard): If the ball last crossed the outermost limits of the immovable *obstruction* at a spot in a *water hazard*, the player is not entitled to relief without penalty. The player must proceed under Rule 26-1.

(iv) On the Putting Green: If the ball last crossed the outermost limits of the immovable *obstruction* at a spot on the *putting green*, the player may *substitute* another ball, without penalty, and take relief as prescribed in Rule 24-2b(iii).

PENALTY
For breach of Rule:
Match play – Loss of hole;
Stroke play – Two strokes.

▶ RULE 24

INCIDENTS

Since 1744, the basic tenets of the Rules have been to play the course as you find it, the ball as it lies and, if you are unsure of the proper procedure, to do what is fair. Harry Bradshaw held true to this spirit at the 1949 Open Championship.

Having shot a stunning first round 68 over Royal St George's, Bradshaw was tied with Roberto De Vicenzo one stroke behind Jimmy Adams. However, playing the 5th hole during the second round, Bradshaw's ball rolled into a discarded beer bottle with a broken neck.

Rather than requesting a ruling for the relief to which he was entitled, Bradshaw determined on his own that he must play the ball as it lay. He took out his sand wedge and made a swing, which shattered the bottle and moved the ball slightly forward. He took a double bogey six.

The result of his playing out of this movable obstruction was that Bradshaw ultimately tied Bobby Locke of South Africa at 283. In the resulting 36-hole play-off, Locke scored 136 to Bradshaw's 147, to win the first of Locke's four Open Championship tournaments.

Under Rule 24-1, because Bradshaw's ball was in a movable obstruction, the ball could have been lifted and cleaned without penalty, the bottle removed and the ball dropped as nearly as possible to the spot directly under the place where the ball lay when it was in the bottle.

In choosing to take relief from an immovable obstruction, the ball must be dropped in a place that avoids interference by the immovable obstruction. Full relief must be taken. Payne Stewart learned this lesson in 1993 during the PGA Tour's annual stop in San Diego.

In taking relief from a cart path, Stewart dropped his ball in a place where, after taking his stance, the heel of his right shoe was still on the cart path from which he was taking relief. The television broadcast showed the breach clearly and Stewart was penalised two strokes for not taking complete relief from the immovable obstruction.

The Exception to Rule 24-2 states clearly that a player may not obtain relief under this Rule if interference would only occur through the use of an abnormal stance, swing or direction of play. This is one of the situations in the Rules where a Referee's judgement is called upon, as David Frost learned during the final round of the 1999 Open Championship at Carnoustie.

Playing with Justin Leonard in the penultimate group, Frost's drive at the 2nd hole was a low hook into the high rough. Near the area where he would stand to play the ball was a road. Frost argued to the attending Rules official that in order to play the ball, which was below his feet, he would have to widen his stance to such an extent that he would be standing on the road and, therefore, he was entitled to relief from an immovable obstruction.

The Referee did not accept the argument and told Frost that such play was not reasonable. It was the official's judgement that had the road not been there, Frost would not have used a stance that would place his left foot on the road. With the final pairing waiting on the tee, time ticked away as confirmation of the official's decision was requested over the radio. It was deemed final, and Frost played the ball as it lay. His shot from this awkward lie came to rest on the road, from where he was then granted relief under Rule 24-2.

In such a situation, the Rules official must consider how the player would attempt the shot if the obstruction in question were not present. In a stroke play situation such as this one, the Rules are there to protect the field and prevent an unfair advantage of one player over all the others.

When the Committee declares an obstruction an integral part of the golf course, it eliminates any argument because there is no free relief. The most famous example of this is on the Road Hole at the Old Course in St Andrews. When a ball lies on the road immediately to the right of the green, it must be played as it lies. As the name of the hole suggests, the road has always been the most important element of the 17th hole and to allow relief would eliminate one of its essential obstacles. Thus, it is an integral part of the golf course.

At the 2005 Caltex Masters in Singapore, the eventual winner, Nick Dougherty, benefited from a ruling at the 16th hole on the final day, while leading the tournament by a single stroke from Colin Montgomerie.

Dougherty's tee shot was pulled to the left and it appeared to have come to rest in a bunker with a large, sleepered face made out of thick wooden planks. However, the Definition of "Bunker" in the Rules of Golf provides that any grass-covered ground bordering or within a bunker is not part of the bunker and what had happened was that the player's ball had run through the bunker and come to rest on grass-covered ground just in front of the sleepers.

Harry Bradshaw views with disbelief his ball, which has rolled into a broken bottle at the 1949 Open Championship.

The sleepers themselves were immovable obstructions and, if Dougherty's ball had been in the bunker, his only options would have been to take relief in the bunker without penalty or drop outside the bunker, back on a line with the flagstick, under penalty of one stroke (Rule 24-2b(ii)). As it was, with the ball lying just outside the bunker, Rule 24-2b(i) allowed Dougherty to ascertain his nearest point of relief from the sleepers outside the bunker and then drop within one club-length of that spot not nearer to the hole. The drop put him in a much more favourable position, as sometimes occurs in free-relief situations, and he then played a superb shot to within three feet of the hole.

Dougherty commented, "I enjoyed a bit of good fortune with the drop, but the shot I played then was the most important of my career so far. I hit a class shot that pitched exactly where I wanted and the ball rolled close to the hole. I felt that shot gave me a valuable psychological edge, with Monty breathing down my neck."

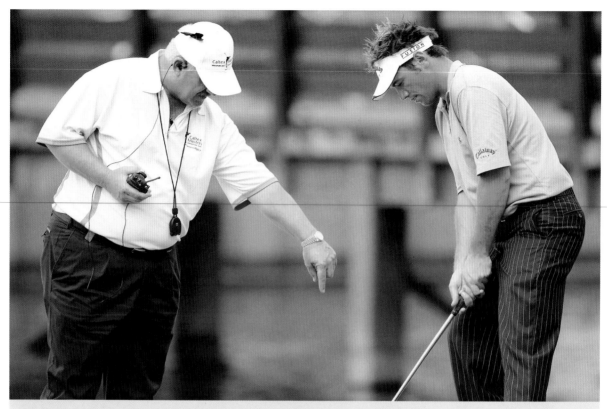

Because Nick Dougherty's ball was lying just in front of some sleepers outside the bunker, he was instructed to drop the ball within one club-length of his nearest relief spot, under Rule 24-2b(i).

► RULE 24

FREQUENTLY ASKED QUESTIONS

Q Should rakes be placed inside or outside bunkers?
A It is recommended that rakes be placed outside bunkers as, on balance, it is felt there is less likelihood of an advantage or disadvantage to the player.

In practice, players who leave rakes in bunkers frequently place them at the side, which tends to stop a ball rolling into the flat part of the bunker, resulting in a much more difficult shot than would otherwise have been the case. This is especially true of small bunkers.

If a ball comes to rest against a rake in the bunker, the player may proceed under Rule 24-1 (Movable Obstruction). However, it may not be possible to replace the ball on the same spot or find a spot in the bunker that is not nearer the hole.

If a rake is left in the middle of the bunker, the only way to get it there is to throw it into the bunker, thus damaging the surface. Also, if a rake is in the middle of

a large bunker it is either not used or the player is obliged to rake a large area of the bunker resulting in unnecessary delay. Therefore, after considering all these aspects, it is recommended that rakes should be left outside bunkers in areas where they are least likely to affect the movement of the ball.

Q May stakes defining a water hazard or lateral water hazard be moved?
A A water hazard stake is an obstruction – see Definition of "obstruction". Consequently, if such a stake is movable, it may be removed without penalty, in accordance with Rule 24-1. A player may remove a movable obstruction anywhere on the course, irrespective of whether his ball lies in a water hazard or not.

► RULE 25

ABNORMAL GROUND CONDITIONS, EMBEDDED BALL AND WRONG PUTTING GREEN

25-1 Abnormal Ground Conditions

25-1 a Interference

Interference by an *abnormal ground condition* occurs when a ball lies in or touches the condition or when the condition interferes with the player's *stance* or the area of his intended swing. If the player's ball lies on the *putting green*, interference also occurs if an *abnormal ground condition* on the *putting green* intervenes on his *line of putt*. Otherwise, intervention on the *line of play* is not, of itself, interference under this Rule.

DEFINITIONS
All defined terms are in *italics* and are listed in the Definitions section – see pages 13–23.

NOTE

The *Committee* may make a Local Rule stating that interference by an *abnormal ground condition* with a player's *stance* is deemed not to be, of itself, interference under this Rule.

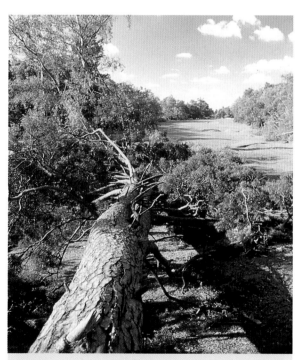

A fallen tree still attached to its stump is not ground under repair, but it can be so declared by the Committee.

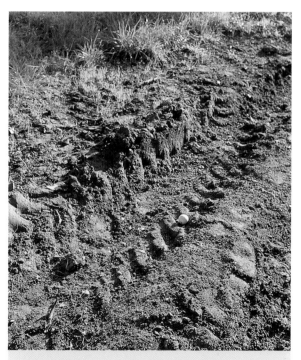

A rut made by a tractor is not ground under repair, but the Committee would be justified in declaring a deep rut to be ground under repair.

AREAS REQUIRING PRESERVATION

If there is an area of the course, such as a plantation of young trees, which requires preservation the Committee should declare it "Ground Under Repair – Play Prohibited".

25-1 b Relief

Except when the ball is in a *water hazard* or a *lateral water hazard*, a player may take relief from interference by an *abnormal ground condition* as follows:

(i) Through the Green: If the ball lies *through the green*, the player must lift the ball and drop it, without penalty, within one club-length of and not nearer the *hole* than the *nearest point of relief*. The *nearest point of relief* must not be in a *hazard* or on a *putting green*. When the ball is dropped within one club-length of the *nearest point of relief*, the ball must first strike a part of the *course* at a spot that avoids interference by the condition and is not in a *hazard* and not on a *putting green*.

(ii) In a Bunker: If the ball is in a *bunker*, the player must lift the ball and drop it either:

(a) Without penalty, in accordance with Clause (i) above, except that the *nearest point of relief* must be in the *bunker* and the ball must be dropped in the *bunker* or, if complete relief is impossible, as near as possible to the spot where the ball lay, but not nearer the *hole*, on a part of the *course* in the *bunker* that affords maximum available relief from the condition; or

(b) Under penalty of one stroke, outside the *bunker* keeping the point where the ball lay directly between the *hole* and the spot on which the ball is dropped, with no limit to how far behind the *bunker* the ball may be dropped.

(iii) On the Putting Green: If the ball lies on the *putting green*, the player must lift the ball and place it, without penalty, at the *nearest point of relief* that is not in a *hazard* or, if complete relief is impossible, at the nearest position to where it lay that affords maximum available relief from the condition, but not nearer the *hole* and not in a *hazard*. The *nearest point of relief* or maximum available relief may be off the *putting green*.

(iv) On the Teeing Ground: If the ball lies on the *teeing ground*, the player must lift the ball and drop it, without penalty, in accordance with Clause (i) above.

The ball may be cleaned when lifted under Rule 25-1b.

(Ball rolling to a position where there is interference by the condition from which relief was taken – see Rule 20-2c(v))

Exception

A player may not take relief under this Rule if **(a)** it is clearly unreasonable for him to make a *stroke* because of interference by anything other than an *abnormal ground condition* or **(b)** interference by an *abnormal ground condition* would occur only through use of an unnecessarily abnormal *stance*, swing or direction of play.

> **NOTE 1**
> If a ball is in a *water hazard* (including a *lateral water hazard*), the player is not entitled to relief, without penalty, from interference by an *abnormal ground condition*. The player must play the ball as it lies (unless prohibited by Local Rule) or proceed under Rule 26-1.
>
> **NOTE 2**
> If a ball to be dropped or placed under this Rule is not immediately recoverable, another ball may be *substituted*.

25-1 c Ball in Abnormal Ground Condition Not Found

It is a question of fact whether a ball that has not been found after having been struck toward an *abnormal ground condition* is in such a condition. In order to apply this Rule, it must be known or virtually certain that the ball is in the *abnormal ground condition*. In the absence of such knowledge or certainty, the player must proceed under Rule 27-1.

CASUAL WATER ON PUTTING GREEN

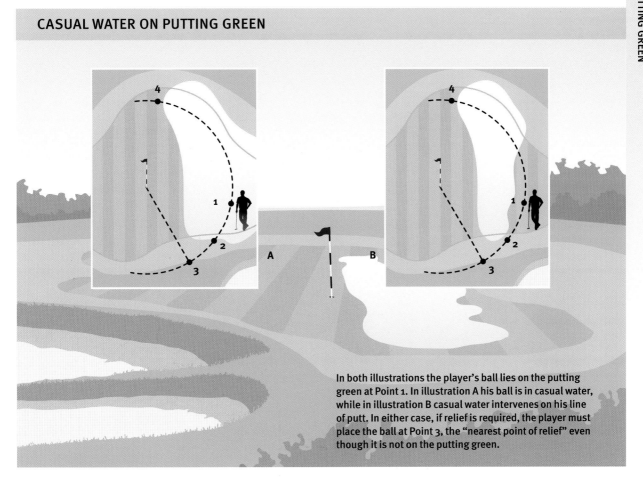

In both illustrations the player's ball lies on the putting green at Point 1. In illustration A his ball is in casual water, while in illustration B casual water intervenes on his line of putt. In either case, if relief is required, the player must place the ball at Point 3, the "nearest point of relief" even though it is not on the putting green.

BALL CLOSE TO CASUAL WATER: LEFT-HANDED STROKE NOT REASONABLE

BALL CLOSE TO CASUAL WATER: LEFT-HANDED STROKE REASONABLE

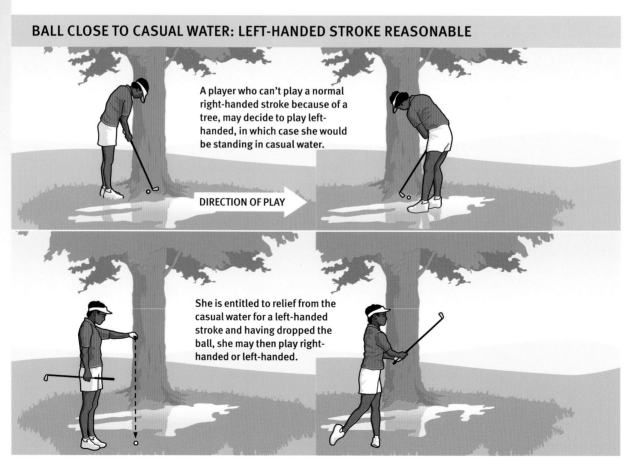

If it is known or virtually certain that a ball that has not been found is in an *abnormal ground condition*, the player may take relief under this Rule. If he elects to do so, the spot where the ball last crossed the outermost limits of the *abnormal ground condition* must be determined and, for the purpose of applying this Rule, the ball is deemed to lie at this spot and the player must proceed as follows:

(i)   **Through the Green:** If the ball last crossed the outermost limits of the *abnormal ground condition* at a spot *through the green*, the player may *substitute* another ball, without penalty, and take relief as prescribed in Rule 25-1b(i).

(ii)   **In a Bunker:** If the ball last crossed the outermost limits of the *abnormal ground condition* at a spot in a *bunker*, the player may *substitute* another ball, without penalty, and take relief as prescribed in Rule 25-1b(ii).

(iii)   **In a Water Hazard (including a Lateral Water Hazard):** If the ball last crossed the outermost limits of the *abnormal ground condition* at a spot in a *water hazard*, the player is not entitled to relief without penalty. The player must proceed under Rule 26-1.

(iv)   **On the Putting Green:** If the ball last crossed the outermost limits of the *abnormal ground condition* at a spot on the *putting green*, the player may *substitute* another ball, without penalty, and take relief as prescribed in Rule 25-1b(iii).

25-2 Embedded Ball

A ball embedded in its own pitch-mark in the ground in any closely-mown area *through the green* may be lifted, cleaned and dropped, without penalty, as near as possible to the spot where it lay but not nearer the *hole*. The ball when dropped must

BALL IN CASUAL WATER IN BUNKER

I am taking relief from this casual water. Must I drop the ball at the nearest point of relief or may I drop it within one club-length of the nearest point of relief not nearer the hole?

As you are able to take complete relief from the casual water, you are allowed to drop within one club-length of the nearest point of relief. However, if complete relief had been impossible and you were taking maximum available relief, the ball would have to be dropped on the spot that gave maximum available relief.

STANCE INTERFERED WITH BY BURROWING ANIMAL HOLE: BALL UNPLAYABLE BECAUSE OF OTHER CONDITION

EMBEDDED BALL

first strike a part of the *course through the green*. "Closely-mown area" means any area of the *course*, including paths through the rough, cut to fairway height or less.

25-3 Wrong Putting Green

25-3 a Interference

Interference by a *wrong putting green* occurs when a ball is on the *wrong putting green*.

Interference to a player's *stance* or the area of his intended swing is not, of itself, interference under this Rule.

25-3 b Relief

If a player's ball lies on a *wrong putting green*, he must not play the ball as it lies. He must take relief, without penalty, as follows:

The player must lift the ball and drop it within one club-length of and not nearer the *hole* than the *nearest point of relief*. The *nearest point of relief* must not be in a *hazard* or on a *putting green*. When dropping the ball within one club-length of the *nearest point of relief*, the ball must first strike a part of the *course* at a spot that avoids interference by the *wrong putting green* and is not in a *hazard* and not on a *putting green*. The ball may be cleaned when lifted under this Rule.

PENALTY
For breach of Rule:
Match play – Loss of hole;
Stroke play – Two strokes.

RELIEF FROM A WRONG PUTTING GREEN

I am going to be standing on this wrong putting green to play my stroke. Must I take relief?

No. Relief must be taken if your ball lies on a wrong putting green, but relief is not available for interference to stance.

▸ RULE 25

INCIDENT

While playing in the penultimate group on the third day of the 2004 Masters Tournament, Ernie Els pulled his tee shot into the trees at the par-4 11th hole. Although the South African managed to find his ball, it was lying badly in among some large, detached tree branches. It looked as if the player's only option would be to deem his ball unplayable, but Els asked Rules officials on the hole whether the branches may have been piled for removal, in which case they would constitute ground under repair (see Definition of "ground under repair") and he may be entitled to free relief. On first look, the officials did not feel that the branches had been piled for removal, but rather had been abandoned, in which case no free relief would be available. However, the officials

agreed to get a second opinion from the Chairman of the Masters Rules Committee.

When the Chairman arrived on the scene he advised the player that the branches had come down in a recent ice storm and had been piled for removal. Els was shown where his nearest point of relief from the branches was and he dropped within one club-length of that point.

A very difficult shot back to the fairway through the trees still faced Els, but he played a great recovery shot and salvaged a bogey. This lucky break allowed Els to maintain his challenge to Phil Mickelson, with the American prevailing by one stroke over Els on the Sunday, after an historic tussle.

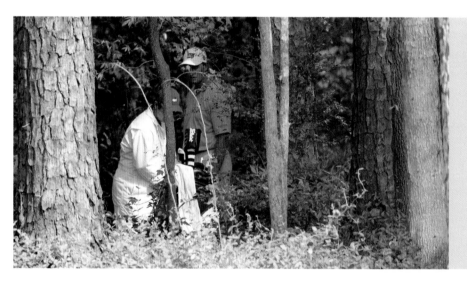

When his tee shot dropped into some branches broken by a recent storm at Augusta National, Ernie Els was allowed free relief.

▸ RULE 25

FREQUENTLY ASKED QUESTION

Q Can I get relief without penalty from a bunker that is completely covered by casual water?
A No. The player may play the ball as it lies, or:
- take relief in accordance with Rule 25-1b(ii)(a), or
- drop the ball behind the bunker under penalty of one stroke as in Rule 25-1b(ii)(b), or
- deem the ball unplayable and proceed in accordance with Rule 28 (see Decision 25-1b/8).

However, prior to a competition commencing, a Committee can declare specific flooded bunkers as ground under repair and "through the green" by Local Rule (Decision 33-8/27). This permits relief without penalty to be taken outside the specified bunkers under Rule 25-1b(i).

► RULE 26

WATER HAZARDS (INCLUDING LATERAL WATER HAZARDS)

26-1 Relief for Ball in Water Hazard

It is a question of fact whether a ball that has not been found after having been struck toward a *water hazard* is in the *hazard*. In order to apply this Rule, it must be known or virtually certain that the ball is in the *hazard*. In the absence of such knowledge or certainty, the player must proceed under Rule 27-1.

If a ball is in a *water hazard* or if it is known or virtually certain that a ball that has not been found is in a *water hazard* (whether the ball lies in water or not), the player may **under penalty of one stroke:**

a.   Play a ball as nearly as possible at the spot from which the original ball was last played (see Rule 20-5); or

b.   Drop a ball behind the *water hazard*, keeping the point at which the original ball last crossed the margin of the *water hazard* directly between the *hole* and the spot on which the ball is dropped, with no limit to how far behind the *water hazard* the ball may be dropped; or

DEFINITIONS
All defined terms are in *italics* and are listed in the Definitions section – see pages 13–23.

Jean Van de Velde's difficulty with the Barry Burn at the 72nd hole of the 1999 Open Championship at Carnoustie resulted in a three-way play-off for the Championship. See the details of his unfortunate brush with Rule 26-1 in the incident on pages 139–140.

c. As additional options available only if the ball last crossed the margin of a *lateral water hazard*, drop a ball outside the *water hazard* within two club-lengths of and not nearer the *hole* than (i) the point where the original ball last crossed the margin of the *water hazard* or (ii) a point on the opposite margin of the *water hazard* equidistant from the *hole*.

When proceeding under this Rule, the player may lift and clean his ball or *substitute* a ball.

(Prohibited actions when ball is in a hazard – see Rule 13-4)

(Ball moving in water in a water hazard – see Rule 14-6)

26-2 Ball Played within Water Hazard

26-2 a Ball Comes to Rest in Same or Another Water Hazard

If a ball played from within a *water hazard* comes to rest in the same or another *water hazard* after the *stroke*, the player may:

(i) proceed under Rule 26-1a. If, after dropping in the *hazard*, the player elects not to play the dropped ball, he may:

(a) proceed under Rule 26-1b, or if applicable Rule 26-1c, adding the **additional penalty of one stroke** prescribed by the Rule and using as the reference point the point where the original ball last crossed the margin of this *hazard* before it came to rest in this *hazard*; or

(b) **add an additional penalty of one stroke** and play a ball as nearly as possible at the spot from which the last *stroke* from outside a *water hazard* was made (see Rule 20-5); or

KNOWN OR VIRTUALLY CERTAIN THAT BALL IS IN WATER HAZARD

BALL CROSSING MARGIN OF WATER HAZARD

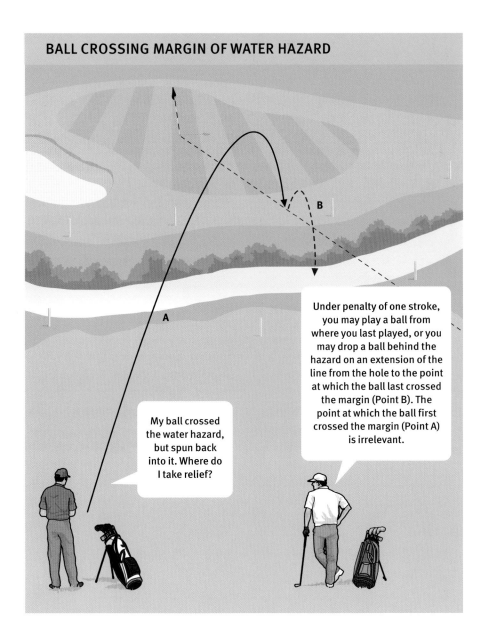

Under penalty of one stroke, you may play a ball from where you last played, or you may drop a ball behind the hazard on an extension of the line from the hole to the point at which the ball last crossed the margin (Point B). The point at which the ball first crossed the margin (Point A) is irrelevant.

My ball crossed the water hazard, but spun back into it. Where do I take relief?

(ii) proceed under Rule 26-1b, or if applicable Rule 26-1c; or
(iii) **under penalty of one stroke**, play a ball as nearly as possible at the spot from which the last *stroke* from outside a *water hazard* was made (see Rule 20-5).

26-2 b Ball Lost or Unplayable Outside Hazard or Out of Bounds

If a ball played from within a *water hazard* is *lost* or deemed unplayable outside the *hazard* or is *out of bounds*, the player may, after taking a **penalty of one stroke** under Rule 27-1 or 28a:

(i) play a ball as nearly as possible at the spot in the *hazard* from which the original ball was last played (see Rule 20-5); or

(ii) proceed under Rule 26-1b, or if applicable Rule 26-1c, **adding the additional penalty of one stroke** prescribed by the Rule and using as the reference point the point where the original ball last crossed the margin of the *hazard* before it came to rest in the *hazard*; or

RELIEF FROM LATERAL WATER HAZARD

The player has played a ball from the tee (Point A) into the lateral water hazard at Point B. It last crossed the margin of the hazard at Point C and the point on the opposite margin, equidistant from the hole is Point E. He may play the ball as it lies or, under penalty of one stroke:
(i) play another ball from the tee – Rule 26-1a;
(ii) drop a ball anywhere on the far side of the hazard on the dotted line from the hole through Point C, e.g. Point D – Rule 26-1b;
(iii) drop a ball in the area on the near side of the hazard, which is all ground within two club-lengths of Point C – Rule 26-1c(i); or
(iv) drop a ball in the area on the far side of the hazard, which is all ground within two club-lengths of Point E – Rule 26-1c(ii).

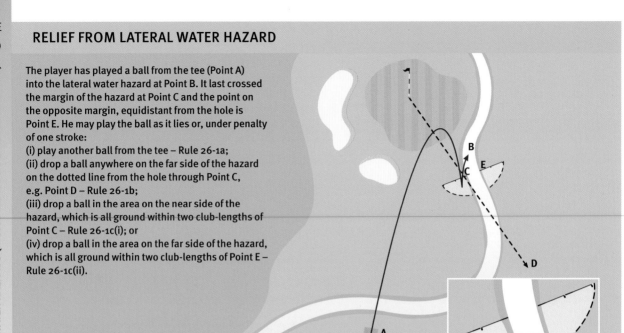

BALL PLAYED FROM WITHIN WATER HAZARD

The player's tee shot at a par-3 hole comes to rest in a water hazard. He plays from the hazard, but fails to get his ball out. He may play the ball as it lies or, under penalty of one stroke:
(i) drop a ball at the spot from which he's just played his second stroke and play again from there;
(ii) drop a ball behind the hazard, anywhere on the dotted line, and play from there; or
(iii) play another ball from the tee.

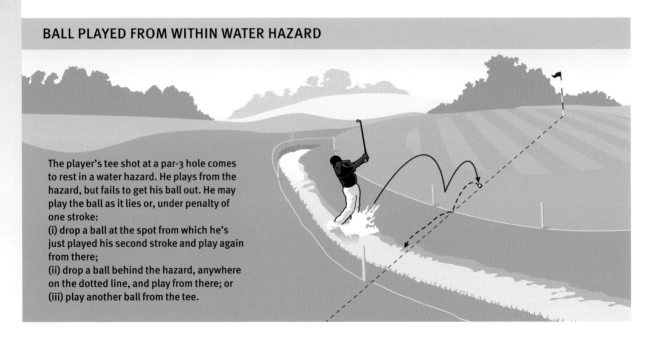

(iii) **add an additional penalty of one stroke** and play a ball as nearly as possible at the spot from which the last *stroke* from outside a *water hazard* was made (see Rule 20-5).

NOTE 1
When proceeding under Rule 26-2b, the player is not required to drop a ball under Rule 27-1 or 28a. If he does drop a ball, he is not required to play it. He may alternatively proceed under Rule 26-2b(ii) or (iii).

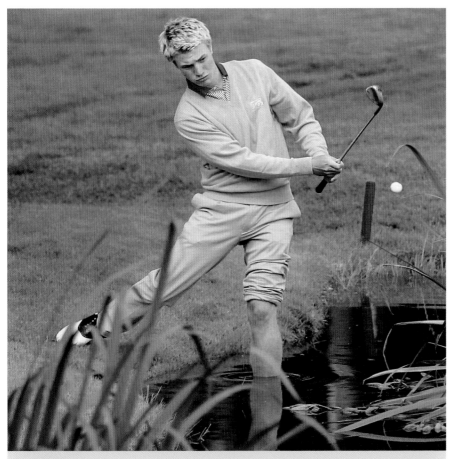

Oliver Fisher plays his ball, which had stopped short of the water hazard. Stakes and lines used to define the margin of or identify a lateral water hazard must be red.

NOTE 2

If a ball played from within a *water hazard* is deemed unplayable outside the *hazard*, nothing in Rule 26-2b precludes the player from proceeding under Rule 28b or c.

PENALTY
For breach of Rule:
Match play – Loss of hole;
Stroke play – Two strokes.

▶ RULE 26
INCIDENTS

Standing on Carnoustie's 18th tee, in the final round of the 1999 Open Championship, Jean Van de Velde needed only a double bogey to become the first Frenchman to win the Championship since 1907.

Minutes later, with his navy blue trousers rolled to his knees, he was standing in the Barry Burn contemplating his fate and his options under Rule 26.

Having played a driver from the tee, the Frenchman's ball had finished well right but safely on a peninsula created by a bend in the burn. Instead of laying up with his second, Van de Velde attempted to play a 2-iron to the distant green. His shot was a bit wayward and it ricocheted off a grandstand railing, the wall of the water hazard and finally settled behind the second crossing of the burn in heavy rough.

Attempting to hit his ball out of the rough and over the burn, he played it badly and the ball finished in the shallow water of the burn. As the stream runs perpendicular to the line of play, it was marked with a yellow line indicating a water hazard.

As such, Van de Velde had three options. He could play the ball without penalty as it lay. Additionally, under penalty of one stroke, he could play again from where he last played, or he could drop behind the hazard keeping the point at which his ball last crossed the margin of the water hazard directly between the hole and the spot on which the ball would be dropped, with no limit to how far behind the hazard he might want to go.

Three in the water, and needing a six to win The Open, the Frenchman contemplated playing out of the hazard in order to avoid the penalty stroke. To make such an assessment, he decided to go into the water to see what the shot required. Having removed his shoes and socks, Van de Velde rolled up his trouser legs and lowered himself down the stone wall into the shallow water.

Van de Velde was left standing alone in the dark water, wedge in hand, assessing his ability to play the submerged ball out of the hazard. After several minutes, discretion became the better part of valour and Van de Velde chose option b under Rule 26-1. He dropped a ball

behind the hazard on the stipulated line, suffered a penalty stroke and played his fifth shot to the right greenside bunker. His up-and-down from the bunker resulted in a score of seven and a play-off between himself, Paul Lawrie and Justin Leonard, which Lawrie went on to win.

Tiger Woods went on to win the 2005 Masters despite putting into Rae's Creek at the 13th hole during his first round.

What was interesting about Tiger's incident was that it was obvious that he knew immediately that he had the option (under Rule 26-1a) of playing again from the spot from which he had initially putted, under penalty of one stroke. While it must have been daunting to face the same lightning-fast putt, his other option, which would have seen him drop on the fairway side of the water hazard (keeping the point where the ball crossed the hazard margin and the flagstick in a direct line), was clearly less desirable.

Another point to note about Tiger's chosen procedure was that, as the next stroke was being made from where the previous stroke had been played, in accordance with Rule 20-5, Woods was required to place a ball on the putting green, rather than drop it. He also chose not to retrieve the original ball from the water and, instead, substituted another ball, which the player is always entitled to do under Rule 26.

▶ RULE 26

FREQUENTLY ASKED QUESTION

Q What differentiates a water hazard from a lateral water hazard?
A A water hazard is any sea, lake, pond, river, ditch, surface drainage ditch or other open water course (whether or not containing water) and anything of a similar nature – see the Definition of "water hazard". If a player's ball lies in a water hazard, he may play the ball as it lies or proceed under Rule 26-1a or b.

A lateral water hazard is a water hazard or that part of a water hazard so situated that it is not possible or is

deemed by the Committee to be impracticable to drop a ball behind the water hazard in accordance with Rule 26-1b – see Definition of "lateral water hazard" – for example, if the area behind the water hazard is out of bounds or is thick with trees. If a player's ball lies in a lateral water hazard, he may, in addition to the options available when in a water hazard, proceed under Rule 26-1c. Stakes and lines defining a water hazard must be yellow. Stakes and lines defining a lateral water hazard must be red.

► RULE 27

BALL LOST OR OUT OF BOUNDS; PROVISIONAL BALL

27-1 Stroke and Distance; Ball Out of Bounds; Ball Not Found Within Five Minutes

27-1 a Proceeding Under Stroke and Distance

At any time, a player may, **under penalty of one stroke**, play a ball as nearly as possible at the spot from which the original ball was last played (see Rule 20-5) i.e., proceed under penalty of stroke and distance.

   Except as otherwise provided in the *Rules*, if a player makes a *stroke* at a ball from the spot at which the original ball was last played, he is deemed to have proceeded **under penalty of stroke and distance.**

27-1 b Ball Out of Bounds

If a ball is *out of bounds*, the player must play a ball, **under penalty of one stroke,** as nearly as possible at the spot from which the original ball was last played (see Rule 20-5).

27-1 c Ball Not Found Within Five Minutes

If a ball is *lost* as a result of not being found or identified as his by the player within five minutes after the player's *side* or his or their *caddies* have begun to search for it, the player must play a ball, **under penalty of one stroke,** as nearly as possible at the spot from which the original ball was last played (see Rule 20-5).

DEFINITIONS
All defined terms are in *italics* and are listed in the Definitions section – see pages 13–23.

PLAYERS UNABLE TO IDENTIFY THEIR BALLS

My ball is a number 3 with black writing.

So is mine. Unless we can identify which is which, both balls are "lost".

Exceptions

1   If it is known or virtually certain that the original ball that has not been found is in an *obstruction* (Rule 24-3) or is in an *abnormal ground condition* (Rule 25-1c), the player may proceed under the applicable Rule.

2   If it is known or virtually certain that the original ball that has not been found has been moved by an *outside agency* (Rule 18-1) or is in a *water hazard*, (Rule 26-1), the player must proceed under the applicable Rule.

PENALTY
For breach of Rule 27-1:
Match play – Loss of hole;
Stroke play – Two strokes.

27-2 Provisional Ball

27-2 a Procedure

If a ball may be *lost* outside a *water hazard* or may be *out of bounds*, to save time the player may play another ball provisionally in accordance with Rule 27-1. The player must inform his opponent in match play or his *marker* or a *fellow-competitor* in stroke play that he intends to play a *provisional ball*, and he must play it before he or his *partner* goes forward to search for the original ball.

   If he fails to do so and plays another ball, that ball is not a *provisional ball* and becomes the *ball in play* **under penalty of stroke and distance** (Rule 27-1); the original ball is *lost*.

(Order of play from teeing ground – see Rule 10-3)

NOTE

If a *provisional ball* played under Rule 27-2a might be *lost* outside a *water hazard* or *out of bounds*, the player may play another *provisional ball*. If another *provisional ball* is played, it bears the same relationship to the previous *provisional ball* as the first *provisional ball* bears to the original ball.

BALL FOUND WITHIN FIVE MINUTES

Thanks for finding my ball and calling me back before I played another ball. We hadn't been looking for it for five minutes, so I'll play it.

That's OK. Your ball wasn't "lost" merely because you went back to play another ball before the five minutes search was up. But if you had played another ball before I called you back that would have become the ball in play and this one would have been "lost". In that situation you couldn't have played on with it.

PROVISIONAL BALL BECOMES BALL IN PLAY

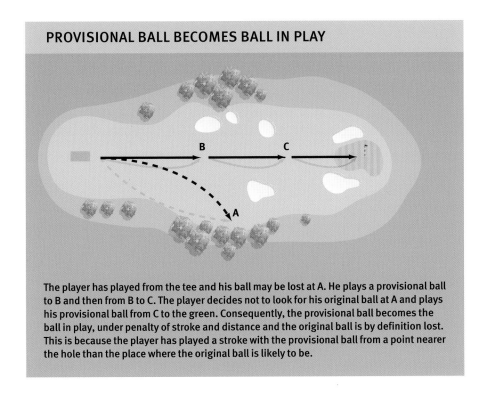

The player has played from the tee and his ball may be lost at A. He plays a provisional ball to B and then from B to C. The player decides not to look for his original ball at A and plays his provisional ball from C to the green. Consequently, the provisional ball becomes the ball in play, under penalty of stroke and distance and the original ball is by definition lost. This is because the player has played a stroke with the provisional ball from a point nearer the hole than the place where the original ball is likely to be.

27-2 b When Provisional Ball Becomes Ball in Play
The player may play a *provisional ball* until he reaches the place where the original ball is likely to be. If he makes a *stroke* with the *provisional ball* from the place where the original ball is likely to be or from a point nearer the *hole* than that place, the original ball is *lost* and the *provisional ball* becomes the *ball in play* **under penalty of stroke and distance** (Rule 27-1).

If the original ball is *lost* outside a *water hazard* or is *out of bounds*, the *provisional ball* becomes the *ball in play*, **under penalty of stroke and distance** (Rule 27-1).

If it is known or virtually certain that the original ball is in a *water hazard,* the player must proceed in accordance with Rule 26-1.

Exception
If it is known or virtually certain that the original ball is in an *obstruction* (Rule 24-3) or an *abnormal ground condition* (Rule 25-1c), the player may proceed under the applicable Rule.

27-2 c When Provisional Ball to be Abandoned
If the original ball is neither *lost* nor *out of bounds*, the player must abandon the *provisional ball* and continue play with the original ball. If he makes any further *strokes* at the *provisional ball*, he is playing a *wrong ball* and the provisions of Rule 15-3 apply.

NOTE
If a player plays a *provisional ball* under Rule 27-2a, the *strokes* made after this Rule has been invoked with a *provisional ball* subsequently abandoned under Rule 27-2c and *penalty strokes* incurred solely by playing that ball are disregarded.

PROVISIONAL BALL PLAYED: ORIGINAL BALL FOUND UNPLAYABLE

A player plays a provisional
ball as his ball may be lost.
The original ball is found
within five minutes and
before the provisional ball
has become the ball in
play, but the ball is
unplayable. The player
must abandon the
provisional ball and
proceed with the original.

► RULE 27

INCIDENTS

During the third round of the 1998 Open Championship
at Royal Birkdale, Mark O'Meara's second shot drifted
too far to the right into knee-high grass and gorse at the
480-yard 6th hole and put into motion a series of events
that led to the introduction of a clarifying Decision.

By the time O'Meara and his caddie reached the area
where they thought his ball had landed, a number of
spectators were already engaged in searching for it.
The Rules observer with the group started the clock for
the five-minute search period when O'Meara and his
caddie arrived.

Several balls were found, but none were O'Meara's.
To everyone in the immediate vicinity, he announced
the type of ball he was using and stated that it was
embossed with his logo.

After searching for approximately four minutes,
O'Meara suspected that his ball was lost. He left the
search area, took another ball from his caddie and
started back down the fairway to play again from where
his original ball had been played.

About 30 seconds later, a spectator announced,
"Here it is. I have it." Someone called to O'Meara, who
apparently did not hear and continued walking. An
official went to where the spectator had found the ball
and saw it was the type O'Meara was using and did have
his logo on it.

By this time, it was nearing the end of the five-minute
search period permitted under the Rules and it was clear
that O'Meara would not be able to get back to the ball in
order to identify it within the five-minute period. The
Definition of "Lost Ball" states that a ball is lost if it is not
"found or identified" within five minutes. If the definition
said "found and identified", the procedure would have
been clear. A radio call was made for a roving Rules
official to make a decision.

The roving official arrived on the scene and brought
O'Meara in a cart back up the fairway where a discussion
took place. A further official arrived and it was
determined that the ball had been found within the five-
minute period, that O'Meara was entitled to identify it

outside the stipulated time period and, if it was his ball, he was entitled to play it, so everyone returned to the area where the ball had been found.

However, during the search, the search area had been trampled and a misguided spectator, who believed the ball had been abandoned, had lifted it. When O'Meara and the official went to the spot, the ball was not there but the spectator was close by and returned the ball to O'Meara who identified it as his. Although the spectator said he knew "exactly" where the ball had been before he lifted it, that turned out to be only an approximation.

Under Rules 18-1 and 20-3c, O'Meara was required to drop as nearly as possible to the spot where the ball had been before being lifted by the spectator. When O'Meara dropped the ball, it rolled more than two club-lengths from the spot where it struck a part of the course thus requiring a re-drop. Upon re-dropping, the ball rolled nearer to the hole and O'Meara, therefore, placed it on the spot where it first struck a part of the course when re-dropped. He then played his shot and continued the round, winning the Championship the following day.

The ambiguity of the Definition of "Lost Ball", in this particular situation, necessitated the addition of Decision 27/5.5. That decision clarifies that if a ball is found within five minutes, the player is allowed enough time to reach the area and identify it even though the identification takes place after the five-minute search period has elapsed.

Another golfer to make a remarkable par recovery from a lost-ball situation was Gary Evans. Having played his way into contention by achieving seven under on the first 16 holes of the final day of the 2002 Open Championship at Muirfield, Evans hooked his second shot at the par-5 17th into deep rough on the outside of the spectator ropes, which sparked a frantic, and ultimately unsuccessful, search.

The clock starts when the player or his caddie has begun to search for a ball, so when spectators started searching for Evans' ball before the player arrived in the area this initial search did not form part of the five-minute period. A player cannot keep away from the area and then claim that, as he has not begun to search, the clock has not started. In such circumstances, a Rules official would have to begin timing when he felt that the player had been given reasonable opportunity to reach the area and begin his search. However, Evans and his caddie got to the area in good time and joined the mass

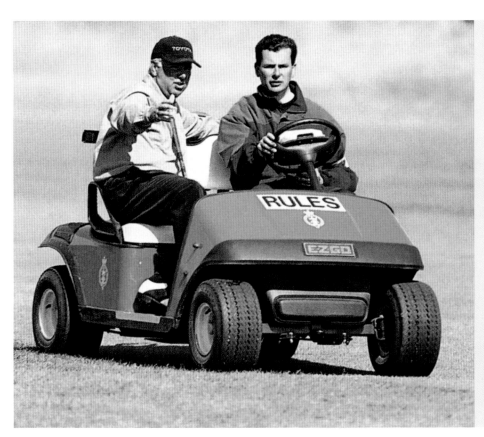

Mark O'Meara returns to identify a ball found within the five-minute search period during the 1998 Open Championship.

Two balls were found when Gary Evans drove into the rough on the 17th hole at Muirfield, but neither of them belonged to him. One in fact was a Titleist 2, which was the same type of ball that Evans was using, but it did not have his identification mark on it. This highlights the importance of putting an identification mark on the ball in order to avoid wrong-ball penalties.

of spectators looking for the ball. Evans could be heard pleading with the crowd to look at the ground rather than looking at him.

Remarkably, with more than 50 people hunting for the ball, it was not to be found. The Rules official walking with the game advised Evans that the five-minute period had elapsed, and Evans had to take the long walk back to where he had played his second shot and put another ball into play under penalty of stroke and distance (Rule 27-1).

At The Open there is a condition of competition that prohibits the use of transport unless authorised by the Committee. If there is a roving Rules official on hand with a cart, a player returning to put another ball into play will be offered a ride by the Rules official, who can authorise this as a member of the Committee. Evans was given this opportunity, but chose to walk back, perhaps in order to gather his thoughts before playing his fourth stroke. This seemed to work, because Evans hit a great shot on to the 17th green and followed that with an amazing putt to save par.

▸ RULE 27
FREQUENTLY ASKED QUESTIONS

Q Can a player take relief from interference by an out-of-bounds fence?
A No. Objects defining out of bounds, such as walls, fences, stakes and railings are considered fixed and are therefore not obstructions.

Q A player hits his ball into some long grass and is unable to find it. May he drop a ball in the area where he thinks his original ball is lost?
A No. The player must return to where he last played and put a ball into play under penalty of stroke and distance – see Rule 27-1.

► RULE 28

BALL UNPLAYABLE

The player may deem his ball unplayable at any place on the *course* except when the ball is in a *water hazard*. The player is the sole judge as to whether his ball is unplayable.

If the player deems his ball to be unplayable, he must **under penalty of one stroke**:

a. Play a ball as nearly as possible at the spot from which the original ball was last played (see Rule 20-5); or

b. Drop a ball behind the point where the ball lay, keeping that point directly between the *hole* and the spot on which the ball is dropped, with no limit to how far behind that point the ball may be dropped; or

c. Drop a ball within two club-lengths of the spot where the ball lay, but not nearer the *hole*.

If the unplayable ball is in a *bunker*, the player may proceed under Clause a, b or c. If he elects to proceed under Clause b or c, a ball must be dropped in the *bunker*.

DEFINITIONS
All defined terms are in *italics* and are listed in the Definitions section – see pages 13–23.

BALL DEEMED UNPLAYABLE

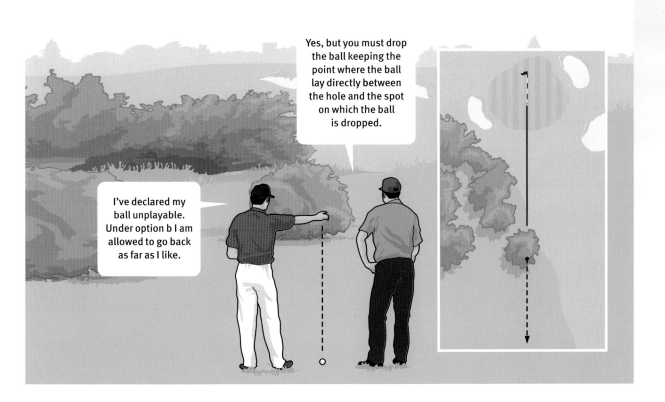

Yes, but you must drop the ball keeping the point where the ball lay directly between the hole and the spot on which the ball is dropped.

I've declared my ball unplayable. Under option b I am allowed to go back as far as I like.

BALL UNPLAYABLE IN BUNKER: PLAYER'S OPTIONS

The player's tee shot comes to rest in a bunker, in an unplayable position. Under penalty of one stroke he may:
(a) play again from where he last played (i.e. the tee); or
(b) drop a ball in the bunker behind the point where the ball lay (1), keeping that point directly between the hole and the spot on which the ball is dropped (i.e. line 1–2); or
(c) drop a ball in the bunker within two club-lengths of where his ball lay (1), but not nearer the hole (i.e. the indicated area).

BALL UNPLAYABLE IN BUSH: PLACE FOR DROPPING

My ball was in the bush. I've declared it unplayable and I'm going to invoke option c and drop the ball within two club-lengths of where it lay.

That's OK. But remember the ball when dropped must strike a part of the course within two club-lengths of where it lay.

When proceeding under this Rule, the player may lift and clean his ball or *substitute* a ball.

PENALTY
For breach of Rule:
Match play – Loss of hole;
Stroke play – Two strokes.

▶ RULE 28
INCIDENT

Former Ryder Cup player Pierre Fulke had an unusual incident at Wentworth's 16th hole during the 2004 PGA Championship. Fulke pulled his tee shot into the trees on the left of the hole and found his ball in an unplayable lie. The option under Rule 28b of dropping back on a line with the flagstick did not provide Fulke with any relief, so he examined the option of dropping within two club-lengths of where the ball lay (Rule 28c). He found that the only place within two club-lengths where he could obtain a playable lie was within a dry lateral water hazard. The player also thought that, if he dropped the ball in the dry ditch and it transpired that he could not play the dropped ball, he would then have the option of dropping out of the hazard under a further penalty of one stroke under Rule 26-1c.

At this point, a Rules official arrived on the scene and was quick to advise Fulke that if he did drop the ball in the lateral water hazard and could not play it, his only option would be to proceed under the stroke and distance element of the water hazard Rule (Rule 26-1a). This is due to the fact that the player would not have a reference point where the ball last crossed the margin of the hazard, as the ball would have been dropped in the hazard rather than entering it as a result of a stroke. The authority for the official's advice is found in Decision 28/4.5, which, remarkably, was introduced in 1998 following an identical incident involving Eamonn Darcy at the very same hole.

Fulke decided that the possibility of incurring two penalty strokes (one under the unplayable ball Rule and one under the water hazard Rule), and then potentially having to return to the tee, was too much of a risk. Consequently, he opted to proceed directly under the stroke and distance option of the unplayable ball Rule (Rule 28a) and returned to the tee, where he played his third shot.

▶ RULE 28
FREQUENTLY ASKED QUESTIONS

Q Where can a player deem his ball unplayable?
A A player can deem his ball unplayable anywhere on the course except when the ball is in a water hazard. The player is the sole judge as to whether his ball is unplayable.

Q If I choose to take relief under Rule 28c – that is, drop a ball within two club-lengths but no nearer the hole, where do I measure the two club-lengths from?
A The area in which to drop a ball under Rule 28c must be measured from where the ball lies, not from the outside edge of the perceived unplayable condition.

149

▶ RULE 29

THREESOMES AND FOURSOMES

29-1 General

In a *threesome* or a *foursome*, during any *stipulated round* the *partners* must play alternately from the *teeing grounds* and alternately during the play of each hole. *Penalty strokes* do not affect the order of play.

29-2 Match Play

If a player plays when his *partner* should have played, **his *side* loses the hole.**

29-3 Stroke Play

If the *partners* make a *stroke* or *strokes* in incorrect order, such *stroke* or *strokes* are cancelled and **the *side* incurs a penalty of two strokes.** The *side* must correct the error by playing a ball in correct order as nearly as possible at the spot from which it first played in incorrect order (see Rule 20-5). If the *side* makes a *stroke* on the next *teeing ground* without first correcting the error or, in the case of the last hole of the round, leaves the *putting green* without declaring its intention to correct the error, **the *side* is disqualified.**

FOURSOMES: ORDER OF PLAY WHEN A PARTNER DRIVES OUT OF BOUNDS

FOURSOMES: WHICH PARTNER DROPS THE BALL

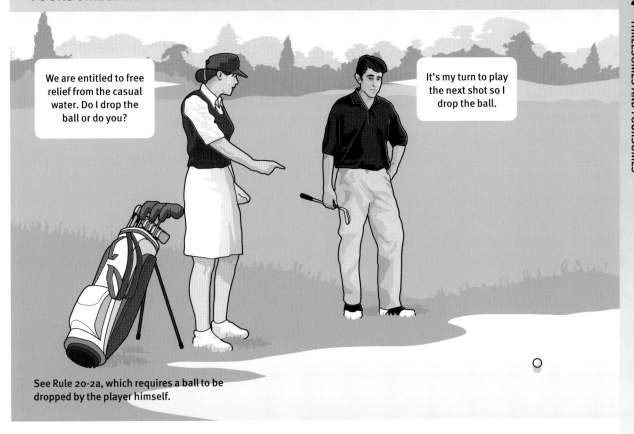

> We are entitled to free relief from the casual water. Do I drop the ball or do you?

> It's my turn to play the next shot so I drop the ball.

See Rule 20-2a, which requires a ball to be dropped by the player himself.

FOURSOMES: ORDER OF PLAY IN 36-HOLE COMPETITION

> Now that we're starting the second 18 holes, are we allowed to change the order of teeing off so that you drive at the evens and I drive at the odds?

> Yes, unless the Committee in charge of the competition has laid down a condition to the contrary.

Rule 29-1. See Definition of "stipulated round".

► RULE 29

INCIDENT

The practice putting green at the Old Course in St Andrews lies just off the course and only a few steps from the 1st tee. Paired together on the second day for the morning foursomes of the 1975 Walker Cup Match, the US side of veteran William C. Campbell and newcomer John Grace reported to the tee a little ahead of time. They had already decided that Grace would drive at the odd-numbered holes, so Campbell decided to use the extra time before the match began to walk to the practice green and hit a few putts.

As the visiting team, Campbell and Grace had the honour. The wind was blowing from the west off St Andrews Bay, which carried the announcement of the match's beginning beyond Campbell's earshot.

As the breeze momentarily died, Campbell heard "the click" of Grace's drive just before striking a practice putt,

and he was unable to interrupt his stroke. He had practised during the play of the hole. Instantly and instinctively recognising his breach, Campbell walked on to the fairway and reported to the referee that the US had lost the 1st hole (Rule 7-2 and Rule 29).

The Referee for the match accepted Campbell's report but made no immediate announcement to the other players. Because play of the hole had ended with the breach of Rule 7-2, Campbell was free to play his side's second from where Grace's good drive lay to the green, as simply more practice.

Walking across the Swilcan Burn, Campbell told Grace what had taken place. "He was incredulous, to say the least," Campbell recalls.

The Americans lost the 1st hole and eventually lost the match to Mark James and Richard Eyles.

► RULE 29

FREQUENTLY ASKED QUESTION

Q Who plays the provisional ball in a foursome competition?
A If there is doubt whether the original ball is out of bounds or lost and a provisional ball is to be played,

the provisional ball must be played by the partner – that is, not by the player who played the original ball.

► RULE 30

THREE-BALL, BEST-BALL AND FOUR-BALL MATCH PLAY

DEFINITIONS
All defined terms are in *italics* and are listed in the Definitions section – see pages 13–23.

30-1 Rules of Golf Apply
The Rules of Golf, so far as they are not at variance with the following specific Rules, apply to *three-ball*, *best-ball* and *four-ball matches*.

30-2 Three-Ball Match Play
30-2 a Ball at Rest Moved by an Opponent
Except as otherwise provided in the *Rules*, if the player's ball is touched or *moved* by an opponent, his *caddie* or *equipment* other than during search, Rule 18-3b applies.

FOUR-BALL MATCH PLAY: BREACH OF RULE BY ONE PARTNER

I'll just remove this twig.

I'm afraid you're disqualified from the hole for removing a loose impediment from the bunker. Fortunately, although I'm in the same bunker I'm not penalised because your breach of Rule 13-4 did not assist my play.

That opponent incurs a penalty of one stroke in his match with the player, but not in his match with the other opponent.

30-2 b Ball Deflected or Stopped by an Opponent Accidentally

If a player's ball is accidentally deflected or stopped by an opponent, his *caddie* or *equipment*, there is no penalty. In his match with that opponent the player may, before another *stroke* is made by either *side*, cancel the *stroke* and play a ball, without penalty, as nearly as possible at the spot from which the original ball was last played (see Rule 20-5) or he may play the ball as it lies. In his match with the other opponent, the ball must be played as it lies.

Exception

Ball striking person attending or holding up *flagstick* or anything carried by him – see Rule 17-3b.
(Ball purposely deflected or stopped by opponent – see Rule 1-2)

30-3 Best-Ball and Four-Ball Match Play

30-3 a Representation of Side

A *side* may be represented by one *partner* for all or any part of a match; all *partners* need not be present. An absent *partner* may join a match between holes, but not during play of a hole.

30-3 b Order of Play

Balls belonging to the same *side* may be played in the order the *side* considers best.

THREE-BALL MATCH PLAY

A John, my ball has struck your bag. What do I do now?
B In your match with me you may either play the ball as it lies or cancel that stroke and replay it. In your match with Jim you must play your original ball as it lies.
A That means I can have two balls in play at the same time at this hole.
B That's right, one in your match against me and one in your match against Jim.

FOUR-BALL: ONE PLAYER MAY REPRESENT SIDE

Your partner's late. Are you disqualified or just your partner?

Fortunately, neither of us. Because this is a four-ball match I am entitled to represent the side. Let's start. My partner is allowed to join us later, at the conclusion of a hole.

30-3 c Wrong Ball

If a player incurs the loss of hole penalty under Rule 15-3a for making a *stroke* at a *wrong ball*, **he is disqualified for that hole,** but his *partner* incurs no penalty even if the *wrong ball* belongs to him. If the *wrong ball* belongs to another player, its owner must place a ball on the spot from which the *wrong ball* was first played.

30-3 d Penalty to Side

A *side* is penalised for a breach of any of the following by any *partner*:

• Rule 4 Clubs
• Rule 6-4 Caddie
• Any Local Rule or Condition of Competition for which the penalty is an adjustment to the state of the match.

30-3 e Disqualification of Side

(i) A *side* is disqualified if any *partner* incurs a penalty of disqualification under any of the following:

• **Rule 1-3** Agreement to Waive Rules
• **Rule 4** Clubs
• **Rule 5-1 or 5-2** The Ball
• **Rule 6-2a** Handicap
• **Rule 6-4** Caddie
• **Rule 6-7** Undue Delay; Slow Play
• **Rule 11-1** Teeing

- **Rule 14-3** Artificial Devices, Unusual Equipment and Unusual Use of Equipment
- **Rule 33-7** Disqualification Penalty Imposed by Committee

(ii) A *side* **is disqualified** if all *partners* incur a penalty of disqualification under any of the following:

- **Rule 6-3** Time of Starting and Groups
- **Rule 6-8** Discontinuance of Play

(iii) In all other cases where a breach of a *Rule* would result in disqualification, **the player is disqualified for that hole only.**

30-3 f Effect of Other Penalties

If a player's breach of a *Rule* assists his *partner*'s play or adversely affects an opponent's play, **the *partner* incurs the applicable penalty in addition to any penalty incurred by the player.**

In all other cases where a player incurs a penalty for breach of a *Rule*, the penalty does not apply to his *partner*. Where the penalty is stated to be loss of hole, the effect is to disqualify the player for that hole.

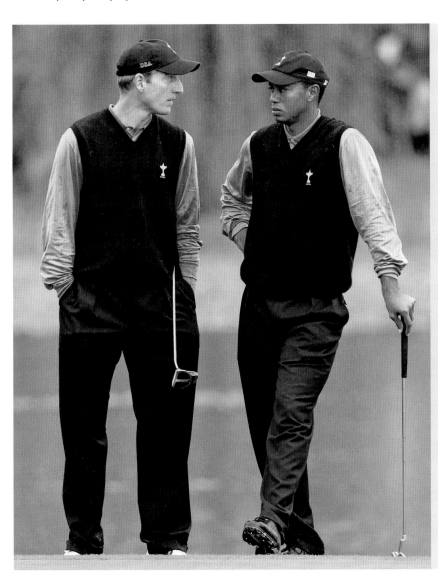

Here Jim Furyk confers with his playing partner Tiger Woods at the 2006 Ryder Cup. Under Rule 30-3b, in match play it is up to each side to decide in which order their balls are played (see incident on page 156).

► RULE 30
INCIDENT

During one of the 2006 Ryder Cup four-ball matches, the American duo Tiger Woods and Jim Furyk were up against Darren Clarke and Lee Westwood, for the European team. While playing the 7th hole at The K Club, Woods hit his second shot into the water behind the green and was not planning to continue the play of the hole, as permitted in match play. Of the remaining three balls, Clarke was farthest away from the hole but Jim Furyk wanted to play first. Although Woods was not going to complete the hole, his ball lying in the water was obviously the farthest away from the hole and, as Rule 30-3b provides that a side may play in the order it considers best, it was Tiger's "honour" and, therefore, Furyk was entitled to play first.

The American duo raised the question of whether Woods had to drop a ball first as he clearly could not play the one in the water. However, the Rules official with the match confirmed that the relevant point for determining the order of play is the spot where the ball lies in the water hazard, not where it might be dropped, so dropping was not necessary (see the Note to Rule 10-1b).

► RULE 30
FREQUENTLY ASKED QUESTION

Q In a four-ball match, the player with the lowest handicap is unable to play. Should the absent partner be disregarded in determining the handicap allowances?

A No. A side may be represented by one partner for all or any part of the match. In determining the handicap allowances, the handicaps of the three players should be reduced by the handicap of the absent player.

► RULE 31
FOUR-BALL STROKE PLAY

DEFINITIONS
All defined terms are in *italics* and are listed in the Definitions section – see pages 13–23.

31-1 General
The Rules of Golf, so far as they are not at variance with the following specific Rules, apply to *four-ball* stroke play.

31-2 Representation of Side
A *side* may be represented by either *partner* for all or any part of a *stipulated round*; both *partners* need not be present. An absent *competitor* may join his *partner* between holes, but not during play of a hole.

31-3 Scoring
The *marker* is required to record for each hole only the gross score of whichever *partner's* score is to count. The gross scores to count must be individually identifiable; otherwise **the *side* is disqualified**. Only one of the *partners* need be responsible for complying with Rule 6-6b.
(Wrong score – see Rule 31-7a)

FOUR-BALL STROKE PLAY

Date __3RD APRIL__ 2009

Competition __SPRING OPEN FOUR-BALL__

PLAYER A __J. SUTHERLAND__ Handicap __16__ Strokes __12__

PLAYER B __W. B. TAYLOR__ Handicap __12__ Strokes __9__

Hole	Length Yards	Par	Stroke Index	Gross Score A	Gross Score B	Net Score A	Net Score B	Won X Lost – Half O	Mar. Score	Hole	Length Yards	Par	Stroke Index	Gross Score A	Gross Score B	Net Score A	Net Score B	Won X Lost – Half O	Mar. Score
1	437	4	4		4		3			10	425	4	3		5		4		
2	320	4	14		4		4			11	141	3	17	3		3			
3	162	3	18		4		4			12	476	5	9	6		5			
4	504	5	7	6		5				13	211	3	11		4		4		
5	181	3	16	4		4				14	437	4	5		5		4		
6	443	4	2		5		4			15	460	4	1		5		4		
7	390	4	8		5		4			16	176	3	15	4		4			
8	346	4	12	5		4				17	340	4	13		4		4		
9	340	4	10	4		3				18	435	4	6	6		5			
Out	3123	35				35				In	3101	34				37			
										Out	3123	35				35			
										T'tl	6224	69				72			
										Handicap									
										Net Score									

Player's Signature ___J. Sutherland___

Marker's Signature ___R. J. Paxton___

Partners' scores to be individually identified

1 The lower score of the partners is the score for the hole (Rule 31).

2 Only one of the partners need be responsible for complying with Rule 6-6b, i.e. recording scores, checking scores, countersigning and returning the card (Rule 31-3).

3 The competitor is solely responsible for the correctness of the gross score recorded. Although there is no objection to the competitor (or his marker) entering the net score, it is the Committee's responsibility to record the better-ball score for each hole, to add up the scores and to apply the handicaps recorded on the card (Rule 33-5). Thus there is no penalty for an error by the competitor (or his marker) for recording an incorrect net score.

4 Scores of the two partners must be kept in separate columns otherwise it is impossible for the Committee to apply the correct handicap. If the scores of both partners, having different handicaps, are recorded in the same column, the Committee has no alternative but to disqualify both partners (Rules 31-7 and 6-6 apply).

5 The Committee is responsible for laying down the conditions under which a competition is to be played (Rule 33-1), including the method of handicapping. In the above illustration the Committee laid down that ¾ handicaps would apply.

31-4 Order of Play
Balls belonging to the same *side* may be played in the order the *side* considers best.

31-5 Wrong Ball
If a *competitor* is in breach of Rule 15-3b for making a *stroke* at a *wrong ball*, **he incurs a penalty of two strokes** and must correct his mistake by playing the correct ball or by proceeding under the *Rules*. His *partner* incurs no penalty even if the *wrong ball* belongs to him.

   If the *wrong ball* belongs to another *competitor*, its owner must place a ball on the spot from which the *wrong ball* was first played.

31-6 Penalty to Side
A *side* **is penalised** for a breach of any of the following by any *partner*:
* **Rule 4** Clubs
* **Rule 6-4** Caddie
* Any Local Rule or Condition of Competition for which there is a maximum penalty per round.

31-7 Disqualification Penalties
31-7 a Breach by One Partner
A *side* **is disqualified from the competition** if either *partner* incurs a penalty of disqualification under any of the following:
* **Rule 1-3** Agreement to Waive Rules
* **Rule 3-4** Refusal to Comply with a Rule
* **Rule 4** Clubs
* **Rule 5-1 or 5-2** The Ball
* **Rule 6-2b** Handicap
* **Rule 6-4** Caddie
* **Rule 6-6b** Signing and Returning Score Card
* **Rule 6-6d** Wrong Score for Hole
* **Rule 6-7** Undue Delay; Slow Play
* **Rule 7-1** Practice Before or Between Rounds
* **Rule 11-1** Teeing
* **Rule 14-3** Artificial Devices, Unusual Equipment and Unusual Use of Equipment
* **Rule 22-1** Ball Assisting Play
* **Rule 31-3** Gross Scores to Count Not Individually Identifiable
* **Rule 33-7** Disqualification Penalty Imposed by Committee

31-7 b Breach by Both Partners
A *side* **is disqualified from the competition**:
(i) if each *partner* incurs a penalty of disqualification for a breach of Rule 6-3 (Time of Starting and Groups) or Rule 6-8 (Discontinuance of Play), or
(ii) if, at the same hole, each *partner* is in breach of a *Rule* the penalty for which is disqualification from the competition or for a hole.

31-7 c For the Hole Only
In all other cases where a breach of a *Rule* would result in disqualification, **the competitor is disqualified only for the hole at which the breach occurred.**

31-8 Effect of Other Penalties

If a *competitor's* breach of a *Rule* assists his *partner's* play, **the *partner* incurs the applicable penalty in addition to any penalty incurred by the *competitor*.**

In all other cases where a *competitor* incurs a penalty for breach of a *Rule*, the penalty does not apply to his *partner*.

▶ RULE 32

BOGEY, PAR AND STABLEFORD COMPETITIONS

32-1 Conditions

Bogey, par and Stableford competitions are forms of stroke play in which play is against a fixed score at each hole. The *Rules* for stroke play, so far as they are not at variance with the following specific Rules, apply.

In handicap bogey, par and Stableford competitions, the *competitor* with the lowest net score at a hole takes the *honour* at the next *teeing ground*.

DEFINITIONS
All defined terms are in *italics* and are listed in the Definitions section – see pages 13–23.

32-1 a Bogey and Par Competitions

The scoring for bogey and par competitions is made as in match play. Any hole for which a *competitor* makes no return is regarded as a loss. The winner is the *competitor* who is most successful in the aggregate of holes.

The *marker* is responsible for marking only the gross number of *strokes* for each hole where the *competitor* makes a net score equal to or less than the fixed score.

NOTE 1

The *competitor's* score is adjusted by **deducting a hole or holes** under the applicable *Rule* when a penalty other than disqualification is incurred under any of the following:

• **Rule 4** Clubs
• **Rule 6-4** Caddie
• Any Local Rule or Condition of Competition for which there is a maximum penalty per round.

The *competitor* is responsible for reporting the facts regarding such a breach to the *Committee* before he returns his score card so that the *Committee* may apply the penalty. If the *competitor* fails to report his breach to the *Committee*, **he is disqualified.**

NOTE 2

If the competitor is in breach of Rule 6-7 (Undue Delay; Slow Play), the *Committee* will **deduct one hole** from the aggregate of holes. For a repeated offence, see Rule 32-2a.

32-1 b Stableford Competitions

The scoring in Stableford competitions is made by points awarded in relation to a fixed score at each hole as follows:

159

Hole Played In	Points
More than one over fixed score or no score returned	0
One over fixed score	1
Fixed score	2
One under fixed score	3
Two under fixed score	4
Three under fixed score	5
Four under fixed score	6

The winner is the *competitor* who scores the highest number of points.

The *marker* is responsible for marking only the gross number of *strokes* at each hole where the *competitor's* net score earns one or more points.

NOTE 1

If a *competitor* is in breach of a *Rule* for which there is a maximum penalty per round, he must report the facts to the *Committee* before returning his score card; if he fails to do so, **he is disqualified**. The *Committee* will, from the total points scored for the round, **deduct two points for each hole at which any breach occurred, with a maximum deduction per round of four points for each *Rule* breached.**

NOTE 2

If the *competitor* is in breach of Rule 6-7 (Undue Delay; Slow Play), the *Committee* will **deduct two points from the total points scored for the round. For a repeat offence, see Rule 32-2a.**

32-2 Disqualification Penalties

32-2 a From the Competition

A *competitor* **is disqualified** from the competition if he incurs a penalty of disqualification under any of the following:

- **Rule 1-3** Agreement to Waive Rules
- **Rule 3-4** Refusal to Comply with a Rule
- **Rule 4** Clubs
- **Rule 5-1 or 5-2** The Ball
- **Rule 6-2b** Handicap
- **Rule 6-3** Time of Starting and Groups
- **Rule 6-4** Caddie
- **Rule 6-6b** Signing and Returning Score Card
- **Rule 6-6d** Wrong Score for Hole, i.e. when the recorded score is lower than actually taken, except that no penalty is incurred when a breach of this Rule does not affect the result of the hole
- **Rule 6-7** Undue Delay; Slow Play
- **Rule 6-8** Discontinuance of Play
- **Rule 7-1** Practice Before or Between Rounds
- **Rule 11-1** Teeing
- **Rule 14-3** Artificial Devices, Unusual Equipment and Unusual Use of Equipment
- **Rule 22-1** Ball Assisting Play
- **Rule 33-7** Disqualification Penalty Imposed by Committee

32-2 b For a Hole

In all other cases where a breach of a *Rule* would result in disqualification, **the competitor is disqualified only for the hole at which the breach occurred.**

▶ RULE 32

FREQUENTLY ASKED QUESTION

Q In a handicap Stableford competition, how is the honour determined?

A At the 1st hole, the honour is determined by the order of the draw. Thereafter, the honour is determined according to the lowest net score at each individual hole.

▶ RULE 33

THE COMMITTEE

33-1 Conditions; Waiving Rule

The *Committee* must establish the conditions under which a competition is to be played.

The *Committee* has no power to waive a Rule of Golf.

Certain specific *Rules* governing stroke play are so substantially different from those governing match play that combining the two forms of play is not practicable and is not permitted. The result of a match played in these circumstances is null and void and, in the stroke play competition, the *competitors* are disqualified.

In stroke play the *Committee* may limit a *referee's* duties.

DEFINITIONS
All defined terms are in *italics* and are listed in the Definitions section – see pages 13–23.

33-2 The Course

33-2 a Defining Bounds and Margins

The *Committee* must define accurately:

(i)   the *course* and *out of bounds*,

(ii) the margins of *water hazards* and *lateral water hazards*,

(iii) *ground under repair*, and

(iv) *obstructions* and integral parts of the *course*.

33-2 b New Holes

New *holes* should be made on the day on which a stroke play competition begins and at such other times as the *Committee* considers necessary, provided all *competitors* in a single round play with each *hole* cut in the same position.

Exception

When it is impossible for a damaged *hole* to be repaired so that it conforms with the Definition, the *Committee* may make a new *hole* in a nearby similar position.

NOTE

Where a single round is to be played on more than one day, the *Committee* may provide, in the conditions of a competition (Rule 33-1), that the *holes* and *teeing*

If the course is not in a playable condition, the Committee may have to temporarily suspend play. In stroke play only, if further play becomes impossible, the Committee may have to declare play null and void.

grounds may be differently situated on each day of the competition, provided that, on any one day, all *competitors* play with each *hole* and each *teeing ground* in the same position.

33-2 c Practice Ground

Where there is no practice ground available outside the area of a competition *course*, the *Committee* should establish the area on which players may practise on any day of a competition, if it is practicable to do so. On any day of a stroke play competition, the *Committee* should not normally permit practice on or to a *putting green* or from a *hazard* of the competition *course*.

33-2 d Course Unplayable

If the *Committee* or its authorised representative considers that for any reason the *course* is not in a playable condition or that there are circumstances that render the proper playing of the game impossible, it may, in match play or stroke play, order a temporary suspension of play or, in stroke play, declare play null and void and cancel all scores for the round in question. When a round is cancelled, all penalties incurred in that round are cancelled.

(Procedure in discontinuing and resuming play – see Rule 6-8)

33-3 Times of Starting and Groups

The *Committee* must establish the times of starting and, in stroke play, arrange the groups in which *competitors* must play.

When a match play competition is played over an extended period, the *Committee* establishes the limit of time within which each round must be completed. When players are allowed to arrange the date of their match within these limits, the *Committee* should announce that the match must be played at a stated time on the last day of the period, unless the players agree to a prior date.

33-4 Handicap Stroke Table

The *Committee* must publish a table indicating the order of holes at which handicap strokes are to be given or received.

33-5 Score Card

In stroke play, the *Committee* must provide each *competitor* with a score card containing the date and the *competitor's* name or, in *foursome* or *four-ball* stroke play, the *competitors'* names.

In stroke play, the Committee is responsible for the addition of scores and application of the handicap recorded on the score card.

In *four-ball* stroke play, the *Committee* is responsible for recording the better-ball score for each hole and in the process applying the handicaps recorded on the score card, and adding the better-ball scores.

In bogey, par and Stableford competitions, the *Committee* is responsible for applying the handicap recorded on the score card and determining the result of each hole and the overall result or points total.

> **NOTE**
> The *Committee* may request that each *competitor* records the date and his name on his score card.

33-6 Decision of Ties

The *Committee* must announce the manner, day and time for the decision of a halved match or of a tie, whether played on level terms or under handicap.

A halved match must not be decided by stroke play. A tie in stroke play must not be decided by a match.

33-7 Disqualification Penalty; Committee Discretion

A penalty of disqualification may in exceptional individual cases be waived, modified or imposed if the *Committee* considers such action warranted.

Any penalty less than disqualification must not be waived or modified.

If a *Committee* considers that a player is guilty of a serious breach of etiquette, it may impose a penalty of disqualification under this Rule.

33-8 Local Rules
33-8 a Policy

The *Committee* may establish Local Rules for local abnormal conditions if they are consistent with the policy set forth in Appendix I.

33-8 b Waiving or Modifying a Rule

A Rule of Golf must not be waived by a Local Rule. However, if a *Committee* considers that local abnormal conditions interfere with the proper playing of the game to the extent that it is necessary to make a Local Rule that modifies the Rules of Golf, the Local Rule must be authorised by the *R&A*.

▶ RULE 33

INCIDENTS

During the first round of the 2007 Open at Carnoustie, Tiger Woods' tee shot at the 10th hole came to rest in the left rough, close to some cables running along the spectator rope line.

The Local Rule for cables adopted at the championship states that, if the cables are "readily movable", Rule 24-1 (Movable Obstruction) applies and the cables may be removed. If, however, the cables are "fixed or not readily movable", they are treated as "immovable obstructions" and the player may lift and drop the ball within one club-length of the nearest point of relief (Rule 24-2; Immovable Obstruction).

Consequently, the ruling for cables will be different depending on whether they are movable or immovable. In addition, in exceptional circumstances, the status of cables may change during the course of play. For example, if a group has many spectators, photographers and TV personnel on golf carts following it (as any group featuring Tiger normally does), there may be hundreds of

people standing on, and golf carts positioned over, the cables. This may result in cables that would otherwise be readily movable, becoming immovable.

In the Woods' case at Carnoustie, the referee walking with the group attempted to move the cables, but having been unable to do so, determined that they were not readily movable. Therefore, Tiger Woods was allowed to lift and drop his ball in accordance with the Rules described above.

A short time later, once the crowds had moved on, the cables were found to be movable, however the decision was entirely correct and in accordance with the Local Rules in effect at the championship, the Rules of Golf and the circumstances that existed at the time of ruling.

In the third round of the 2000 Weetabix Women's British Open Championship at Royal Birkdale Golf Club, Karrie Webb took incorrect relief from a fixed sprinkler head on her line of play.

Tiger Woods proceeds to take relief from interference from cables lying on the ground under the watchful eye of a referee at the 2007 Open Championship.

Webb was entitled to relief from the fixed sprinkler head within two club-lengths of the putting green by a Local Rule and together with her fellow-competitor, Trish Johnson, Webb referred to the wording of the Local Rule contained in Appendix I of the Rules of Golf. Having read the Local Rule, Webb confirmed that she was entitled to relief. She determined her nearest point of relief but then mistakenly measured a one club-length area within which to drop the ball. Webb was required to drop at the nearest point of relief, therefore having dropped and played the ball from within one club-length of this point rather than at it, Webb was in breach of the Local Rule and incurred a penalty of two strokes.

Rules officials noticed the infringement on the television coverage but could not prevent the breach occurring. Webb was advised of the infringement and resulting penalty at the end of her round but before she signed her score card, thereby avoiding a disqualification for signing for a score lower than actually taken.

The importance of Rule 33-6, that is, of establishing a method of settling ties prior to a stroke play competition, was emphasised at the 2006 Women's World Amateur Team Championship held in Stellenbosch, South Africa. The biennial Championships involve three-player teams playing four days of stroke play, with the best two scores counting each day. Due to daylight constraints, a team play-off was not feasible and, consequently, it was necessary for the Committee to establish a method of breaking a tie for first place should one occur.

At the conclusion of the Championship, the women's teams from Sweden and South Africa were tied on 10 under par, and this brought the tie-breaking method into play. The first criteria for determining the order if two or more teams were tied for first place was to take into account the non-counting score for the final round. However, the non-counting scores on the last day for Sweden and South Africa were 75 and, therefore, the second criteria of the non-counting score on the third day had to be relied upon. With South Africa's non-counting score on the third day being a 73 to Sweden's 77, the South African women were crowned champions. This highlighted the importance of having a fool-proof method of settling a tie.

▶ RULE 33
FREQUENTLY ASKED QUESTIONS

Q Can a player be disqualified for an omission or error in adding his score or Stableford points on his score card?
A A competitor is responsible only for the correctness of the score recorded for each hole (Rule 6-6d) and the Committee is responsible for the addition of scores or points (Rule 33-5). If a total recorded by a competitor is incorrect, it is the responsibility of the Committee to correct the error, without penalty to the competitor.

Q Can I use a motorised cart?
A Unless the use of a motorised cart is prohibited by the Committee in the conditions of competition (Rule 33-1), a player may use such equipment during a competition.

It is a policy of The R&A to encourage golfers with physical difficulties to play the game if at all possible. However, it is important that Clubs and Committees consider the issues surrounding the use of golf carts and any relevant legislation, as well as health and safety issues, weather and ground conditions. They should also decide whether the layout of the course dictates that the use of carts is impracticable.

If a Club or Committee does decide to permit the use of golf carts in competition, they may wish to consider putting restrictions on their use: for example, that golf carts would be permitted only for competitors with medical certificates or for competitors over a certain age who would otherwise be unable to participate due to physical limitations as a result of their age.

It is a matter for individual Clubs and Committees to decide and to be separately advised as to their legal position. It would be sensible for Clubs to ensure that they are aware of the relevant disability discrimination issues and of any guidance given by the Government or related bodies.

If a Club permits the use of golf carts, it would be prudent to ensure that appropriate insurance cover is in operation in the event of any accident or personal injury occurring as a result of their use.

It was only after the exceptional consideration of South Africa's and Sweden's non-counting team scores on the third day of play that officials were able to declare South Africa the winners of the 2006 Women's World Amateur Team Championship.

Q May a junior compete in adult club competitions and be eligible for prizes?

A It is the responsibility of the Committee in charge of the competition to establish the conditions under which the competition is played (Rule 33-1). For example, who is eligible to play, handicap restrictions, age, gender, format, and so on. Therefore, it is for the Committee to decide whether juniors are eligible to enter and win any prizes in certain competitions.

Q Is the player responsible for completing the score card with the competition details, date, and so on?

A It is the responsibility of the Committee to issue each competitor with a score card containing his name and the date of the competition (Rule 33-5). A Committee may ask the competitors to complete this information in order to assist in the administration of the event, but it cannot require players to do so. Ultimately it is the Committee's responsibility, and a player cannot be penalised for failing to do so.

► RULE 34

DISPUTES AND DECISIONS

DEFINITIONS
All defined terms are in *italics* and are listed in the Definitions section – see pages 13–23.

34-1 Claims and Penalties

34-1 a Match Play

If a claim is lodged with the *Committee* under Rule 2-5, a decision should be given as soon as possible so that the state of the match may, if necessary, be adjusted. If a claim is not made in accordance with Rule 2-5, it must not be considered by the *Committee*.

There is no time limit on applying the disqualification penalty for a breach of Rule 1-3.

34-1 b Stroke Play

In stroke play, a penalty must not be rescinded, modified or imposed after the competition has closed. A competition is closed when the result has been officially announced or, in stroke play qualifying followed by match play, when the player has teed off in his first match.

Exceptions

A penalty of disqualification must be imposed after the competition has closed if a *competitor*:

(i)   was in breach of Rule 1-3 (Agreement to Waive Rules); or

(ii)   returned a score card on which he had recorded a handicap that, before the competition closed, he knew was higher than that to which he was entitled, and this affected the number of strokes received (Rule 6-2b); or

(iii) returned a score for any hole lower than actually taken (Rule 6-6d) for any reason other than failure to include a penalty that, before the competition closed, he did not know he had incurred; or

(iv) knew, before the competition closed, that he had been in breach of any other *Rule* for which the penalty is disqualification.

34-2 Referee's Decision

If a *referee* has been appointed by the *Committee*, his decision is final.

34-3 Committee's Decision

In the absence of a *referee*, any dispute or doubtful point on the *Rules* must be referred to the *Committee*, whose decision is final.

If the *Committee* cannot come to a decision, it may refer the dispute or doubtful point to the Rules of Golf Committee of The R&A, whose decision is final.

If the dispute or doubtful point has not been referred to the Rules of Golf Committee, the player or players may request that an agreed statement be referred through a duly authorised representative of the *Committee* to the Rules of Golf Committee for an opinion as to the correctness of the decision given. The reply will be sent to this authorised representative.

If play is conducted other than in accordance with the Rules of Golf, the Rules of Golf Committee will not give a decision on any question.

► RULE 34

INCIDENTS

The 2004 Open Championship featured an incident that emphasised the importance of timing in terms of discovering a possible breach of the Rules. At the 14th hole on the final day, eventual winner Todd Hamilton putted to a few feet from the hole. When he marked and lifted his ball, he tapped his ball-marker down three times with his ball, replaced the ball and holed the putt.

Hamilton was already involved in the 1st hole of his four-hole play-off with Ernie Els when a television viewer made contact with The R&A Rules Office at the Championship and advised that he thought he had seen Hamilton touch his line of putt in breach of Rule 16-1a on the 14th hole.

As any such reports have to be followed up, the footage of the incident was closely reviewed. Had

Hamilton breached Rule 16-1a, he would have been liable to a penalty of two strokes at the 14th hole. However, as he had returned his score card for that round – without any penalty included for that hole – and the competition had not yet closed (see Rule 34-1b), he would have been subject to a penalty of disqualification for returning a score for a hole lower than had actually been taken, in breach of Rule 6-6d. A further twist was that, had there been a breach but it had not come to light until after the competition was closed, in view of Rule 34-1b, which provides that no penalty can be waived, modified or imposed after a competition has closed, there would have been no penalty.

As it transpired, the replays confirmed that Hamilton had not breached the Rules at the 14th hole, and the American went on to defeat Ernie Els and lift the Claret Jug.

South African Dawie Van der Walt was disqualified from the 2007 Russian Open two weeks after the event when it emerged that he had signed for a four at the 13th hole of his third round, instead of the five he actually took. He recorded a total of 68 for the third round, rather than 69.

Only in limited exceptional circumstances may a penalty of disqualification be imposed after the competition has closed, one of those circumstances being where the competitor has returned a score for any hole that is lower than actually taken for any reason other than failure to include a penalty that, before the competition closed, he did not know he had incurred (Rule 34-1b(iii)). The wrong score was not recorded because the player failed to take account of a penalty – it was simply an innocent, but costly mistake. Van der Walt finished fourth in the event, but had to return his cheque for £48,361 on being disqualified.

▸ RULE 34

FREQUENTLY ASKED QUESTIONS

Q What are the Rules for Greensomes and Texas Scrambles?
A These are not recognised forms of play and thus are not covered by the Rules of Golf. Therefore, it is a matter for the Committee in charge of the competition to decide upon any matters that may arise and its decision shall be final (Rule 34-3).

Q When is a record score officially recognised as a "course record"?
A The term "course record" is not defined in the Rules of Golf. Therefore it is a matter for the Committee in charge of the competition to decide whether it recognises a score as a course record.

It is recommended that a record score should be recognised only if made in an individual stroke play competition (excluding a Stableford or a par/bogey competition) with the holes and tee-markers in their championship positions and when a Local Rule on preferred lies is not in operation.

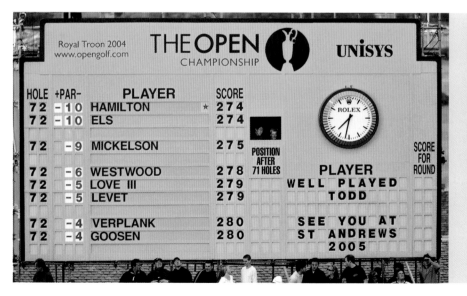

While Todd Hamilton was in the course of his four-hole play-off against Ernie Els for the Claret Jug, a possible Rules infringement on the 14th hole was lodged against him with The R&A Rules Office at Royal Troon. Fortunately for Hamilton it was not upheld, and he went on to become The Open winner for 2004.

► APPENDICES

▶ APPENDIX I
Local Rules; Conditions of Competition

Definitions
All defined terms are in *italics* and are listed in the Definitions section – see pages 13–23.

PART A Local Rules

As provided in Rule 33-8a, the *Committee* may make and publish Local Rules for local abnormal conditions if they are consistent with the policy established in this Appendix. In addition, detailed information regarding acceptable and prohibited Local Rules is provided in "Decisions on the Rules of Golf" under Rule 33-8 and in "Guidance on Running a Competition".

If local abnormal conditions interfere with the proper playing of the game and the *Committee* considers it necessary to modify a Rule of Golf, authorisation from the *R&A* must be obtained.

1 Defining Bounds and Margins
Specifying means used to define *out of bounds*, *water hazards*, *lateral water hazards*, *ground under repair*, *obstructions* and integral parts of the *course* (Rule 33-2a).

2 Water Hazards
a Lateral Water Hazards
Clarifying the status of *water hazards* that may be *lateral water hazards* (Rule 26).
b Ball Played Provisionally Under Rule 26-1
Permitting play of a ball provisionally under Rule 26-1 for a ball that may be in a *water hazard* (including a *lateral water hazard*) of such character that, if the original ball is not found, it is known or virtually certain that it is in the *water hazard* and it would be impracticable to determine whether the ball is in the *hazard* or to do so would unduly delay play.

3 Areas of the Course Requiring Preservation; Environmentally-Sensitive Areas
Assisting preservation of the *course* by defining areas, including turf nurseries, young plantations and other parts of the *course* under cultivation, as *ground under repair* from which play is prohibited.

When the *Committee* is required to prohibit play from environmentally-sensitive areas that are on or adjoin

the *course*, it should make a Local Rule clarifying the relief procedure.

4 Course Conditions – Mud, Extreme Wetness, Poor Conditions and Protection of Course
a Lifting an Embedded Ball, Cleaning
Temporary conditions that might interfere with proper playing of the game, including mud and extreme wetness, warranting relief for an embedded ball anywhere *through the green* or permitting lifting, cleaning and replacing a ball anywhere *through the green* or on a closely-mown area *through the green*.
b "Preferred Lies" and "Winter Rules"
Adverse conditions, including the poor condition of the *course* or the existence of mud, are sometimes so general, particularly during winter months, that the *Committee* may decide to grant relief by temporary Local Rule either to protect the *course* or to promote fair and pleasant play. The Local Rule should be withdrawn as soon as the conditions warrant.

5 Obstructions
a General
Clarifying status of objects that may be *obstructions* (Rule 24).

Declaring any construction to be an integral part of the *course* and, accordingly, not an *obstruction*, e.g., built-up sides of *teeing grounds*, *putting greens* and *bunkers* (Rules 24 and 33-2a).
b Stones in Bunkers
Allowing the removal of stones in *bunkers* by declaring them to be movable *obstructions* (Rule 24-1).
c Roads and Paths
(i) Declaring artificial surfaces and sides of roads and paths to be integral parts of the *course*, or
(ii) Providing relief of the type afforded under Rule 24-2b from roads and paths not having artificial surfaces and sides if they could unfairly affect play.
d Immovable Obstructions Close to Putting Green
Providing relief from intervention by immovable *obstructions* on or within two club-lengths of the *putting green* when the ball lies within two club-lengths of the immovable *obstruction*.
e Protection of Young Trees
Providing relief for the protection of young trees.
f Temporary Obstructions
Providing relief from interference by temporary *obstructions* (e.g., grandstands, television cables and equipment, etc).

6 Dropping Zones

Establishing special areas on which balls may or must be dropped when it is not feasible or practicable to proceed exactly in conformity with Rule 24-2b or 24-3 (Immovable Obstruction), Rule 25-1b or 25-1c (Abnormal Ground Conditions), Rule 25-3 (Wrong Putting Green), Rule 26-1 (Water Hazards and Lateral Water Hazards) or Rule 28 (Ball Unplayable).

PART B Specimen Local Rules

Within the policy established in Part A of this Appendix, the *Committee* may adopt a Specimen Local Rule by referring, on a score card or notice board, to the examples given below. However, Specimen Local Rules of a temporary nature should not be printed on a score card.

1 Water Hazards, Ball Played Provisionally Under Rule 26-1

If a *water hazard* (including a *lateral water hazard*) is of such size and shape and/or located in such a position that:

(i) it would be impracticable to determine whether the ball is in the *hazard* or to do so would unduly delay play, and

(ii) if the original ball is not found, it is known or virtually certain that it is in the *water hazard*,

the *Committee* may introduce a Local Rule permitting the play of a ball provisionally under Rule 26-1. The ball is played provisionally under any of the applicable options under Rule 26-1 or any applicable Local Rule. In such a case, if a ball is played provisionally and the original ball is in a *water hazard*, the player may play the original ball as it lies or continue with the ball played provisionally, but he may not proceed under Rule 26-1 with regard to the original ball.

In these circumstances, **the following Local Rule is recommended:**

"If there is doubt whether a ball is in or is *lost* in the *water hazard* (specify location), the player may play another ball provisionally under any of the applicable options in Rule 26-1.

If the original ball is found outside the *water hazard*, the player must continue play with it.

If the original ball is found in the *water hazard*, the player may either play the original ball as it lies or continue with the ball played provisionally under Rule 26-1.

If the original ball is not found or identified within the five-minute search period, the player must continue with the ball played provisionally.

PENALTY FOR BREACH OF LOCAL RULE:
Match Play – Loss of hole;
Stroke Play – Two strokes."

2 Areas of the Course Requiring Preservation; Environmentally-Sensitive Areas
a Ground Under Repair; Play Prohibited
If the *Committee* wishes to protect any area of the *course*, it should declare it to be *ground under repair* and prohibit play from within that area. **The following Local Rule is recommended:**

"The _____(defined by _____) is *ground under repair* from which play is prohibited. If a player's ball lies in the area, or if it interferes with the player's *stance* or the area of his intended swing, the player must take relief under Rule 25-1.

PENALTY FOR BREACH OF LOCAL RULE:
Match play – Loss of hole;
Stroke play – Two strokes."

b Environmentally-Sensitive Areas
If an appropriate authority (i.e. a Government Agency or the like) prohibits entry into and/or play from an area on or adjoining the *course* for environmental reasons, the *Committee* should make a Local Rule clarifying the relief procedure.

The *Committee* has some discretion in terms of whether the area is defined as *ground under repair*, a *water hazard* or *out of bounds*. However, it may not simply define the area to be a *water hazard* if it does not meet the Definition of a *"Water Hazard"* and it should attempt to preserve the character of the hole. **The following Local Rule is recommended:**
"I Definition
An environmentally-sensitive area (ESA) is an area so declared by an appropriate authority, entry into and/or play from which is prohibited for environmental reasons. These areas may be defined as *ground under repair*, a *water hazard*, a *lateral water hazard* or *out of bounds* at the discretion of the *Committee*, provided that in the case of an ESA that has been defined as a *water hazard* or a *lateral water hazard*, the area is, by definition, a *water hazard*.

171

NOTE

The *Committee* may not declare an area to be environmentally sensitive.

II Ball in Environmentally-Sensitive Area
a Ground Under Repair

If a ball is in an ESA, defined as *ground under repair*, a ball must be dropped in accordance with Rule 25-1b.

If it is known or virtually certain that a ball that has not been found is in an ESA defined as *ground under repair*, the player may take relief without penalty as prescribed in Rule 25-1c.

b Water Hazards and Lateral Water Hazards

If it is known or virtually certain that a ball that has not been found is in an ESA defined as a *water hazard* or *lateral water hazard*, the player must, under penalty of one stroke, proceed under Rule 26-1.

NOTE

If a ball, dropped in accordance with Rule 26 rolls into a position where the ESA interferes with the player's *stance* or the area of his intended swing, the player must take relief as provided in Clause III of this Local Rule.

c Out of Bounds

If a ball is in an ESA defined as *out of bounds*, the player must play a ball, under penalty of one stroke, as nearly as possible at the spot from which the original ball was last played (see Rule 20-5).

III Interference with Stance or Area of Intended Swing

Interference by an ESA occurs when the ESA interferes with the player's *stance* or the area of his intended swing. If interference exists, the player must take relief as follows:

(a) Through the Green: If the ball lies *through the green*, the point on the *course* nearest to where the ball lies must be determined that (a) is not nearer the *hole*, (b) avoids interference by the ESA and (c) is not in a *hazard* or on a *putting green*. The player must lift the ball and drop it, without penalty, within one club-length of the point so determined on a part of the *course* that fulfils (a), (b) and (c) above.

(b) In a Hazard: If the ball is in a *hazard*, the player must lift the ball and drop it either:

(i) Without penalty, in the *hazard*, as near as possible to the spot where the ball lay, but not nearer the *hole*, on a part of the *course* that provides complete relief from the ESA; or

(ii) Under penalty of one stroke, outside the *hazard*, keeping the point where the ball lay directly between the *hole* and the spot on which the ball is dropped, with no limit to how far behind the *hazard* the ball may be dropped. Additionally, the player may proceed under Rule 26 or 28 if applicable.

(c) On the Putting Green: If the ball lies on the *putting green*, the player must lift the ball and place it, without penalty, in the nearest position to where it lay that affords complete relief from the ESA, but not nearer the *hole* or in a *hazard*.

The ball may be cleaned when lifted under Clause III of this Local Rule.

EXCEPTION

A player may not take relief under Clause III of this Local Rule if **(a)** it is clearly unreasonable for him to make a *stroke* because of interference by anything other than an ESA or **(b)** interference by an ESA would occur only through use of an unnecessarily abnormal *stance*, swing or direction of play.

PENALTY FOR BREACH OF LOCAL RULE:
Match play – Loss of hole;
Stroke play – Two strokes.

NOTE

In the case of a serious breach of this Local Rule, the *Committee* may impose a penalty of disqualification."

3 Protection of Young Trees

When it is desired to prevent damage to young trees, **the following Local Rule is recommended:**

"Protection of young trees identified by _____. If such a tree interferes with a player's *stance* or the area of his intended swing, the ball must be lifted, without penalty, and dropped in accordance with the procedure prescribed in Rule 24-2b (Immovable Obstruction). If the ball lies in a *water hazard*, the player must lift and drop the ball in accordance with Rule 24-2b(i), except that the *nearest point of relief* must be in the *water hazard* and the ball must be dropped in the *water hazard* or the player may proceed under Rule 26. The ball may be cleaned when lifted under this Local Rule.

RELIEF FROM STAKED TREES

EXCEPTION

A player may not obtain relief under this Local Rule if **(a)** it is clearly unreasonable for him to make a *stroke* because of interference by anything other than the tree or **(b)** interference by the tree would occur only through use of an unnecessarily abnormal *stance*, swing or direction of play.

PENALTY FOR BREACH OF LOCAL RULE:
Match play – Loss of hole;
Stroke play – Two strokes."

4 Course Conditions – Mud, Extreme Wetness, Poor Conditions and Protection of the Course

a Relief for Embedded Ball

Rule 25-2 provides relief, without penalty, for a ball embedded in its own pitch-mark in any closely-mown area *through the green*. On the *putting green*, a ball may be lifted and damage caused by the impact of a ball may be repaired (Rules 16-1b and c). When permission to take relief for an embedded ball anywhere *through the green* would be warranted, **the following Local Rule is recommended:**
"*Through the green*, a ball that is embedded in its own pitch-mark in the ground may be lifted, without penalty, cleaned and dropped as near as possible to where it lay but not nearer the *hole*. The ball when dropped must first strike a part of the *course through the green*.

EXCEPTIONS

1 A player may not take relief under this Local Rule if the ball is embedded in sand in an area that is not closely mown.

2 A player may not take relief under this Local Rule if it is clearly unreasonable for him to make a *stroke* because of interference by anything other than the condition covered by this Local Rule.

PENALTY FOR BREACH OF LOCAL RULE:
Match play – Loss of hole;
Stroke play – Two strokes."

b Cleaning Ball

Conditions, such as extreme wetness causing significant amounts of mud to adhere to the ball, may be such that permission to lift, clean and replace the ball would be appropriate. In these circumstances, **the following Local Rule is recommended:**
"(Specify area) a ball may be lifted, cleaned and replaced without penalty.

NOTE

The position of the ball must be marked before it is lifted under this Local Rule – see Rule 20-1.

PENALTY FOR BREACH OF LOCAL RULE:
Match play – Loss of hole;
Stroke play – Two strokes."

c "Preferred Lies" and "Winter Rules"

Ground under repair is provided for in Rule 25 and occasional local abnormal conditions that might interfere with fair play and are not widespread should be defined as *ground under repair*.

However, adverse conditions, such as heavy snows, spring thaws, prolonged rains or extreme heat can make fairways unsatisfactory and sometimes prevent use of heavy mowing equipment. When such conditions are so general throughout a *course* that the *Committee* believes "preferred lies" or "winter rules" would promote fair play or help protect the *course*, **the following Local Rule is recommended:**

"A ball lying on a closely-mown area *through the green* [or specify a more restricted area, e.g. at the 6th hole] may be lifted, without penalty, and cleaned. Before lifting the ball, the player must mark its position. Having lifted the ball, he must place it on a spot within [specify area, e.g. six inches, one club-length, etc.] of and not nearer the *hole* than where it originally lay, that is not in a *hazard* and not on a *putting green*.

A player may place his ball only once, and it is *in play* when it has been placed (Rule 20-4). If the ball fails to come to rest on the spot on which it is placed, Rule 20-3d applies. If the ball when placed comes to rest on the spot on which it is placed and it subsequently

moves, there is no penalty and the ball must be played as it lies, unless the provisions of any other *Rule* apply.

If the player fails to mark the position of the ball before lifting it or *moves* the ball in any other manner, such as rolling it with a club, he incurs a penalty of one stroke.

NOTE

"Closely-mown area" means any area of the *course*, including paths through the rough, cut to fairway height or less.

* PENALTY FOR BREACH OF LOCAL RULE:
Match play – Loss of hole;
Stroke play – Two strokes.
* If a player incurs the general penalty for a breach of this Local Rule, no additional penalty under the Local Rule is applied."

d Aeration Holes

When a *course* has been aerated, a Local Rule permitting relief, without penalty, from an aeration hole may be warranted. **The following Local Rule is recommended:**

"*Through the green*, a ball that comes to rest in or on an aeration hole may be lifted, without penalty, cleaned and dropped, as near as possible to the spot where it lay but not nearer the *hole*. The ball when dropped must first strike a part of the course *through the green*.

On the *putting green*, a ball that comes to rest in or on an aeration hole may be placed at the nearest spot not nearer the *hole* that avoids the situation.

PENALTY FOR BREACH OF LOCAL RULE:
Match play – Loss of hole;
Stroke play – Two strokes."

e Seams of Cut Turf

If a *Committee* wishes to allow relief from seams of cut turf, but not from the cut turf itself, **the following Local Rule is recommended:**

"*Through the green*, seams of cut turf (not the turf itself) are deemed to be *ground under repair*. However, interference by a seam with the player's *stance* is deemed not to be, of itself, interference under Rule 25-1. If the ball lies in or touches the seam or the seam interferes with the area of intended swing, relief is available under Rule 25-1. All seams within the cut turf area are considered the same seam.

PREFERRED LIES

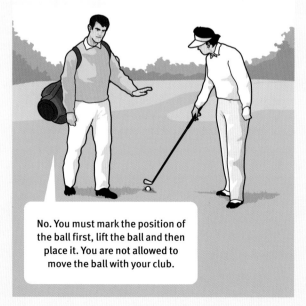

Preferred Lies are in operation, so I'll just move the ball with my club.

No. You must mark the position of the ball first, lift the ball and then place it. You are not allowed to move the ball with your club.

PENALTY FOR BREACH OF LOCAL RULE:
Match play – Loss of hole;
Stroke play – Two strokes."

5 Stones in Bunkers

Stones are, by definition, *loose impediments* and, when a player's ball is in a *hazard*, a stone lying in or touching the *hazard* may not be touched or moved (Rule 13-4). However, stones in *bunkers* may represent a danger to players (a player could be injured by a stone struck by the player's club in an attempt to play the ball) and they may interfere with the proper playing of the game.

When permission to lift a stone in a *bunker* is warranted, **the following Local Rule is recommended:**

"Stones in *bunkers* are movable *obstructions* (Rule 24-1 applies)."

6 Immovable Obstructions Close to Putting Green

Rule 24-2 provides relief, without penalty, from interference by an immovable *obstruction*, but it also provides that, except on the *putting green*, intervention on the *line of play* is not, of itself, interference under this Rule.

However, on some courses, the aprons of the *putting greens* are so closely mown that players may wish to putt from just off the green. In such conditions, immovable *obstructions* on the apron may interfere with the proper playing of the game and the introduction of the following Local Rule providing additional relief, without penalty, from intervention by an immovable *obstruction* would be warranted:

"Relief from interference by an immovable *obstruction* may be obtained under Rule 24-2. In addition, if a ball lies off the *putting green* but not in a *hazard* and an immovable *obstruction* on or within two club-lengths of the *putting green* and within two club-lengths of the ball intervenes on the *line of play* between the ball and the *hole*, the player may take relief as follows:

The ball must be lifted and dropped at the nearest point to where the ball lay that **(a)** is not nearer the *hole*, **(b)** avoids intervention and **(c)** is not in a *hazard* or on a *putting green*. The ball may be cleaned when lifted.

Relief under this Local Rule is also available if the player's ball lies on the *putting green* and an immovable *obstruction* within two club-lengths of the *putting green* intervenes on his *line of putt*. The player may take relief as follows:

The ball must be lifted and placed at the nearest point to where the ball lay that **(a)** is not nearer the *hole*, **(b)** avoids intervention and **(c)** is not in a *hazard*. The ball may be cleaned when lifted."

PENALTY FOR BREACH OF LOCAL RULE:
Match play – Loss of hole;
Stroke play – Two strokes."

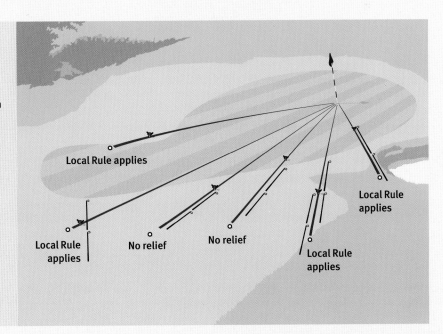

A player is entitled to relief from an immovable obstruction under Rule 24-2. If the specimen Local Rule is introduced, a player is also entitled to relief for intervention to his line of play provided: (a) (i) the immovable obstruction is on or within two club-lengths of the putting green, and (ii) the ball lies within two club-lengths of the immovable obstruction; or (b) the ball lies on the putting green and the immovable obstruction within two club-lengths of the putting green intervenes on his line of play.

Local Rule applies

Local Rule applies

No relief

No relief

Local Rule applies

Local Rule applies

7 Temporary Obstructions

When temporary obstructions are installed on or adjoining the course, the *Committee* should define the status of such obstructions as movable, immovable or temporary immovable obstructions.

a Temporary Immovable Obstructions

If the *Committee* defines such obstructions as temporary immovable obstructions, **the following Local Rule is recommended:**

"I Definition

A temporary immovable obstructions (TIO) is a non-permanent artificial object that is often erected in conjunction with a competition and is fixed or not readily movable.

Examples of TIOs include, but are not limited to, tents, scoreboards, grandstands, television towers and lavatories.

Supporting guy wires are part of the TIO, unless the *Committee* declares that they are to be treated as elevated power lines or cables.

II Interference

Interference by a TIO occurs when **(a)** the ball lies in front of and so close to the TIO that the TIO interferes with the player's *stance* or the area of his intended swing, or **(b)** the ball lies in, on, under or behind the TIO so that any part of the TIO intervenes directly between the player's ball and the *hole* and is on his *line of play*; interference also exists if the ball lies within one club-length of a spot equidistant from the *hole* where such intervention would exist.

NOTE

A ball is under a TIO when it is below the outer most edges of the TIO, even if these edges do not extend downwards to the ground.

III Relief

A player may obtain relief from interference by a TIO, including a TIO that is *out of bounds*, as follows:
(a) Through the Green: If the ball lies *through the green*, the point on the *course* nearest to where the ball lies must be determined that **(a)** is not nearer the *hole*, **(b)** avoids interference as defined in Clause II and **(c)** is not in a *hazard* or on a *putting green*. The player must lift the ball and drop it, without penalty, within one club-length of the point so determined on a part of the *course* that fulfils **(a)**, **(b)** and **(c)** above.

(b) In a Hazard: If the ball is in a *hazard*, the player must lift and drop the ball either:
(i) Without penalty, in accordance with Clause III(a) above, except that the nearest part of the *course* affording complete relief must be in the *hazard* and the ball must be dropped in the *hazard* or, if complete relief is impossible, on a part of the *course* within the *hazard* that affords maximum available relief; or
(ii) Under penalty of one stroke, outside the *hazard* as follows: the point on the *course* nearest to where the ball lies must be determined that **(a)** is not nearer the *hole*, **(b)** avoids interference as defined in Clause II and **(c)** is not in a *hazard*. The player must drop the ball within one club-length of the point so determined on a part of the *course* that fulfils **(a)**, **(b)** and **(c)** above.

The ball may be cleaned when lifted under Clause III.

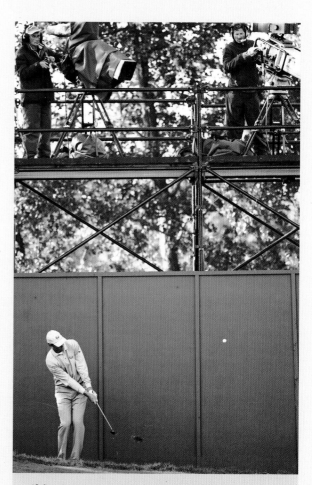

If there are temporary immovable obstructions, such as TV towers, on the course, the Committee should introduce a Local Rule providing for relief from such temporary immovable obstructions.

NOTE 1

If the ball lies in a *hazard*, nothing in this Local Rule precludes the player from proceeding under Rule 26 or Rule 28, if applicable.

NOTE 2

If a ball to be dropped under this Local Rule is not immediately recoverable, another ball may be *substituted*.

NOTE 3

A *Committee* may make a Local Rule (a) permitting or requiring a player to use a dropping zone when taking relief from a TIO or (b) permitting a player, as an additional relief option, to drop the ball on the opposite side of the TIO from the point established under Clause III, but otherwise in accordance with Clause III.

EXCEPTIONS

If a player's ball lies in front of or behind the TIO (not in, on or under the TIO), he may not obtain relief under Clause III if:

1 It is clearly unreasonable for him to make a *stroke* or, in the case of intervention, to make a *stroke* such that the ball could finish on a direct line to the *hole*, because of interference by anything other than the TIO;

2 Interference by the TIO would occur only through use of an unnecessarily abnormal *stance*, swing or direction of play; or

3 In the case of intervention, it would be clearly unreasonable to expect the player to be able to strike the ball far enough towards the *hole* to reach the TIO.

A player not entitled to relief due to these exceptions may proceed under Rule 24-2, if applicable.

IV   Ball in TIO Not Found

If it is known or virtually certain that a ball that has not been found is in, on or under a TIO, a ball may be dropped under the provisions of Clause III or Clause V, if applicable. For the purpose of applying Clauses III and V, the ball is deemed to lie at the spot where it last crossed the outermost limits of the TIO (Rule 24-3).

V   Dropping Zones

If the player has interference from a TIO, the *Committee* may permit or require the use of a dropping zone. If the

player uses a dropping zone in taking relief, he must drop the ball in the dropping zone nearest to where his ball originally lay or is deemed to lie under Clause IV (even though the nearest dropping zone may be nearer the *hole*).

NOTE

A *Committee* may make a Local Rule prohibiting the use of a dropping zone that is nearer the *hole*.

PENALTY FOR BREACH OF LOCAL RULE:

Match play – Loss of hole;

Stroke play – Two strokes."

b   Temporary Power Lines and Cables

When temporary power lines, cables or telephone lines are installed on the *course*, **the following Local Rule is recommended:**

"Temporary power lines, cables, telephone lines and mats covering or stanchions supporting them are *obstructions*:

1 If they are readily movable, Rule 24-1 applies.

2 If they are fixed or not readily movable, the player may, if the ball lies *through the green* or in a *bunker*, obtain relief as provided in Rule 24-2b. If the ball lies in a *water hazard*, the player may lift and drop the ball in accordance with Rule 24-2b(i) except that the *nearest point of relief* must be in the *water hazard* and the ball must be dropped in the *water hazard* or the player may proceed under Rule 26.

3 If a ball strikes an elevated power line or cable, the *stroke* must be cancelled and replayed, without penalty (see Rule 20-5). If the ball is not immediately recoverable another ball may be *substituted*.

NOTE

Guy wires supporting a temporary immovable *obstruction* are part of the temporary immovable obstruction unless the *Committee*, by Local Rule, declares that they are to be treated as elevated power lines or cables.

EXCEPTION

A *stroke* that results in a ball striking an elevated junction section of cable rising from the ground must not be replayed.

4 Grass-covered cable trenches are *ground under repair*, even if not marked, and Rule 25-1b applies."

8 Dropping Zones

If the *Committee* considers that it is not feasible or practicable to proceed in accordance with a Rule providing relief, it may establish dropping zones in which balls may or must be dropped when taking relief. Generally, such dropping zones should be provided as an additional relief option to those available under the Rule itself, rather than being mandatory.

Using the example of a dropping zone for a *water hazard*, when such a dropping zone is established, **the following Local Rule is recommended:**

"If a ball is in or it is known or virtually certain that a ball that has not been found is in the *water hazard* (specify location), the player may:

(i)   proceed under Rule 26; or

(ii) as an additional option, drop a ball, under penalty of one stroke, in the dropping zone.

PENALTY FOR BREACH OF LOCAL RULE:

Match play – Loss of hole;

Stroke play – Two strokes."

NOTE

When using a dropping zone the following provisions apply regarding the dropping and re-dropping of the ball:

(a) The player does not have to stand within the dropping zone when dropping the ball.

(b) The dropped ball must first strike a part of the *course* within the dropping zone.

(c) If the dropping zone is defined by a line, the line is within the dropping zone.

(d) The dropped ball does not have to come to rest within the dropping zone.

(e) The dropped ball must be re-dropped if it rolls and comes to rest in a position covered by Rule 20-2c(i-vi).

(f) The dropped ball may roll nearer the *hole* than the spot where it first struck a part of the course provided it comes to rest within two club-lengths of that spot and not into any of the positions covered by (e).

(g) Subject to the provisions of (e) and (f), the dropped ball may roll and come to rest nearer the *hole* than:

- its original position or estimated position (see Rule 20-2b);
- the *nearest point of relief* or maximum available relief (Rule 24-2, 24-3, 25-1 or 25-3); or
- the point where the original ball last crossed the margin of the *water hazard* or *lateral water hazard* (Rule 26-1).

9 Distance-Measuring Devices

If the *Committee* wishes to act in accordance with the Note under Rule 14-3, **the following wording is recommended:**

DISTANCE-MEASURING DEVICES

As the Local Rule permitting the use of distance-measuring devices is in operation, I'll use my range finder to measure how close I am to the hole.

That's fine, as long as the device cannot measure other conditions such as gradient, windspeed and temperature.

"[Specify as appropriate, e.g. In this competition, or For all play at this course, etc.], a player may obtain distance information by using a device that measures distance only. If, during a *stipulated round*, a player uses a distance-measuring device that is designed to gauge or measure other conditions that might affect his play (e.g. gradient, windspeed, temperature, etc.), the player is in breach of Rule 14-3, for which the penalty is disqualification, regardless of whether any such additional function is actually used."

PART C Conditions of the Competition

Rule 33-1 provides, "The *Committee* must establish the conditions under which a competition is to be played." The conditions should include many matters such as method of entry, eligibility, number of rounds to be played, etc. which it is not appropriate to deal with in the Rules of Golf or this Appendix. Detailed information regarding these conditions is provided in "Decisions on the Rules of Golf" under Rule 33-1 and in "Guidance on Running a Competition".

However, there are a number of matters that might be covered in the Conditions of the Competition to which the *Committee's* attention is specifically drawn. These are:

1 Specification of Clubs and the Ball
The following conditions are recommended only for competitions involving expert players:

a List of Conforming Driver Heads
On its web site (www.randa.org) the *R&A* periodically issues a List of Conforming Driver Heads that lists driving clubheads that have been evaluated and found to conform with the Rules of Golf. If the *Committee* wishes to limit players to drivers that have a clubhead, identified by model and loft, that is on the List, the List should be made available and **the following condition of competition used:**

"Any driver the player carries must have a clubhead, identified by model and loft, that is named on the current List of Conforming Driver Heads issued by the *R&A*.

EXCEPTION
A driver with a clubhead that was manufactured prior to 1999 is exempt from this condition.

* PENALTY FOR CARRYING, BUT NOT MAKING STROKE WITH, CLUB OR CLUBS IN BREACH OF CONDITION:
Match play – At the conclusion of the hole at which the breach is discovered, the state of the match is adjusted by deducting one hole for each hole at which a breach occurred; maximum deduction per round – Two holes.
Stroke play – Two strokes for each hole at which any breach occurred; maximum penalty per round – Four strokes.
Match or stroke play – In the event of a breach between the play of two strokes, the penalty applies to the next hole.
Bogey and par competitions – See Note 1 to Rule 32-1a.
Stableford competitions – See Note 1 to Rule 32-1b.
* Any club or clubs carried in breach of this condition must be declared out of play by the player to his opponent in match play or his *marker* or a *fellow-competitor* in stroke play immediately upon discovery that a breach has occurred. If he fails to do so, he is disqualified.

PENALTY FOR MAKING STROKE WITH CLUB IN BREACH OF CONDITION:
Disqualification."

b List of Conforming Golf Balls
On its website (www.randa.org) the *R&A* periodically issues a List of Conforming Golf Balls that lists balls that have been tested and found to conform with the Rules of Golf. If the Committee wishes to require players to play a model of golf ball on the List, the List should be made available and **the following condition of competition used:**

"The ball the player plays must be named on the current List of Conforming Golf Balls issued by the *R&A*.

PENALTY FOR BREACH OF CONDITION:
Disqualification."

c One Ball Condition
If it is desired to prohibit changing brands and models of golf balls during a *stipulated round*, **the following condition is recommended:**

"Limitation on Balls Used During Round: (Note to Rule 5-1)

(i) "One Ball" Condition

During a *stipulated round*, the balls a player plays must be of the same brand and model as detailed by a single entry on the current List of Conforming Golf Balls.

NOTE

If a ball of a different brand and/or model is dropped or placed it may be lifted, without penalty, and the player must then proceed by dropping or placing a proper ball (Rule 20-6).

PENALTY FOR BREACH OF CONDITION:

Match play – At the conclusion of the hole at which the breach is discovered, the state of the match must be adjusted by deducting one hole for each hole at which a breach occurred; maximum deduction per round – Two holes.

Stroke play – Two strokes for each hole at which any breach occurred; maximum penalty per round – Four strokes.

(ii) Procedure When Breach Discovered

When a player discovers that he has played a ball in breach of this condition, he must abandon that ball before playing from the next *teeing ground* and complete the round with a proper ball; otherwise, the player is disqualified. If discovery is made during play of a hole and the player elects to *substitute* a proper ball before completing that hole, the player must place a proper ball on the spot where the ball played in breach of the condition lay."

2 Time of Starting (Note to Rule 6-3a)

If the *Committee* wishes to act in accordance with the Note, **the following wording is recommended:**

"If the player arrives at his starting point, ready to play, within five minutes after his starting time, in the absence of circumstances that warrant waiving the penalty of disqualification as provided in Rule 33-7, the penalty for failure to start on time is loss of the first hole to be played in match play or two strokes in stroke play. Penalty for lateness beyond five minutes is disqualification."

3 Caddie (Note to Rule 6-4)

Rule 6-4 permits a player to use a *caddie* provided he has only one *caddie* at any one time. However, there may be circumstances where a *Committee* may wish to prohibit *caddies* or restrict a player in his choice of *caddie*, e.g. professional golfer, sibling, parent, another player in the competition, etc. In such cases, **the following wording is recommended:**

Use of Caddie Prohibited

"A player is prohibited from using a *caddie* during the *stipulated round*."

Restriction on Who May Serve as Caddie

"A player is prohibited from having _____ serve as his *caddie* during the *stipulated round*.

PENALTY FOR BREACH OF CONDITION:

Match play – At the conclusion of the hole at which the breach is discovered, the state of the match is adjusted by deducting one hole for each hole at which a breach occurred; maximum deduction per round – Two holes.

Stroke play – Two strokes for each hole at which any breach occurred; maximum penalty per round – Four strokes.

Match or stroke play – In the event of a breach between the play of two holes, the penalty applies to the next hole. A player having a *caddie* in breach of this condition must immediately upon discovery that a breach has occurred ensure that he conforms with this condition for the remainder of the *stipulated round*. Otherwise, the player is disqualified."

4 Pace of Play (Note 2 to Rule 6-7)

The *Committee* may establish pace of play guidelines to help prevent slow play, in accordance with Note 2 to Rule 6-7.

5 Suspension of Play Due to a Dangerous Situation (Note to Rule 6-8b)

As there have been many deaths and injuries from lightning on golf courses, all clubs and sponsors of golf competitions are urged to take precautions for the protection of persons against lightning. Attention is called to Rules 6-8 and 33-2d. If the *Committee* desires to adopt the condition in the Note under Rule 6-8b, **the following wording is recommended:**

"When play is suspended by the *Committee* for a dangerous situation, if the players in a match or group are between the play of two holes, they must not resume play until the *Committee* has ordered a resumption of play. If they are in the process of playing a hole, they must discontinue play immediately and not resume play until the *Committee* has ordered a resumption of play. If a player fails to discontinue play

SUSPENSION OF PLAY DUE TO A DANGEROUS SITUATION

immediately, he is disqualified, unless circumstances warrant waiving the penalty as provided in Rule 33-7.

The signal for suspending play due to a dangerous situation will be a prolonged note of the siren."

The following signals are generally used and it is recommended that all *Committees* do similarly:

DISCONTINUE PLAY IMMEDIATELY: One prolonged note of siren.

DISCONTINUE PLAY: Three consecutive notes of siren, repeated.

RESUME PLAY: Two short notes of siren, repeated.

6 Practice

a General

The *Committee* may make regulations governing practice in accordance with the Note to Rule 7-1, Exception (c) to Rule 7-2, Note 2 to Rule 7 and Rule 33-2c.

b Practice Between Holes (Note 2 to Rule 7)

If the *Committee* wishes to act in accordance with Note 2 to Rule 7-2 **the following wording is recommended**:

"Between the play of two holes, a player must not make any practice *stroke* on or near the *putting green* of the hole last played and must not test the surface of the *putting green* of the hole last played by rolling a ball.

PENALTY FOR BREACH OF CONDITION:

Match play – Loss of next hole.

Stroke play – Two strokes at the next hole.

Match or stroke play – In the case of a breach at the last hole of the *stipulated round*, the player incurs the penalty at that hole."

7 Advice in Team Competitions (Note to Rule 8)

If the *Committee* wishes to act in accordance with the Note under Rule 8, **the following wording is recommended**:

"In accordance with the Note to Rule 8 of the Rules of Golf, each team may appoint one person (in addition to the persons from whom *advice* may be asked under that Rule) who may give *advice* to members of that team. Such person (if it is desired to insert any restriction on who may be nominated insert such restriction here) must be identified to the *Committee* before giving *advice*."

8 New Holes (Note to Rule 33-2b)

The *Committee* may provide, in accordance with the Note to Rule 33-2b, that the *holes* and *teeing grounds* for a single-round competition being held on more than one day may be differently situated on each day.

9 Transportation

If it is desired to require players to walk in a competition, **the following condition is recommended:**

    "Players must not ride on any form of transportation during a *stipulated round* unless authorised by the *Committee*.

PENALTY FOR BREACH OF CONDITION:

Match play – At the conclusion of the hole at which the breach is discovered, the state of the match is adjusted by deducting one hole for each hole at which a breach occurred; maximum deduction per round – Two holes.

Stroke play – Two strokes for each hole at which any breach occurred; maximum penalty per round – Four strokes.

Match or stroke play – In the event of a breach between the play of two holes, the penalty applies to the next hole. Use of any unauthorised form of transportation must be discontinued immediately upon discovery that a breach has occurred. Otherwise, the player is disqualified."

10 Anti-Doping

The *Committee* may require, in the conditions of competition, that players comply with an anti-doping policy.

11 How to Decide Ties

In both match play and stroke play, a tie can be an acceptable result. However, when it is desired to have a sole winner, the *Committee* has the authority, under Rule 33-6, to determine how and when a tie is decided. The decision should be published in advance.

The *R&A* recommends:

Match Play

A match that ends all square should be played off hole by hole until one *side* wins a hole. The play-off should start on the hole where the match began. In a handicap match, handicap strokes should be allowed as in the *stipulated round*.

Stroke Play

(a) In the event of a tie in a scratch stroke play competition, a play-off is recommended. The play-off may be over 18 holes or a smaller number of holes as specified by the *Committee*. If that is not feasible or there is still a tie, a hole-by-hole play-off is recommended.

(b) In the event of a tie in a handicap stroke play competition, a play-off with handicaps is recommended. The play-off may be over 18 holes or a smaller number of holes as specified by the *Committee*. It is recommended that any such play-off consist of at least three holes.

In competitions where the handicap stroke allocation table is not relevant, if the play-off is less than 18 holes, the percentage of 18 holes played should be applied to the players' handicaps to determine their play-off handicaps. Handicap stroke fractions of one-half stroke or more should count as a full stroke and any lesser fractions should be disregarded.

In competitions where the handicap stroke table is relevant, such as four-ball stroke play and bogey, par

General Numerical Draw

UPPER HALF	LOWER HALF	UPPER HALF	LOWER HALF	UPPER HALF	LOWER HALF
64 qualifiers		**32 qualifiers**		**16 qualifiers**	
1 vs. 64	2 vs. 63	1 vs. 32	2 vs. 31	1 vs. 16	2 vs. 15
32 vs. 33	31 vs. 34	16 vs. 17	15 vs. 18	8 vs. 9	7 vs. 10
16 vs. 49	15 vs. 50	8 vs. 25	7 vs. 26	4 vs. 13	3 vs. 14
17 vs. 48	18 vs. 47	9 vs. 24	10 vs. 23	5 vs. 12	6 vs. 11
8 vs. 57	7 vs. 58	4 vs. 29	3 vs. 30		
25 vs. 40	26 vs. 39	13 vs. 20	14 vs. 19	UPPER HALF	LOWER HALF
9 vs. 56	10 vs. 55	5 vs. 28	6 vs. 27	**8 qualifiers**	
24 vs. 41	23 vs. 42	12 vs. 21	11 vs. 22	1 vs. 8	2 vs. 7
4 vs. 61	3 vs. 62			4 vs. 5	3 vs. 6
29 vs. 36	30 vs. 35				
13 vs. 52	14 vs. 51				
20 vs. 45	19 vs. 46				
5 vs. 60	6 vs. 59				
28 vs. 37	27 vs. 38				
12 vs. 53	11 vs. 54				
21 vs. 44	22 vs. 43				

and Stableford competitions, handicap strokes should be taken as they were assigned for the competition using the players' respective stroke allocation table(s).

(c) If a play-off of any type is not feasible, matching score cards is recommended. The method of matching cards should be announced in advance and should also provide what will happen if this procedure does not produce a winner. An acceptable method of matching cards is to determine the winner on the basis of the best score for the last nine holes. If the tying players have the same score for the last nine, determine the winner on the basis of the last six holes, last three holes and finally the 18th hole. If this method is used in a competition with a multiple tee start, it is recommended that the "last nine holes, last six holes, etc." is considered to be holes 10–18, 13–18, etc.

For competitions where the handicap stroke table is not relevant, such as individual stroke play, if the last nine, last six, last three holes scenario is used, one-half, one-third, one-sixth, etc. of the handicaps should be deducted from the score for those holes. In terms of the use of fractions in such deductions, the *Committee* should act in accordance with the recommendations of the relevant handicapping authority.

In competitions where the handicap stroke table is relevant, such as *four-ball* stroke play and bogey, par and Stableford competitions, handicap strokes should be taken as they were assigned for the competition, using the players' respective stroke allocation table(s).

12 Draw for Match Play

Although the draw for match play may be completely blind or certain players may be distributed through different quarters or eighths, the General Numerical Draw (see page 182) is recommended if matches are determined by a qualifying round.

General Numerical Draw

For purposes of determining places in the draw, ties in qualifying rounds other than those for the last qualifying place are decided by the order in which scores are returned, with the first score to be returned receiving the lowest available number, etc. If it is impossible to determine the order in which scores are returned, ties are determined by a blind draw.

► APPENDIX I

INCIDENTS

A Local Rule that is frequently introduced at events played on links courses relates to immovable obstructions close to the putting green, the most common example of such immovable obstructions being fixed sprinkler heads.

The Local Rule provides additional relief to that found in the Rules of Golf, by enabling a player, whose ball lies off the putting green but not in a hazard, to take a drop if an obstruction, which lies within two club-lengths of the putting green, is within two club-lengths of the player's ball and also on his line of play. When taking relief, the player must drop his ball at the nearest point where there is no intervention from the obstruction, which is not in a hazard and not on a putting green. It is important to note that there is not a one club-length dropping area, as is normally the case when free relief is given from an immovable obstruction, although the ball, when dropped, can roll up to two club-lengths without a re-drop being required (Rule 20-2c).

The introduction of this Local Rule is appropriate on courses where players may frequently elect to putt from off the green and, consequently, the Local Rule is used at The Open Championship.

In the final round at Royal Troon in 2004, Tiger Woods utilised the Local Rule when his ball lay close to the 18th green. However, matters were complicated when, in dropping the ball at the nearest point of relief, the ball rolled into a bunker. In this situation, Rule 20-2c(ii) comes into play and the player is required to re-drop the ball. Tiger did so and the same thing happened. Rule 20-2c then provides that the ball must be placed as near as possible to the spot where it first struck the course when re-dropped.

US pro and former Walker Cup player, Erik Compton, has already had two heart transplants, his last being in May 2008. Only six months later he was at the US PGA Tour Qualifying School. On the Tour there is a condition of competition prohibiting the use of any transportation, unless permitted by the Committee – for example, when a player is given a lift back to the tee because his ball is lost.

Given his exceptional circumstances, Compton was given a special dispensation by the Tour to use a cart for six months until his strength returned. Compton narrowly missed out on reaching the second stage of the Tour School by one stroke, but continues to compete on the Tour through sponsors' invitations.

Shortly after finishing at The Honda Classic in March 2009, where Compton walked all four rounds and finished tied for 44th at three over, he remarked, "My desire is to walk and to play, to be normal. I have the talent; it's obvious the health has been a huge problem. I just think I'll continue to get better in the next few years."

Michelle Wie (seeded second) and Maru Martinez (seeded 63rd) were playing in the first round of match play at the 2003 US Women's Amateur at Philadelphia Country Club when Martinez made a quick stop in the clubhouse, after completing the 9th hole. She was two up at the time. Martinez then received a ride from a club volunteer from the clubhouse to the 10th tee.

However, the USGA had adopted a condition that players shall walk at all times during a stipulated round, and it was at that point that confusion set in about how the penalty should be applied. The initial ruling had Martinez incurring a loss of hole penalty, so the players picked up from the 10th fairway and started walking to the next tee. However, before the players reached the tee, the officials came over the radio to state that the penalty was actually an adjustment to the state of the match. Therefore, the players returned to the drive zone where their tee shots came to rest, then continued play of the hole. Wie won the 10th hole with a conceded birdie,

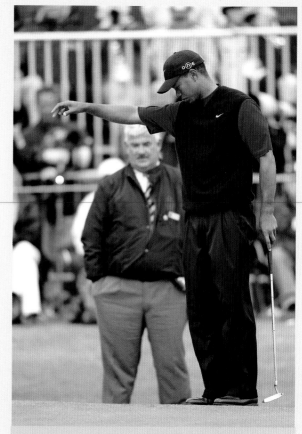

Tiger Woods at the 2004 Open Championship drops his ball when taking relief under the Local Rule for immovable obstructions close to the putting green.

and with the state of the match adjustment the match was now all square. Martinez commented, "I was very mad but I just said I've got to start all over again. It was my responsibility." She went on to win the match one up.

▸ APPENDIX I

FREQUENTLY ASKED QUESTION

Q How is a tie in stroke play decided?
A It is up to the Committee to determine how ties are to be decided, and the Committee should announce the

procedure in advance. The R&A recommendation can be found in Appendix I, Part C, 11.

APPENDICES II AND III

The *R&A* reserves the right, at any time, to change the Rules relating to clubs and balls and make or change the interpretations relating to these Rules. For up-to-date information, please contact the *R&A* or refer to: www.randa.org/equipmentrules.

Any design in a club or ball which is not covered by the *Rules*, which is contrary to the purpose and intent of the *Rules*, or which might significantly change the nature of the game, will be ruled on by the *R&A*. The dimensions and limits contained in Appendices II and III are given in the units by which conformance is determined. An equivalent imperial/metric conversion is also referenced for information, calculated using a conversion rate of 1 inch = 25.4 mm.

► APPENDIX II
Design of Clubs

A player in doubt as to the conformity of a club should consult the *R&A*. A manufacturer should submit to the *R&A* a sample of a club to be manufactured for a ruling as to whether the club conforms with the *Rules*. The sample becomes the property of the *R&A* for reference purposes. If a manufacturer fails to submit a sample or, having submitted a sample, fails to await a ruling before manufacturing and/or marketing the club, the manufacturer assumes the risk of a ruling that the club does not conform with the *Rules*.

The following paragraphs prescribe general regulations for the design of clubs, together with specifications and interpretations. Further information relating to these regulations and their proper interpretation is provided in "A Guide to the Rules on Clubs and Balls".

Where a club, or part of a club, is required to meet a specification within the *Rules*, it must be designed and manufactured with the intention of meeting that specification.

1 Clubs
a General
A club is an implement designed to be used for striking the ball and generally comes in three forms: woods, irons and putters distinguished by shape and intended use. A putter is a club with a loft not exceeding 10 degrees designed primarily for use on the *putting green*.

The club must not be substantially different from the traditional and customary form and make. The club must be composed of a shaft and a head and it may also have material added to the shaft to enable the player to obtain a firm hold (see 3 below). All parts of the club must be fixed so that the club is one unit, and it must have no external attachments. Exceptions may be made for attachments that do not affect the performance of the club.

b Adjustability
All clubs may incorporate mechanisms for weight adjustment. Other forms of adjustability may also be permitted upon evaluation by the *R&A*. The following requirements apply to all permissible methods of adjustment:

(i) the adjustment cannot be readily made;

(ii) all adjustable parts are firmly fixed and there is no reasonable likelihood of them working loose during a round; and

(iii) all configurations of adjustment conform with the *Rules*.

During a *stipulated round*, the playing characteristics of a club must not be purposely changed by adjustment or by any other means (see Rule 4-2a).

c Length
The overall length of the club must be at least 18 inches (0.457 m) and, except for putters, must not exceed 48 inches (1.219 m). For irons and woods, the measurement of length is taken when the club is lying on a horizontal plane and the sole is set against a 60-degree plane as shown in Fig. I. The length is defined as the distance from the point of the intersection between the two planes to the top of the grip. For putters, the measurement of length is taken from the top of the grip along the axis of the shaft or a straight line extension of it to the sole of the club.

d Alignment
When the club is in its normal address position the shaft must be so aligned that:

(i) the projection of the straight part of the shaft on to the vertical plane through the toe and heel must diverge from the vertical by at least 10 degrees (see Fig. II). If the overall design of the club is such that the player can effectively use the club in a vertical or close-to-vertical position, the shaft may be required to diverge from the vertical in this plane by as much as 25 degrees.

FIG I

60°

club length

FIG II

10° min

Shaft axis

Toe

Heel

Sole

Shaft axis

0.625" max

Shaft axis

FIG IV

Sole

Sole

FIG III

10° max

20° max

Back

Face

0.625" max

Sole

Shaft straightness measurement ends here

Bent shaft axis 5" max

FIG V

Sole

Neck or socket measurement starts here

Neck or socket axis 5" max

FIG VI

Sole

Dotted line shows neck and socket measurement to the sole

5" max

Sole

186

(ii) the projection of the straight part of the shaft on to the vertical plane along the intended *line of play* must not diverge from the vertical by more than 20 degrees forwards or 10 degrees backwards (see Fig. III).

Except for putters, all of the heel portion of the club must lie within 0.625 inches (15.88 mm) of the plane containing the axis of the straight part of the shaft and the intended (horizontal) *line of play* (see Fig. IV).

2 Shaft

a Straightness
The shaft must be straight from the top of the grip to a point not more than 5 inches (127 mm) above the sole, measured from the point where the shaft ceases to be straight along the axis of the bent part of the shaft and the neck and/or socket (see Fig. V).

b Bending and Twisting Properties
At any point along its length, the shaft must:
(i) bend in such a way that the deflection is the same regardless of how the shaft is rotated about its longitudinal axis; and
(ii) twist the same amount in both directions.

c Attachment to Clubhead
The shaft must be attached to the clubhead at the heel either directly or through a single plain neck and/or socket. The length from the top of the neck and/or socket to the sole of the club must not exceed 5 inches (127 mm), measured along the axis of, and following any bend in, the neck and/or socket (see Fig. VI).
Exception for Putters: The shaft or neck or socket of a putter may be fixed at any point in the head.

3 Grip (see Fig. VII)
The grip consists of material added to the shaft to enable the player to obtain a firm hold. The grip must be fixed to the shaft, must be straight and plain in form, must extend to the end of the shaft and must not be moulded for any part of the hands. If no material is added, that portion of the shaft designed to be held by the player must be considered the grip.
(i) For clubs other than putters the grip must be circular in cross-section, except that a continuous, straight, slightly raised rib may be incorporated along the full length of the grip, and a slightly indented spiral is permitted on a wrapped grip or a replica of one.
(ii) A putter grip may have a non-circular cross-section, provided the cross-section has no concavity, is symmetrical and remains generally similar throughout the length of the grip. (See Clause (v) below.)
(iii) The grip may be tapered but must not have any bulge or waist. Its cross-sectional dimensions measured in any direction must not exceed 1.75 inches (44.45 mm).
(iv) For clubs other than putters the axis of the grip must coincide with the axis of the shaft.
(v) A putter may have two grips provided each is circular in cross-section, the axis of each coincides with the axis of the shaft, and they are separated by at least 1.5 inches (38.1 mm).

4 Clubhead

a Plain in Shape
The clubhead must be generally plain in shape. All parts must be rigid, structural in nature and functional. The clubhead or its parts must not be designed to resemble any other object. It is not practicable to define plain in shape precisely and comprehensively. However, features that are deemed to be in breach of this requirement and are therefore not permitted include, but are not limited to:

(i) All Clubs
- holes through the face;
- holes through the head (some exceptions may be made for putters and cavity back irons);
- features that are for the purpose of meeting dimensional specifications;
- features that extend into or ahead of the face;
- features that extend significantly above the top line of the head;
- furrows in or runners on the head that extend into the face (some exceptions may be made for putters); and
- optical or electronic devices.

(ii) Woods and Irons
- all features listed in (i) above;
- cavities in the outline of the heel and/or the toe of the head that can be viewed from above;
- severe or multiple cavities in the outline of the back of the head that can be viewed from above;
- transparent material added to the head with the intention of rendering conforming a feature that is not otherwise permitted; and
- features that extend beyond the outline of the head when viewed from above.

FIG VII

Circular cross-section

Non-circular cross-section (putters only)

Waist (not permitted)

Bulge (not permitted)

Axis of symmetry

Groove width (max 0.035")

Groove depth (max 0.020")

30°   30°   Converging   Asymmetric

Conforming   Non-Conforming

FIG XI Examples of groove cross-sections

A

Face   Back

FIG VIII

Toe   Crown

60°

Heel

B

0.875"

C   Sole

FIG X

Illustrative impact area

b Dimensions, Volume and Moment of Inertia
(i) Woods
When the club is in a 60-degree lie angle, the dimensions of the clubhead must be such that:

- the distance from the heel to the toe of the clubhead is greater than the distance from the face to the back;
- the distance from the heel to the toe of the clubhead is not greater than 5 inches (127 mm); and
- the distance from the sole to the crown of the clubhead, including any permitted features, is not greater than 2.8 inches (71.12 mm).

These dimensions are measured on horizontal lines between vertical projections of the outermost points of:

- the heel and the toe; and
- the face and the back (see Fig. VIII, dimension A);

and on vertical lines between the horizontal projections of the outermost points of the sole and the crown (see Fig. VIII, dimension B). If the outermost point of the heel is not clearly defined, it is deemed to be 0.875 inches (22.23 mm) above the horizontal plane on which the club is lying (see Fig. VIII, dimension C).

The volume of the clubhead must not exceed 460 cubic centimetres (28.06 cubic inches), plus a tolerance of 10 cubic centimetres (0.61 cubic inches).

When the club is in a 60-degree lie angle, the moment of inertia component around the vertical axis through the clubhead's centre of gravity must not exceed 5900 g cm² (32.259 oz in²), plus a test tolerance of 100 g cm² (0.547 oz in²).

(ii) Irons
When the clubhead is in its normal address position, the dimensions of the head must be such that the distance from the heel to the toe is greater than the distance from the face to the back.

(iii) Putters (see Fig. IX)
When the clubhead is in its normal address position, the dimensions of the head must be such that:

- the distance from the heel to the toe is greater than the distance from the face to the back;
- the distance from the heel to the toe of the head is less than or equal to 7 inches (177.8 mm);

- the distance from the heel to the toe of the face is greater than or equal to two-thirds of the distance from the face to the back of the head;
- the distance from the heel to the toe of the face is greater than or equal to half of the distance from the heel to the toe of the head; and
- the distance from the sole to the top of the head, including any permitted features, is less than or equal to 2.5 inches (63.5 mm).

For traditionally shaped heads, these dimensions will be measured on horizontal lines between vertical projections of the outermost point of:

- the heel and the toe of the head;
- the heel and the toe of the face; and
- the face and the back;

and on vertical lines between the horizontal projections of the outermost points of the sole and the top of the head.

For unusually shaped heads, the toe to heel dimension may be made at the face.

c. Spring Effect and Dynamic Properties

The design, material and/or construction of, or any treatment to, the clubhead (which includes the club face) must not:

(i) have the effect of a spring which exceeds the limit set forth in the Pendulum Test Protocol on file with the *R&A*; or

(ii) incorporate features or technology including, but not limited to, separate springs or spring features, that have the intent of, or the effect of, unduly influencing the clubhead's spring effect; or

(iii) unduly influence the movement of the ball.

NOTE

(i) above does not apply to putters.

d. Striking Faces

The clubhead must have only one striking face, except that a putter may have two such faces if their characteristics are the same, and they are opposite each other.

5 Club Face

a General

The face of the club must be hard and rigid and must not impart significantly more or less spin to the ball than a standard steel face (some exceptions may be made for putters). Except for such markings listed

FIG IX

TOP VIEW

$A \leq 7''$
$B \geq \frac{2}{3} C$
$B \geq \frac{1}{2} A$
$A \geq C$
$D \leq 2.5''$

FACE VIEW

below, the club face must be smooth and must not have any degree of concavity.

b Impact Area Roughness and Material

Except for markings specified in the following paragraphs, the surface roughness within the area where impact is intended (the "impact area") must not exceed that of decorative sandblasting, or of fine milling (see Fig. X).

The whole of the impact area must be of the same material (exceptions may be made for clubheads made of wood).

c Impact Area Markings

If a club has grooves and/or punch marks in the impact area, they must be designed to meet the following specifications:

(i) Grooves

- Grooves must not have sharp edges or raised lips (test on file).
- Grooves must be straight and parallel.
- Grooves must have a symmetrical cross-section and have sides which do not converge (see Fig. XI).
- The width, spacing and cross-section of the grooves must be consistent throughout the impact area.
- Any rounding of groove edges must be in the form of a radius which does not exceed 0.020 inches (0.508 mm).
- The width of each groove must not exceed 0.035 inches (0.9 mm), using the 30-degree method of measurement on file with the *R&A*.
- The distance between edges of adjacent grooves must not be less than three times the width of the grooves, and not less than 0.075 inches (1.905 mm).
- The depth of each groove must not exceed 0.020 inches (0.508 mm).

(ii) Punch Marks

- The area of any punch mark must not exceed 0.0044 square inches (2.84 sq mm).
- The distance between adjacent punch marks (or between punch marks and grooves) must not be less than 0.168 inches (4.27 mm), measured from centre to centre.
- The depth of any punch mark must not exceed 0.040 inches (1.02 mm).
- Punch marks must not have sharp edges or raised lips (test on file).

d Decorative Markings

The centre of the impact area may be indicated by a design within the boundary of a square whose sides are 0.375 inches (9.53 mm) in length. Such a design must not unduly influence the movement of the ball. Decorative markings are permitted outside the impact area.

e Non-Metallic Club Face Markings

The above specifications do not apply to clubheads made of wood on which the impact area of the face is of a material of hardness less than the hardness of metal and whose loft angle is 24 degrees or less, but markings which could unduly influence the movement of the ball are prohibited.

f Putter Face Markings

Any markings on the face of a putter must not have sharp edges or raised lips. The specifications with regard to roughness, material and markings in the impact area do not apply.

▶ APPENDIX II

FREQUENTLY ASKED QUESTIONS

Q Are there any limits on club length?
A Yes. The overall length of the club shall be at least 0.457 m (18 inches) and, except for putters, must not exceed 1.219 m (48 inches).

Q Can a "chipper" have two striking faces?
A No. The Rules relating to iron clubs, and not putters, apply to the design of chippers. Decision 4-1/3 provides that a "chipper" is an iron club designed primarily for use off the putting green, generally with a loft greater than 10 degrees. As most players adopt a "putting stroke" when using a chipper, there can be a tendency to design the club as if it was a putter. To eliminate confusion, the Rules which apply to "chippers" include:
(1) The shaft must be attached to the clubhead at the heel (Appendix II, 2c);
(2) The grip must be circular in cross-section (Appendix II, 3(i)) and only one grip is permitted (Appendix II, 3(v));
(3) The clubhead must be generally plain in shape (Appendix II, 4a) and have only one striking face (Appendix II, 4d); and
(4) The face of the club must conform to specifications with regard to hardness, surface roughness, material and markings in the impact area (Appendix II, 5).

Q Can a golf club be designed to be adjustable?
A Yes, any club may be designed to be adjustable. However, the adjustment mechanism must conform to the following conditions set forth in Appendix II, 4b:
(i) The adjustment cannot be readily made. This means that the adjustment must require the use of a special tool rather than purely the hands or something that would commonly be kept in a golfer's pocket or golf bag (for example, a coin or a pitch-mark repair tool).
(ii) All adjustable parts must be firmly fixed and there must be no reasonable likelihood of them working loose during a round. Mechanisms that are fixed by friction fit alone would not normally be permitted.
(iii) All configurations of adjustment must conform to the Rules. Therefore, if a putter is designed to be adjustable for lie, it must not be possible to position the shaft at an angle less than 10 degrees from the vertical (see Appendix II, 1d).

Q What are the Rules relating to the "spring" effect of driving clubs?

A The R&A's interpretation of "spring" effect in driving clubs is a measure of clubhead flexibility (or Characteristic Time). This is measured using the Pendulum Test, which consists of a steel mass suspended on a pendulum being released from varying heights to strike the club face. The amount of time these two objects are in contact is the basis for the test, and the conformance limit has been set at 239 microseconds, plus a test tolerance of 18 microseconds.

A list of Conforming Driver Heads and the List of Non-conforming Driving Clubs are published on The R&A's website (www.randa.org). Further details on the situation regarding driving clubs is available on The R&A's website, including information on the Driving Club Condition of Competition and a copy of the full test protocol.

The rules, specifications and interpretations relating to clubs and balls can be found on The R&A's website and in The R&A's publication *A Guide to the Rules on Clubs and Balls*.

Q How do I find out if an item of golfing equipment I have designed conforms to the Rules or not?

A The R&A can only render a formal ruling on an item of golfing equipment if a sample is submitted for examination. However, informal opinions, based on a description, diagrams and/or photographs can sometimes be given. The R&A strongly recommends that new design ideas should be communicated or submitted as early as possible in the development process and certainly prior to beginning production of any golf club, device or component. Even though a final ruling cannot be made without the benefit of a sample, costly errors can be prevented if communication with The R&A is made as soon as possible. If a manufacturer fails to submit a sample or begins manufacturing and/or marketing an item of equipment prior to receiving an R&A ruling, the manufacturer assumes the risk of a possible ruling that the item of equipment does not conform with the Rules. Equipment submissions or enquiries should be directed to: Equipment Standards, The R&A, St Andrews, Fife, KY16 9JD, Scotland

▶ APPENDIX III
The Ball

1 General
The ball must not be substantially different from the traditional and customary form and make. The material and construction of the ball must not be contrary to the purpose and intent of the *Rules*.

2 Weight
The weight of the ball must not be greater than 1.620 ounces avoirdupois (45.93 g).

3 Size
The diameter of the ball must not be less than 1.680 inches (42.67 mm). This specification will be satisfied if, under its own weight, a ball falls through a 1.680-inch diameter ring gauge in fewer than 25 out of 100 randomly selected positions, the test being carried out at a temperature of 23 +/-1°C.

4 Spherical symmetry
The ball must not be designed, manufactured or intentionally modified to have properties which differ from those of a spherically symmetrical ball.

5 Initial Velocity
The initial velocity of the ball must not exceed the limit specified (test on file) when measured on apparatus approved by the *R&A*.

6 Overall Distance Standard
The combined carry and roll of the ball, when tested on apparatus approved by the *R&A*, must not exceed the distance specified under the conditions set forth in the Overall Distance Standard for golf balls on file with the *R&A*.

HANDICAPS
The Rules of Golf do not legislate for the allocation and adjustment of handicaps. Such matters are within the jurisdiction of the National Union concerned and queries should be directed accordingly.

ACKNOWLEDGEMENTS

Photographic acknowledgements:
Action Plus Glyn Kirk 184; **Corbis** Bettmann 51 a; **Getty Images** 63, 86, 102, 125, 127 l, 166; Andrew Redington 37, 38, 51 b, 67 a, 75, 134, 164; Craig Jones 116; David Cannon 20, 34, 61, 73, 81, 114, 145, 146; David Frost 122; Donald Miralle 10, 39, 176; Hulton Archive 29; Jeff Gross 101; Jeff Haynes 155; Richard Heathcote 42, 67 b, 95, 104, 126; Ross Kinnaird 78, 97; Martin Hayhow 22; S Greenwood 45; Stephen Dunn 72; Stephen Munday 15; Stuart Franklin 14 a & b; Warren Little 139, 168; **Michael G Leemhuis**/Congressional Country Club 162; **Peter Dazeley** 127 r; **Phil Sheldon** 135.

Illustration by Sudden Impact Media

An Hachette UK Company
www.hachette.co.uk

First published in Great Britain in 2003

This revised and updated edition published in 2009 by Hamlyn, a division of Octopus Publishing Group Ltd
2–4 Heron Quays, London E14 4JP
www.octopusbooks.co.uk

Text copyright © R&A Rules Limited 2003, 2005, 2008, 2009
Design copyright © Octopus Publishing Group Ltd 2003, 2005, 2008, 2009

ISBN: 978-0-600-62044-0

A CIP catalogue record of this book is available from the British Library.

Printed and bound in China

10 9 8 7 6 5 4 3